Deploying Node.js

Learn how to build, test, deploy, monitor, and maintain your Node.js applications at scale

Sandro Pasquali

[PACKT] **open source**
PUBLISHING   community experience distilled

BIRMINGHAM - MUMBAI

Deploying Node.js

First published: July 2015

Production reference: 1170715

Published by Packt Publishing Ltd.
Livery Place
35 Livery Street
Birmingham B3 2PB, UK.

ISBN 978-1-78398-140-3

www.packtpub.com

Credits

Author
Sandro Pasquali

Reviewers
Benjamin Bahrenburg
Nikola Brežnjak
Félix Saparelli
Jim Schubert

Commissioning Editor
Edward Gordon

Acquisition Editor
Meeta Rajani

Content Development Editor
Rohit Kumar Singh

Technical Editor
Humera Shaikh

Copy Editor
Sarang Chari

Project Coordinator
Mary Alex

Proofreader
Safis Editing

Indexer
Mariammal Chettiyar

Production Coordinator
Conidon Miranda

Cover Work
Conidon Miranda

About the Author

Sandro Pasquali, in 1997, formed `Simple.com`, a technology company that sold the world's first JavaScript-based application development framework and was awarded several patents for deployment and advertising technologies that anticipated the future of Internet-based software. Node represents, for him, the natural next step in the inexorable march toward the day when JavaScript powers nearly every level of software development.

Sandro has led the design of enterprise-grade applications for some of the largest companies in the world, including Nintendo, Major League Baseball, Bang and Olufsen, LimeWire, AppNexus, Conde Nast, and others. He has displayed interactive media exhibits during the Venice Biennial, won design awards, built knowledge management tools for research institutes and schools, and started and run several start-ups. Always seeking new ways to blend design excellence and technical innovation, he has made significant contributions across all levels of software architecture, from data management and storage tools to innovative user interfaces and frameworks.

He is the author of *Mastering Node.js*, also by Packt Publishing, which takes you on a deep dive into Node, teaching you how to use it to build modern, fast, and scalable networked software.

Sandro runs a software development company in New York and trains corporate development teams interested in using Node and JavaScript to improve their products. He spends the rest of his time entertaining his beautiful daughter and his wife.

About the Reviewers

Benjamin Bahrenburg is an author, blogger, speaker, and technology director. Over the last decade, he has designed and implemented innovative enterprise-scale solutions to meet the technology challenges of numerous Fortune 100 organizations. Ben specializes in cross-platform mobile solutions built upon full-stack JavaScript solutions.

Ben is the author of *Appcelerator Titanium Business Application Development Cookbook* by Packt Publishing, and he is a frequent speaker on Mobile JavaScript techniques. He spends much of his time blogging about JavaScript and mobile development at `bencoding.com`.

For more information, you can contact Ben on Twitter at `@bencoding`.

Nikola Brežnjak is an engineer at heart and a "jack of all trades" kind of guy. He lives in Croatia with his lovely wife and daughter. For those who care about titles, he has a master's degree in computing from FER (`http://www.fer.unizg.hr/en/education/msc_study/comp/piis`). Over the past 7 years, he has worked in the betting software industry, where he made use of his knowledge in areas ranging from full-stack (web and desktop) development to game development through Linux and database administration and the use of various languages (C#, PHP, and JavaScript, to name just a few). Lately, he's been interested in the MEAN stack, the Ionic framework, and Unity3D. Also, he likes to help out on StackOverflow, where he's currently in the top 1 percent. He self-published the book *Getting MEAN with MEMEs* at `https://leanpub.com/meantodo`.

You can find out more about him through his blog at `http://www.nikola-breznjak.com/blog`.

I would like to thank my wife and daughter for supporting me in all my geeky endeavors. Also, I would like to thank my parents, who taught me the power of hard and consistent work.

Félix Saparelli is a software developer at McKay Software, based in northern New Zealand. His role as a full-stack developer covers the design and development of elegant industrial solutions.

He has travelled the world by boat and studied architecture. He speaks two languages and has visited over 25 countries (and counting). He enjoys tea, despises rain, and appreciates fan fiction. Over this time, he's developed a passion for all things computing. He's spent the last 7 years programming and interacting with the open source community.

To find out more about him, visit his website at `https://passcod.name`. You can also find him on Twitter at `@passcod`.

Jim Schubert is an applications and web developer from Richmond, VA. He has previously held positions with GE Healthcare, Primescape Solutions, Enghouse Interactive, and Expedia. He is currently a senior systems analyst at Integrated Business Systems, Inc., where he contributes to the design and construction of complete club management systems. He is mainly proficient in C#, Scala, and JavaScript. While at Expedia, he helped drive the success of an internally consumed Node.js API before moving on to construct a Scala API designed for both internal and external consumption. When not blogging about C# or AngularJS or self-publishing books about software, he is usually reading any book related to software construction he can get his hands on.

I'd like to say thanks to my beautiful wife, Crystal, and our handsome son, Jack.

www.PacktPub.com

Support files, eBooks, discount offers, and more

For support files and downloads related to your book, please visit www.PacktPub.com.

Did you know that Packt offers eBook versions of every book published, with PDF and ePub files available? You can upgrade to the eBook version at www.PacktPub.com and as a print book customer, you are entitled to a discount on the eBook copy. Get in touch with us at service@packtpub.com for more details.

At www.PacktPub.com, you can also read a collection of free technical articles, sign up for a range of free newsletters and receive exclusive discounts and offers on Packt books and eBooks.

https://www2.packtpub.com/books/subscription/packtlib

Do you need instant solutions to your IT questions? PacktLib is Packt's online digital book library. Here, you can search, access, and read Packt's entire library of books.

Why subscribe?

- Fully searchable across every book published by Packt
- Copy and paste, print, and bookmark content
- On demand and accessible via a web browser

Free access for Packt account holders

If you have an account with Packt at www.PacktPub.com, you can use this to access PacktLib today and view 9 entirely free books. Simply use your login credentials for immediate access.

Table of Contents

Preface

Over the past few years, Node.js has found its way into the technology stack of Fortune 500 companies, mobile-first start-ups, successful Internet-based businesses, and other enterprises. In addition to validating its power as a platform, this success has exposed a shortage of tools for managing, deploying, and monitoring Node.js applications. Even though the Node.js community is open and collaborative, comprehensive information on how professional Node developers design, test, and push their code into production environments is hard to find.

This book is an attempt to close that gap in knowledge by explaining and documenting techniques and tools that working Node.js developers can use to create scalable, smart, robust, and maintainable software for the enterprise.

After a brief introduction to Node and the philosophy behind its design, you will learn how to install and update your applications on local servers and across the cloud. This foundation is then built upon by proceeding step by step through load balancing and other scaling techniques, explaining how to handle sudden changes in traffic volume and shape, implement version control, and design memory-efficient, stateful, distributed applications.

Once you've completed the groundwork essential to creating production-ready systems, you will need to test and deploy them. Filled with real-world code examples, this book is structured as a progressive workbook explaining strategies for success to be used during each stage of the testing, deploying, monitoring, and maintaining marathon that every successful piece of software runs.

When you've finished this book, you will have learned a set of reusable patterns directly applicable to solving the problems that you are dealing with today and will have laid the foundation to make confident decisions about how to build and deploy your next project.

What this book covers

Chapter 1, Appreciating Node, goes into the thinking behind Node.js, helping you to think clearly about what Node.js is good at, what it is less good at, and how to leverage Node.js to solve real-world challenges.

Chapter 2, Installing and Virtualizing Node Servers, teaches you how to create a basic Node.js application and get it running on a server. You will also learn how to do the same thing on certain popular cloud-hosting providers, such as DigitalOcean and Heroku, additionally learning how to use Docker to create lightweight, easily replicable, virtual machines.

Chapter 3, Scaling Node, explores both vertical and horizontal scaling techniques. You will learn how to use the cluster module to maximize Node's effectiveness on a single server and how to coordinate many distributed Node.js servers to handle increasing network traffic, learning about Nginx load balancing, setting up proxies using message queues, and coordinating interprocess communication in the process.

Chapter 4, Managing Memory and Space, demonstrates how good engineering practices never go out of style. We start with a discussion of microservices, introducing general techniques to design systems composed of small, focused, communicating processes. Next comes a deep exploration of how to optimize JavaScript, particularly for the V8 compiler. Beginning with several examples of memory-efficient ways to store and retrieve event data in Redis, we look at caching strategies, session management, and using CDNs to reduce server load.

Chapter 5, Monitoring Applications, explains strategies to effectively monitor your application once it has been deployed. Examples of using various third-party monitoring tools are included as well as examples outlining how you can build your own custom system sampling and logging modules. Finally, we look at debugging techniques, examining several tools and strategies to help you find and prevent runtime bottlenecks.

Chapter 6, Building and Testing, introduces certain considerations when creating a build pipeline for your application. Full examples of using Gulp, Browserify, and npm to create build tools are provided as well as information on testing with Mocha, mocking with Sinon, and using PhantomJS for headless browser testing.

Chapter 7, Deploying and Maintaining, walks you through the entire deployment pipleline, from setting up virtualized development environments to building continuous integration into your workflow. You will learn about using GitHub webhooks and Vagrant and using Jenkins to automate your deployment process. Additionally, the npm package manager will be fully dissected, and strategies for dependency management will be discussed.

What you need for this book

You will need to install Node v. 0.12.5 or higher, preferably on a Unix-based operating system, such as Linux or Mac OS X. You will also need to install several tools primarily to set up development and deployment examples:

- Use Node Version Manager (nvm) to install Node.js (and npm): https://github.com/creationix/nvm
- Git: http://git-scm.com/book/en/Getting-Started-Installing-Git
- Redis: http://redis.io/topics/quickstart
- MongoDB: http://docs.mongodb.org/manual/installation/
- Nginx: http://wiki.nginx.org/Install
- Docker: https://docs.docker.com/installation/
- PhantomJS: http://phantomjs.org/download.html
- Jenkins: https://wiki.jenkins-ci.org/display/JENKINS/Installing+Jenkins
- Vagrant: http://docs.vagrantup.com/v2/installation/
- In addition, these npm packages must be installed globally (npm install <packagename> -g):
    - gulp
    - pm2
    - mocha

Further installation and configuration instructions for these and other packages will be provided, when necessary, as you work through the book.

Who this book is for

This book is designed for Node.js developers who are ready to deploy large Node.js applications in production environments. It is designed to teach intermediate Node.js developers about the platform in more detail by situating examples in realistic contexts, focusing on modular design, and using extensive testing, active monitoring, and team-focused maintenance strategies. Those who are interested in improving the quality and efficiency of the JavaScript/Node programs they write and in delivering robust systems that withstand enterprise-level traffic, will enjoy this book. DevOps engineers without experience with the Node.js platform will also gain valuable information on how the techniques they already know are being implemented by the Node.js community.

Conventions

In this book, you will find a number of text styles that distinguish between different kinds of information. Here are some examples of these styles and an explanation of their meaning.

Code words in text, database table names, folder names, filenames, file extensions, pathnames, dummy URLs, user input, and Twitter handles are shown as follows: "Therefore, once we have the page loaded, we send keystrokes (sendKeys) into the #source input box with the Italian word "Ciao"."

A block of code is set as follows:

```
variable = produceAValue()
print variable
// some value is output when #produceAValue is finished.
```

Any command-line input or output is written as follows:

```
> This happens first

> Then the contents are available, [file contents shown]
```

New terms and **important words** are shown in bold. Words that you see on the screen, for example, in menus or dialog boxes, appear in the text like this: "You should see **You just deployed some Node!** displayed."

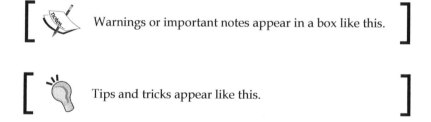

Warnings or important notes appear in a box like this.

Tips and tricks appear like this.

Reader feedback

Feedback from our readers is always welcome. Let us know what you think about this book—what you liked or disliked. Reader feedback is important for us as it helps us develop titles that you will really get the most out of.

To send us general feedback, simply e-mail feedback@packtpub.com, and mention the book's title in the subject of your message.

If there is a topic that you have expertise in and you are interested in either writing or contributing to a book, see our author guide at www.packtpub.com/authors.

Customer support

Now that you are the proud owner of a Packt book, we have a number of things to help you to get the most from your purchase.

Downloading the example code

You can download the example code files from your account at `http://www.packtpub.com` for all the Packt Publishing books you have purchased. If you purchased this book elsewhere, you can visit `http://www.packtpub.com/support` and register to have the files e-mailed directly to you.

Errata

Although we have taken every care to ensure the accuracy of our content, mistakes do happen. If you find a mistake in one of our books—maybe a mistake in the text or the code—we would be grateful if you could report this to us. By doing so, you can save other readers from frustration and help us improve subsequent versions of this book. If you find any errata, please report them by visiting `http://www.packtpub.com/submit-errata`, selecting your book, clicking on the **Errata Submission Form** link, and entering the details of your errata. Once your errata are verified, your submission will be accepted and the errata will be uploaded to our website or added to any list of existing errata under the Errata section of that title.

To view the previously submitted errata, go to `https://www.packtpub.com/books/content/support` and enter the name of the book in the search field. The required information will appear under the **Errata** section.

Piracy

Piracy of copyrighted material on the Internet is an ongoing problem across all media. At Packt, we take the protection of our copyright and licenses very seriously. If you come across any illegal copies of our works in any form on the Internet, please provide us with the location address or website name immediately so that we can pursue a remedy.

Please contact us at `copyright@packtpub.com` with a link to the suspected pirated material.

We appreciate your help in protecting our authors and our ability to bring you valuable content.

Questions

If you have a problem with any aspect of this book, you can contact us at questions@packtpub.com, and we will do our best to address the problem.

1
Appreciating Node

At the time of writing this book, Node is approaching its fifth year of existence, and its usage has grown in each of those five years. The opportunity for Node to fail has come, and passed. Node is a serious technology built by a highly skilled core team and very active community focused on constantly improving its speed, security, and usefulness.

Every day, developers face some of the problems that NodeJS aims to solve. Some of them are as follows:

- Scaling networked applications beyond a single server
- Preventing I/O bottlenecks (database, file, and network access)
- Monitoring system usage and performance
- Testing the integrity of system components
- Managing concurrency safely and reliably
- Pushing code changes and bug fixes into live environments

In this book, we will look at techniques of deploying, scaling, monitoring, testing, and maintaining your Node applications. The focus will be on how Node's event-driven, nonblocking model can be applied in practice to these aspects of software design and deployment.

On February 28, 2014, Eran Hammer delivered the keynote address to attendees of NodeDay, a large developer conference organized and sponsored by PayPal. He began his address by reciting some numbers relevant to his employer, Walmart:

- 11,000 stores
- Half a trillion dollars of net sales per year
- 2.2 million employees
- The largest private employer in the world

He continued:

> "55 percent of our Black Friday traffic, which is our Superbowl of the year…we do about 40 percent of annual revenues on Black Friday. 55 percent came on mobile… that 55 percent of traffic went 100 percent through Node. […] We were able to deliver…this massive traffic with the equivalent of two CPUs and 30 Gigs of RAM. That's it. That's what Node needed to handle 100 percent of mobile Node traffic on Black Friday. […] Walmart global e-commerce is a 10-billion-dollar business, and by the end of this year, all 10 billion will go through Node."
>
> *Eran Hammer, Senior Architect, Walmart Labs*

Modern network software, for various reasons, is growing in complexity and, in many ways, changing how we think about application development. Most new platforms and languages are attempting to address these changes. Node is no exception—and JavaScript is no exception.

Learning about Node means learning about event-driven programming, composing software out of modules, creating and linking data streams, and producing and consuming events and their related data. Node-based architectures are often composed of many small processes and/or services communicating with events—internally, by extending the EventEmitter interface and using callbacks and externally, over one of several common transport layers (for example, HTTP, TCP) or through a thin messaging layer covering one of these transport layers (for example, 0MQ, Redis PUBSUB, and Kafka). It is likely that these processes are composed of several free, open source, and high-quality **npm** modules, each distributed with unit tests and/or examples and/or documentation.

In this chapter, we will take a quick tour of Node, highlighting the problems it aims to solve, the solutions implied by its design, and what this means to you. We will also briefly discuss some of the core topics we will explore more comprehensively in later chapters, such as how to structure efficient and stable Node servers, how to make the best use of JavaScript for your application and your team, and how to think about and use Node for best results.

Let's start with understanding the how and why of Node's design.

Understanding Node's unique design

I/O operations (disk and network) are clearly more expensive. The following table shows clock cycles consumed by typical system tasks (from Ryan Dahl's original presentation of Node—https://www.youtube.com/watch?v=ztspvPYybIY):

L1-cache	3 cycles
L2-cache	14 cycles
RAM	250 cycles
Disk	41,000,000 cycles
Network	240,000,000 cycles

The reasons are clear enough: a disk is a physical device, a spinning metal platter—storing and retrieving that data is much slower than moving data between solid-state devices (such as microprocessors and memory chips) or indeed optimized on-chip L1/L2 caches. Similarly, data does not move from point to point on a network instantaneously. Light itself needs 0.1344 seconds to circle the globe! In a network used by many billions of people regularly interacting across great distances at speeds much slower than the speed of light, with many detours and few straight lines, this sort of latency builds up.

When our software ran on personal computers on our desks, little or no communication was happening over the network. Delays or hiccups in our interactions with a word processor or spreadsheet had to do with disk access time. Much work was done to improve disk access speeds. Data storage and retrieval became faster, software became more responsive, and users now expect this responsiveness in their tools.

With the advent of cloud computing and browser-based software, your data has left the local disk and exists on a remote disk, and you access this data via a network—the Internet. Data access times have slowed down again, dramatically. Network I/O is slow. Nevertheless, more companies are migrating sections of their applications into the *cloud*, with some software being entirely network-based.

Node is designed to make I/O fast. It is designed for this new world of networked software, where data is in many places and must be assembled quickly. Many of the traditional frameworks to build web applications were designed at a time when a single user working on a desktop computer used a browser to periodically make HTTP requests to a single server running a relational database. Modern software must anticipate tens of thousands of simultaneously connected clients concurrently altering enormous, shared data pools via a variety of network protocols on any number of unique devices. Node is designed specifically to help those building that kind of network software.

What do concurrency, parallelism, asynchronous execution, callbacks, and events mean to the Node developer?

Concurrency

Running code procedurally, or in order, is a reasonable idea. We tend to do that when we execute tasks and, for a long time, programming languages were naturally procedural. Clearly, at some point, the instructions you send to a processor must be executed in a predictable order. If I want to multiply 8 by 6, divide that result by 144 divided by 12, and then add the total result to 10, the order of those operations must proceed sequentially:

```
( (8x6) / (144/12) ) + 10
```

The order of operations must not be as follows:

```
(8x6) / ( (144/12) + 10 )
```

This is logical and easy to understand. Early computers typically had one processor, and processing one instruction blocked the processing of subsequent instructions. But things did not stay that way, and we have moved far beyond single-core computers.

If you think about the previous example, it should be obvious that calculating `144/12` and `8x6` can be done independently—one need not wait for the other. A problem can be divided into smaller problems and distributed across a pool of available people or workers to work on in parallel, and the results can be combined into a correctly ordered final calculation.

Multiple processes, each solving one part of a single mathematical problem simultaneously, are an example of **parallelism**.

Rob Pike, co-inventor of Google's Go programming language, defines **concurrency** in this way:

> *"Concurrency is a way to structure a thing so that you can, maybe, use parallelism to do a better job. But parallelism is not the goal of concurrency; concurrency's goal is a good structure."*

Concurrency is not parallelism. A system demonstrating concurrency allows developers to compose applications *as if* multiple independent processes are simultaneously executing many possibly related things. Successful high-concurrency application development frameworks provide an easy-to-reason-about vocabulary to describe and build such a system.

Node's design suggests that achieving its primary goal—to provide an easy way to build scalable network programs—includes simplifying how the execution order of coexisting processes is structured and composed. Node helps a developer reasoning about a program, within which many things are happening at once (such as serving many concurrent clients), to better organize his or her code.

Let's take a look at the differences between parallelism and concurrency, threads and processes, and the special way that Node absorbs the best parts of each into its own unique design.

Parallelism and threads

The following diagram describes how a traditional microprocessor might execute the simple program discussed previously:

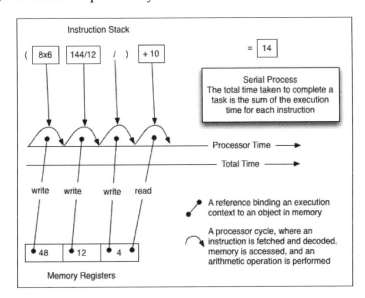

The program is broken up into individual instructions that are executed in order. This works but does require that instructions be processed in a serial fashion, and, while any one instruction is being processed, subsequent instructions must wait. This is a blocking process — executing any one segment of this chain blocks the execution of subsequent segments. There is a **single thread** of execution in play.

However, there is some good news. The processor has (literally) total control of the board, and there is no danger of another processor nulling memory or overriding any other state that this primary processor might manipulate. Speed is sacrificed for stability and safety.

We do like speed; however, the model discussed earlier rapidly became obsolete as chip designers and systems programmers worked to introduce parallel computing. Rather than having one blocking thread, the goal was to have multiple cooperating threads.

This improvement definitely increased the speed of calculation but introduced some problems, as described in the following schematic:

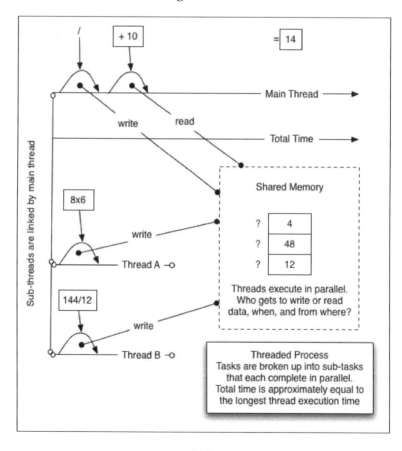

This diagram illustrates cooperating threads executing in parallel within a single process, which reduces the time necessary to perform the given calculation. Distinct threads are employed to break apart, solve, and compose a solution. As many subtasks can be completed independently, the overall completion time can be reduced dramatically.

Threads provide parallelism within a single process. A single thread represents a single sequence of (serially executed) instructions. A process can contain any number of threads.

Difficulties arise out of the complexity of thread synchronization. It is very difficult to model highly concurrent scenarios using threads, especially models in which the state is shared. It is difficult to anticipate all the ways in which an action taken in one thread will affect all the others if it is never clear when an asynchronously executing thread will complete:

- The shared memory and the locking behavior this requires lead to systems that are very difficult to reason about as they grow in complexity.

- Communication between tasks requires the implementation of a wide range of synchronization primitives, such as mutexes and semaphores, condition variables, and so on. An already challenging environment requires highly complex tools, expanding the level of expertise necessary to complete even relatively simple systems.

- Race conditions and deadlocks are a common pitfall in these sorts of systems. Contemporaneous read/write operations within a shared program space lead to problems of sequencing, where two threads may be in an unpredictable *race* for the right to influence a state, event, or other key system characteristic.

- Because maintaining dependable boundaries between threads and their states is so difficult, ensuring that a library (for Node, it would be a *package* or *module*) is thread safe occupies a great deal of the developer's time. Can I know that this library will not destroy some part of my application? Guaranteeing thread safety requires great diligence on the part of a library's developer, and these guarantees may be conditional: for example, a library may be thread safe when reading—but not when writing.

We want the power of parallelization provided by threads but could do without the mind-bending world of semaphores and mutexes. In the Unix world, there is a concept that is sometimes referred to as the **Rule of Simplicity**: *Developers should design for simplicity by looking for ways to break up program systems into small, straightforward cooperating pieces. This rule aims to discourage developers' affection for writing 'intricate and beautiful complexities' that are, in reality, bug-prone programs.*

Concurrency and processes

Parallelism within a single process is a complicated illusion that is achieved deep within mind-bendingly complex chipsets and other hardware. The question is really about appearances—about how the activity of the system appears to, and can be programmed by, a developer. Threads offer hyper-efficient parallelism, but make concurrency difficult to reason about.

Rather than have the developer struggle with this complexity, Node itself manages I/O threads, simplifying this complexity by demanding only that control flow be managed between events. There is a need to *micromanage* I/O threading; one simply designs an application to establish data availability points (callbacks) and the instructions to be executed once the said data is available. A single stream of instructions that explicitly takes and relinquishes control in a clear, collision-free, and predictable way aids development:

- Instead of concerning themselves with arbitrary locking and other collisions, developers can focus on constructing execution chains, the ordering of which is predictable.

- Parallelization is accomplished through the use of multiple processes, each with an individual and distinct memory space, due to which communication between processes remains uncomplicated—via the *Rule of Simplicity*, we achieve not only simple and bug-free components, but also easier interoperability.

- The state is not (arbitrarily) shared between individual Node processes. A single process is automatically protected from surprise visits from other processes bent on memory reallocation or resource monopolization. Communication is through clear channels using basic protocols, all of which make it very hard to write programs that make unpredictable changes across processes.

- Thread safety is one less concern for developers to waste time worrying about. Because single-threaded concurrency obviates the collisions present in multithreaded concurrency, development can proceed more quickly and on surer ground.

A single thread describing asynchronous control flow efficiently managed by an event loop brings stability, maintainability, readability, and resilience to Node programs. The big news is that Node continues to deliver the speed and power of multithreading to its developers—the brilliance of Node's design makes such power transparent, reflecting one part of Node's stated aim of bringing the most power to the most people with the least difficulty.

Events

Many JavaScript extensions in Node emit events. These are instances of `events.EventEmitter`. Any object can extend `EventEmitter`, which gives the developer an elegant toolkit to build tight, asynchronous interfaces to their object methods.

Work through this example demonstrating how to set an `EventEmitter` object as the prototype of a function constructor. As each constructed instance now has the `EventEmitter` object exposed to its prototype chain, `this` provides a natural reference to the event's **Application Programming Interface (API)**. The `counter` instance methods can, therefore, emit events, and these can be listened for. Here, we emit the latest count whenever the `counter.increment` method is called and bind a callback to the "incremented" event, which simply prints the current counter value to the command line:

```
var EventEmitter = require('events').EventEmitter;
var util = require('util');

var Counter = function(init) {
  this.increment = function() {
    init++;
    this.emit('incremented', init);
  }
}

util.inherits(Counter, EventEmitter);

var counter = new Counter(10);

var callback = function(count) {
  console.log(count);
}
counter.addListener('incremented', callback);

counter.increment(); // 11
counter.increment(); // 12
```

Downloading the example code

You can download the example code files for all Packt books you have purchased from your account at http://www.packtpub.com. If you purchased this book elsewhere, you can visit http://www.packtpub.com/support and register to have the files e-mailed directly to you.

To remove the event listeners bound to `counter`, use `counter.removeListener('incremented', callback)`.

`EventEmitter`, as an extensible object, adds to the expressiveness of JavaScript. For example, it allows I/O data streams to be handled in an event-oriented manner in keeping with Node's principle of asynchronous, nonblocking programming:

```
var stream = require('stream');
var Readable = stream.Readable;
var util = require('util');

var Reader = function() {
  Readable.call(this);
  this.counter = 0;
}

util.inherits(Reader, Readable);

Reader.prototype._read = function() {
  if(++this.counter > 10) {
    return this.push(null);
  }
  this.push(this.counter.toString());
};

// When a #data event occurs, display the chunk.
//
var reader = new Reader();
reader.setEncoding('utf8');
reader.on('data', function(chunk) {
  console.log(chunk);
});
reader.on('end', function() {
  console.log('--finished--');
});
```

In this program, we have a `Readable` stream pushing out a set of numbers—with listeners on that stream's data event catching numbers as they are emitted and logging them—and finishing with a message when the stream has ended. It is plain that the listener is called once per number, which means that running this set did not block the event loop. Because Node's event loop need only commit resources to handling callbacks, many other instructions can be processed in the downtime of each event.

The event loop

The code seen in non-networked software is often synchronous or blocking. I/O operations in the following pseudo-code are also blocking:

```
variable = produceAValue()
print variable
// some value is output when #produceAValue is finished.
```

The following iterator will read one file at a time, dump its contents, and then read the next until it is done:

```
fileNames = ['a','b','c']
while(filename = fileNames.shift()) {
  fileContents = File.read(filename)
  print fileContents
}
// > a
// > b
// > c
```

This is a fine model for many cases. However, what if these files are very large? If each takes 1 second to fetch, all will take 3 seconds to fetch. The retrieval on one file is always waiting on another retrieval to finish, which is inefficient and slow. Using Node, we can initiate file reads on all files simultaneously:

```
var fs = require('fs');
var fileNames = ['a','b','c'];
fileNames.forEach(function(filename) {
  fs.readFile(filename, {encoding:'utf8'}, function(err, content)
    {
    console.log(content);
  });
});
// > b
// > a
// > c
```

The Node version will read all three files at once, each call to `fs.readFile` returning its result at some unknowable point in the future. This is why we can't always expect the files to be returned in the order they were arrayed. We can expect that all three will be returned in roughly the time it took for one to be retrieved—something less than 3 seconds. We have traded a predictable execution order for speed, and, as with threads, achieving synchronization in concurrent environments requires extra work. How do we manage and describe unpredictable data events so that our code is both easy to understand *and* efficient?

The key design choice made by Node's designers was the implementation of an event loop as a concurrency manager. The following description of event-driven programming (taken from http://www.princeton.edu/~achaney/tmve/wiki100k/docs/Event-driven_programming.html) clearly not only describes the event-driven paradigm, but also introduces us to how events are handled in Node and how JavaScript is an ideal language for such a paradigm:

> *"In computer programming, event-driven programming or event-based programming is a programming paradigm in which the flow of the program is determined by events — that is, sensor outputs or user actions (mouse clicks, key presses) or messages from other programs or threads.*
>
> *Event-driven programming can also be defined as an application architecture technique in which the application has a main loop that is clearly divided down to two sections: the first is event selection (or event detection), and the second is event handling [...]*
>
> *Event-driven programs can be written in any language although the task is easier in languages that provide high-level abstractions, such as closures."*

As we've seen in the preceding quote, single-threaded execution environments block and can, therefore, run slowly. V8 provides a single thread of execution for JavaScript programs.

How can this single thread be made more efficient?

Node makes a single thread more efficient by delegating many blocking operations to OS subsystems to process, bothering the main V8 thread only when there is data available for use. The main thread (your executing Node program) expresses interest in some data (such as via fs.readFile) by passing a callback and is notified when that data is available. Until that data arrives, no further burden is placed on V8's main JavaScript thread. How? Node delegates I/O work to **libuv**, as quoted at http://nikhilm.github.io/uvbook/basics.html#event-loops:

> *"In event-driven programming, an application expresses interest in certain events and responds to them when they occur. The responsibility of gathering events from the operating system or monitoring other sources of events is handled by libuv, and the user can register callbacks to be invoked when an event occurs."*

The user in the preceding quote is the Node process executing a JavaScript program. *Callbacks* are JavaScript functions, and managing callback invocation for the user is accomplished by Node's event loop. Node manages a queue of I/O requests populated by libuv, which is responsible for polling the OS for I/O data events and handing off the results to JavaScript callbacks.

Consider the following code:

```
var fs = require('fs');
fs.readFile('foo.js', {encoding:'utf8'}, function(err,
  fileContents) {
  console.log('Then the contents are available', fileContents);
});
console.log('This happens first');
```

This program will result in the following output:

```
> This happens first
> Then the contents are available, [file contents shown]
```

Here's what Node does when executing this program:

- Node loads the `fs` module. This provides access to `fs.binding`, which is *a static type map defined in src/node.cc that provides glue between C++ and JS code.* (`https://groups.google.com/forum/#!msg/nodejs/R5fDzBr0eEk/lrCKaJX_6vIJ`).

- The `fs.readFile` method is passed instructions and a JavaScript callback. Through `fs.binding`, libuv is notified of the file read request and is passed a specially prepared version of the callback sent by the original program.

- libuv invokes the OS-level functions necessary to read a file within its own thread pool.

- The JavaScript program continues, printing `This happens first`. Because there is a callback outstanding, the event loop continues to spin, waiting for that callback to resolve.

- When the file descriptor has been fully read by the OS, libuv (via internal mechanisms) is informed and the callback passed to libuv is invoked, which essentially prepares the original JavaScript callback for re-entrance into the main (V8) thread.

- The original JavaScript callback is pushed onto the event loop queue and is invoked on the next tick of the loop.

- The file contents are printed to the console.

- As there are no further callbacks in flight, the process exits.

Here, we see the key ideas that Node implements to achieve fast, manageable, and scalable I/O. If, for example, there were 10 read calls made for 'foo.js' in the preceding program, the execution time would, nevertheless, remain roughly the same. Each call would have been made *in parallel* in its *own thread* within the libuv thread pool. Even though we wrote our code "in JavaScript", we are actually deploying a very efficient multithreaded execution engine *while avoiding the difficulties of thread management.*

Let's close with more details on how exactly libuv results are returned into the main thread's event loop.

When data becomes available on a socket or other stream interface, we cannot simply execute our callback immediately. JavaScript is single threaded, so results must be synchronized. We can't suddenly change the state in the middle of an event loop tick — this would create some of the classic multithreaded application problems of race conditions, memory access conflicts, and so on.

Upon entering an event loop, Node (in effect) makes a copy of the current instruction queue (also known as **stack**), empties the original queue, and executes its copy. The processing of this instruction queue is referred to as a *tick*. If libuv, asynchronously, receives results while the chain of instructions copied at the start of this tick are being processed on the single main thread (V8), these results (wrapped as callbacks) are queued. Once the current queue is emptied and its last instruction has completed, the queue is again checked for instructions to execute *on the next tick*. This pattern of checking and executing the queue will repeat (loop) until the queue is emptied, and no further data events are expected, at which point the Node process exits.

> This discussion at `https://github.com/joyent/node/issues/5798` among some core Node developers about the `process.nextTick` and `setImmediate` implementations offers very precise information on how the event loop operates.

The following are the sorts of I/O events fed into the queue:

- **Execution blocks**: These are blocks of JavaScript code comprising the Node program; they could be expressions, loops, functions, and so on. This includes `EventEmitter` events emitted within the current execution context.

- **Timers**: These are callbacks deferred to a time in the future specified in milliseconds, such as `setTimeout` and `setInterval`.

- **I/O**: These are prepared callbacks returned to the main thread after being delegated to Node's managed thread pool, such as filesystem calls and network listeners.

- **Deferred execution blocks**: These are mainly the functions slotted on the stack according to the rules of `setImmediate` and `process.nextTick`.

There are two important things to remember:

- You don't start and/or stop the event loop. The event loop starts as soon as a process starts and ends when no further callbacks remain to be performed. The event loop may, therefore, run forever.
- The event loop executes on a single thread but delegates I/O operations to libuv, which manages a thread pool that parallelizes these operations, notifying the event loop when results are available. An easy-to-reason-about single-threaded programming model is reinforced with the efficiency of multithreading.

To learn more about how Node is bound to libuv and other core libraries, parse through the `fs` module code at `https://github.com/joyent/node/blob/master/lib/fs.js`. Compare the `fs.read` and the `fs.readSync` methods to observe the difference between how synchronous and asynchronous actions are implemented—note the `wrapper` callback that is passed to the native `binding.read` method in `fs.read`.

To take an even deeper dive into the very heart of Node's design, including the queue implementation, read through the Node source at `https://github.com/joyent/node/tree/master/src`. Follow `MakeCallback` within `fs_event_wrap.cc` and `node.cc`. Investigate the `req_wrap` class, a wrapper for the V8 engine, deployed in `node_file.cc` and elsewhere and defined in `req_wrap.h`.

The implications of Node's design on system architects

Node is a new technology. At the time of writing this, it has yet to reach its 1.0 version. Security flaws have been found and fixed. Memory leaks have been found and fixed. Eran Hammer, mentioned at the beginning of this chapter, and his entire team at Walmart Labs actively contribute to the Node codebase—in particular when they find flaws! This is true of many other large companies committed to Node, such as PayPal.

If you have chosen Node, and your application has grown to such a size that you feel you need to read a book on how to deploy Node, you have the opportunity to not only benefit from the community, but have a part, perhaps, in literally designing aspects of the environment based on your particular needs. Node is open source, and you can submit pull requests.

In addition to events, there are two key design aspects that are important to understand if you are going to do advanced Node work: build your systems out of small parts and use evented streams when piping data between them.

Building large systems out of small systems

In his book, *The Art of Unix Programming*, Eric Raymond proposed the **Rule of Modularity**:

> *"Developers should build a program out of simple parts connected by well-defined interfaces, so problems are local, and parts of the program can be replaced in future versions to support new features. This rule aims to save time on debugging complex code that is complex, long, and unreadable."*

This idea of building complex systems out of "small pieces, loosely joined" is seen in management theory, theories of government, manufacturing, and many other contexts. In terms of software development, it advises developers to contribute only the simplest, most useful component necessary within a larger system. Large systems are hard to reason about, especially if the boundaries of their components are fuzzy.

One of the primary difficulties when constructing scalable JavaScript programs is the lack of a standard interface to assemble a coherent program out of many smaller ones. For example, a typical web application might load dependencies using a sequence of <script> tags in the <head> section of a **HyperText Markup Language (HTML)** document:

```
<head>
  <script src="fileA.js"></script>
  <script src="fileB.js"></script>
</head>
```

There are many problems with this sort of system:

- All potential dependencies must be declared prior to their being needed—dynamic inclusion requires complicated *hacks*.

- The introduced scripts are not forcibly encapsulated—nothing stops both files from writing to the same global object. Namespaces can easily collide, which makes arbitrary injection dangerous.

- fileA cannot address fileB as a collection—an addressable context, such as fileB.method, isn't available.

- The <script> method itself isn't systematic, precluding the design of useful module services, such as dependency awareness and version control.

- Scripts cannot be easily removed or overridden.

- Because of these dangers and difficulties, sharing is not effortless, thus diminishing opportunities for collaboration in an open ecosystem.

Ambivalently inserting unpredictable code fragments into an application frustrates attempts to predictably shape functionality. What is needed is a standard way to load and share discreet program modules.

Accordingly, Node introduced the concept of the **package**, following the CommonJS specification. A package is a collection of program files bundled with a manifest file describing the collection. Dependencies, authorship, purpose, structure, and other important metadata is exposed in a standard way. This encourages the construction of large systems from many small, interdependent systems. Perhaps, even more importantly, it encourages sharing:

> *"What I'm describing here is not a technical problem. It's a matter of people getting together and making a decision to step forward and start building up something bigger and cooler together."*

> *– Kevin Dangoor, creator of CommonJS*

In many ways, the success of Node is due to the growth in the number and quality of packages available to the developer community that are distributed via Node's package management system, **npm**. This system has done much to help make JavaScript a viable, professional option for systems programming.

 A good introduction to npm for anyone new to Node can be found at: https://www.npmjs.org/doc/developers.html.

Streams

In his book, *The C++ Programming Language, Third Edition*, Bjarne Stoustrup states:

> *"Designing and implementing a general input/output facility for a programming language is notoriously difficult. [...] An I/O facility should be easy, convenient, and safe to use; efficient and flexible; and, above all, complete."*

It shouldn't surprise anyone that a design team focused on providing efficient and easy I/O has delivered such a facility through Node. Through a symmetrical and simple interface, which handles data buffers and stream events so that the implementer does not have to, Node's `Stream` module is the preferred way to manage asynchronous data streams for both internal modules and, hopefully, for the modules that developers will create.

An excellent tutorial on the `Stream` module can be found at
`https://github.com/substack/stream-handbook`. Also, the
Node documentation is comprehensive at `http://nodejs.org/`
`api/stream.html`.

A stream in Node is simply a sequence of bytes or, if you like, a sequence of
characters. At any time, a stream contains a buffer of bytes, and this buffer has a
length of zero or more.

Because each character in a stream is well defined, and because every type of digital
data can be expressed in bytes, any part of a stream can be redirected, or *piped*, to any
other stream, different chunks of the stream can be sent to different handlers. In this
way, stream input and output interfaces are both flexible and predictable and can be
easily coupled.

In addition to events, Node is distinctive for its comprehensive use of streams.
Continuing the idea of composing applications out of many small processes
emitting events or reacting to events, several Node I/O modules and features are
implemented as streams. Network sockets, file readers and writers, stdin and stdout,
Zlib, and so on, are all data producers and/or consumers that are easily connected
through the abstract `Stream` interface. Those familiar with Unix pipes will see some
similarities.

Five distinct base classes are exposed via the abstract `Stream` interface: `Readable`,
`Writable`, `Duplex`, `Transform`, and `PassThrough`. Each base class inherits from
`EventEmitter`, which we know to be an interface to which event listeners and
emitters can be bound. Streams in Node are evented streams, and sending data
between processes is commonly done using streams. Because streams can be
easily chained and otherwise combined, they are fundamental tools for the Node
developer.

It is recommended that you develop a clear understanding of what streams are and
how they are implemented in Node before going further as we will use streams
extensively throughout this book.

Using full-stack JavaScript to maximum effect

JavaScript has become a full-stack language. A native JavaScript runtime exists in all browsers. V8, the JavaScript interpreter used by Node, is the same engine powering Google's Chrome browser. And the language has gone even further than covering both the client and server layers of the software stack. JavaScript is used to query the CouchDB database, do map/reduce with MongoDB, and find data in ElasticSearch collections. The wildly popular **JavaScript Object Notation (JSON)** data format simply represents data as a JavaScript object.

When different languages are used within the same application, the cost of *context switching* goes up. If a system is composed of parts described in different languages, the system architecture becomes more difficult to describe, understand, and extend. If different parts of a system *speak* differently, every cross-dialect conversation will require expensive translation.

Inefficiencies in comprehension lead to larger costs and more brittle systems. The members of the engineering team for this system must each be fluent in these many languages or be grouped by different skill sets; engineers are expensive to find and/ or train. When the inner workings of significant parts of a system become opaque to all but a few engineers, it is likely that cross-team collaboration will decrease, making product upgrades and additions more difficult and likely leading to more errors.

What new opportunities open up when these difficulties are reduced or eliminated?

Hot code

Because your clients and servers will speak the same language, each can pass code to be natively executed on the other. If you are building a web application, this opens up very interesting (and unique) opportunities.

For example, consider an application that allows one client to make changes to another's environment. This tool allows a software developer to make changes to the JavaScript powering a website and allows their clients to see those changes in real time in their browsers. What this application must do is transform live code in many browsers so that it reflects changes. One way to do this would be to capture a change set into a transform function, pass that function across to all connected clients, and have that function executed in their local environment, updating it to reflect the *canonical* view. One application evolves, it emits a *genetic* update in the code of JavaScript, and the rest of its species similarly evolves. We will use one such technology in *Chapter 7, Deploying and Maintaining*.

Since Node shares the same JavaScript code base, a Node server, on its own initiative, can take this action. The network itself can broadcast code for its clients to execute. Similarly, clients can send code to the server for execution. It is easy to see how this allows hot code pushes, where a Node process sends a unique packet of raw JavaScript to specific clients for execution.

When **Remote Procedure Calls (RPC)** no longer require a broker layer to translate between communicating contexts, code can exist anywhere in the network for as long or as brief a period as necessary and can execute in multiple contexts, which are chosen for reasons of load balancing, data awareness, computational power, geographic precision, and so on.

Browserify

JavaScript is the language common to Node and the browser. However, Node significantly extends the JavaScript language, adding many commands and other constructs that are not available to the client-side developer. For example, there is no equivalent of the core Node `stream` module in JavaScript.

Additionally, the npm repository is rapidly growing, and, at the time of writing, contains more than 80,000 Node packages. Many of these packages are equally useful on the client as well as within Node. The spread of JavaScript to the server has, in effect, created two cooperating threads producing enterprise-grade JavaScript libraries and modules.

Browserify was developed to make it easy to share **npm** modules and core Node modules seamlessly with the client. Once a package has been *browserified*, it is easily imported into a browser environment using the standard `<script>` tag. Installing Browserify is simple:

```
npm install -g browserify
```

Let's build an example. Create a file, `math.js`, written as you would write an npm module:

```
module.exports = function() {
  this.add = function(a, b) {
    return a + b;
  }
  this.subtract = function(a, b) {
    return a - b;
  }
};
```

Next, create a program file, `add.js`, that uses this module:

```
var Math = require('./math.js');
var math = new Math;

console.log(math.add(1,3)); // 4
```

Executing this program using Node on the command line (`> node add.js`) will result in 4 being printed to your terminal. What if we wanted to use our math module in the browser? Client-side JavaScript doesn't have a `require` statement, so we browserify it:

browserify math.js -o bundle.js

Browserify walks through your code, finding `require` statements and automatically bundling those dependencies (and the dependencies of those dependencies) into one file that you load into your client application:

```
<script src="bundle.js"></script>
```

As an added bonus, this bundle automatically introduces some useful Node globals to your browser environment: `__filename`, `__dirname`, `process`, `Buffer`, and `global`. This means you have, for example, `process.nextTick` available in the browser.

> The creator of Browserify, James Halliday, is a prolific contributor to the Node community. Visit him at `https://github.com/substack`. Also, there exists an online service for testing out browserified npm modules at http://requirebin.com. The full documentation can be found at `https://github.com/substack/node-browserify#usage`.
>
> Another exciting project that, like Browserify, leverages Node to enhance the JavaScript available to browser-based JavaScript is **Component**. The authors describe it this way: *Component is currently a stopgap for ES6 modules and Web Components. When all modern browsers start supporting these features, Component will begin focusing more on semantic versioning and server-side bundling as browsers would be able to handle the rest.* The project is still in flux but worth a look. Here's the link: `https://github.com/componentjs/guide`.

Summary

In this chapter, we went on a whirlwind tour of Node. You learned something about why it is designed the way it is and why this event-driven environment is a good solution to modern problems in networked software. Having explained the event loop and the related ideas around concurrency and parallelism, we talked a bit about the Node philosophy of composing software from *small pieces loosely joined*. You learned about the special advantages that full-stack JavaScript provides and explored new possibilities of applications made possible because of them.

You now have a good understanding of the kind of applications we will be deploying, and this understanding will help you see the unique concerns and considerations faced when building and maintaining Node applications. In the next chapter, we'll dive right in with building servers with Node, options for hosting these applications, and ideas around building, packaging, and distributing them.

2
Installing and Virtualizing Node Servers

Recall the story from *Chapter 1*, *Appreciating Node*, about how Walmart ran all of its *Black Friday* mobile traffic through Node, which was deployed across *the equivalent of 2 CPUs and 30 gigs of RAM*. This demonstrates that Node processes I/O so efficiently that even Walmart-level traffic on *Black Friday* can be handled with only a few servers. This means that, for many people, running your Node application on a single server is all you'll ever need to do.

Nevertheless, it is often good to have several servers at your disposal, such as redundant servers to ensure failover recovery, a distinct database server, specialized media servers, one hosting a message queue, and so on. In keeping with the idea of separating concerns into many independent processes, Node-based applications are often composed of many lightweight servers spread across a data center, possibly even spread across several data centers.

In this chapter, we will look at the basics of setting up single Node servers concretely and virtually. The goal is to explore your options for *mass producing* servers in response to scaling needs and to see how you can connect these together. You will learn how to set up an HTTP/S server yourself as well as how to do tunneling and proxying with Node. We'll then look at a few popular cloud-hosting solutions and how to set up Node servers on those. We'll close with a discussion on **Docker**, an exciting new technology to create lightweight virtual services.

Getting a basic Node server up and running

HTTP is a data transfer protocol built upon a request/response model. Normally, a client makes a request to a server, receives a response, makes another request, and so on. HTTP is stateless, which simply means that each request or response maintains no information on previous requests or responses. Facilitating this sort of rapid-pattern network communication is the sort of I/O that Node is designed to excel at. While Node represents a much more interesting technology stack overall, it does help engineers in creating networked protocol servers. In this section, we will move through a general overview of how to set up a basic HTTP server and then into a few more specialized uses of the protocol.

Hello world

An HTTP server responds to connection attempts and manages data as it arrives and as it is sent along. A Node server is typically created using the `createServer` method of the HTTP module:

```
var http = require('http');

var server = http.createServer(function(request, response) {
  console.log('Got Request Headers: ');
  console.log(request.headers);
  response.writeHead(200, {
    'Content-Type': 'text/plain'
  });
  response.write('PONG');
  response.end();
}).listen(8080);
```

The object returned by `http.createServer` is an instance of `http.Server`, which extends `EventEmitter` and broadcasts network events as they occur, such as a client connection or request. Most server implementations using Node use this method of instantiation. However, listening for event broadcasts by an `http.Server` instance can be a more useful, even natural, way to organize server/client interactions within a Node program.

Here, we create a basic server that simply reports when a connection is made and when it is terminated:

```
var http = require('http');
var server = new http.Server();

server.on("connection", function(socket) {
  console.log("Client arrived: " + new Date());
  socket.on("end", function() {
    console.log("Client left: " + new Date());
  });
})

server.listen(8080);
```

When building multiuser systems, especially authenticated multiuser systems, this point in the server-client transaction is an excellent place for client validation and a tracking code. Cookies can be set and read, along with other session variables. A client arrival event can be broadcast to other concurrent clients interacting within real-time applications.

By adding a listener for requests, we arrive at the more common request/response pattern, handled as a `Readable` stream. When a client posts data, we can catch that data, as shown here:

```
server.on("request", function(request, response) {
  request.setEncoding("utf8");
  request.on("readable", function() {
    console.log(request.read())
  });
});
```

Send this server some data using **curl**:

```
curl http://localhost:8080 -d "Here is some data"
```

Using connection events, we can nicely separate our connection-handling code, grouping it into clearly defined functional domains, which are correctly described as executing in response to particular events.

For example, we can set timers on server connections. Here, we can terminate client connections that fail to send new data within a roughly 2-second window:

```
server.setTimeout(2000, function(socket) {
  socket.write("Too Slow!", "utf8");
  socket.end();
});
```

Making HTTP requests

HTTP servers are often called upon to perform HTTP services for clients making requests. Most commonly, this sort of proxying was done on behalf of web applications running in browsers with restrictions on cross-domain requests. Node provides an easy interface to make external HTTP calls.

For example, the following code will fetch the front page of google.com:

```
var http = require('http');

http.request({
  host: 'www.google.com',
  method: 'GET',
  path: "/"
}, function(response) {
  response.setEncoding('utf8');
  response.on('readable', function() {
    console.log(response.read())
  });
}).end();
```

Here, we simply dump a Readable stream to the terminal, but this stream could easily be piped to a Writable stream, perhaps bound to a file handle. Note that you must always signify that you're done with a request using the request.end method.

A popular Node module to manage HTTP requests is Mikeal Rogers' **request**:

https://github.com/mikeal/request

Because it is common to use `HTTP.request` in order to GET external pages, Node offers a shortcut:

```
http.get("http://www.google.com/", function(response) {
  console.log("Status: " + response.statusCode);
}).on('error', function(err) {
  console.log("Error: " + err.message);
});
```

Let's now look at a few more advanced implementations of HTTP servers, where we perform general network services for clients.

Proxying and tunneling

Sometimes, it is useful to provide a means for one server to function as a proxy, or broker, for other servers. This would allow one server to distribute requests to other servers, for example. Another use would be to provide access to a secured server to users who are unable to connect to that server directly—this is often seen in countries that place restrictions on Internet access. It is also common to have one server answering for more than one URL using a proxy; that one server can forward requests to the right recipient.

Because Node has consistent network interfaces implemented as evented streams, we can build a simple HTTP proxy in just a few lines of code. For example, the following program will set up an HTTP server on port `8080`, which will respond to any request by fetching the front page of Google and piping that back to the client:

```
var http = require('http');
var server = new http.Server();

server.on("request", function(request, socket) {
  http.request({
    host: 'www.google.com',
    method: 'GET',
    path: "/",
    port: 80
  }, function(response) {
    response.pipe(socket);
  }).end();
});

server.listen(8080);
```

Once this server receives the client socket, it is free to push content from any readable stream back to the client. Here, the result of the GET of www.google.com is so streamed. One can easily see how an external content server managing a caching layer for your application might become a proxy endpoint.

Using similar ideas, we can create a tunneling service using Node's native CONNECT support:

```
var http = require('http');
var net = require('net');
var url = require('url');
var proxy = new http.Server();

proxy.on('connect', function(request, clientSocket, head) {
  var reqData = url.parse('http://' + request.url);
  var remoteSocket = net.connect(reqData.port, reqData.hostname,
    function() {
    clientSocket.write('HTTP/1.1 200 \r\n\r\n');
    remoteSocket.write(head);

    // The bi-directional tunnel
    remoteSocket.pipe(clientSocket);
    clientSocket.pipe(remoteSocket);
  });
}).listen(8080, function() {
```

We've set up a proxy server that responds to clients requesting an HTTP CONNECT method [on("connect")], which contains the request object, the network socket-binding client and server, and the 'head' (the first packet) of the tunneling stream. When a CONNECT request is received from a client, we parse out request.url, fetch the requested host information, and open the requested network socket. By piping remote data to the client and client data to the remote connection, a bidirectional data tunnel is established. Now we need only make the CONNECT request to our proxy, as follows:

```
var request = http.request({
  port: 8080,
  hostname: 'localhost',
  method: 'CONNECT',
  path: 'www.google.com:80'
});
request.end();
```

Once a status 200 confirmation of our CONNECT request is received, we can push request packets down this tunnel, catching responses and dumping those to `stdout`:

```
request.on('connect', function(res, socket, head) {
  socket.setEncoding("utf8");
  socket.write('GET / HTTP/1.1\r\nHost:
    www.google.com:80\r\nConnection: close\r\n\r\n');
  socket.on('readable', function() {
    console.log(socket.read());
  });
  socket.on('end', function() {
    proxy.close();
  });
});
});
```

HTTPS, TLS (SSL), and securing your server

Web applications have grown in size, importance, and complexity. The security of web applications has, therefore, become an important topic. For one reason or another, early web applications were allowed to venture into the experimental world of client-side business logic, unsecured password transmission, and open web services while shielded by only a diaphanous curtain. This is becoming harder to find among users interested in the security of their information.

As Node is regularly deployed as a web server, it is imperative that the community begins to accept responsibility for securing these servers. HTTPS is a secure transmission protocol—essentially, encrypted HTTP formed by layering the HTTP protocol on top of the SSL/TLS protocol. Let's learn how to secure our Node deployments.

Creating a self-signed certificate for development

In order to support SSL connections, a server will need a properly signed certificate. While developing, it is much easier to simply create a self-signed certificate, allowing us to use Node's HTTPS module.

These are the steps needed to create a certificate for development. Remember that this process does not create a real certificate, and the generated certificate is *not secure*—it simply allows us to develop within an HTTPS environment from a terminal:

```
openssl genrsa -out server-key.pem 2048

openssl req -new -key server-key.pem -out server-csr.pem

openssl x509 -req -in server-csr.pem -signkey server-key.pem -out server-cert.pem
```

These keys can now be used to develop HTTPS servers. The contents of these files need simply be passed along as options to a Node server running on the (default) SSL port 443:

```
var https = require('https');
var fs = require('fs');

https.createServer({
  key: fs.readFileSync('server-key.pem'),
  cert: fs.readFileSync('server-cert.pem')
}, function(req,res) {
  ...
}).listen(443)
```

 Free **low-assurance** SSL certificates are available from http://www.startssl.com/ for cases where self-signed certificates are not ideal during development.

Installing a real SSL certificate

In order to move a secure application out of a development environment and into an Internet-exposed environment, a real certificate will need to be purchased. The prices of these certificates have been dropping year by year, and it should be easy to find providers of reasonably priced certificates with a high enough level of security. Some providers even offer free personal-use certificates.

Setting up a professional certificate simply requires changing the HTTPS options we introduced previously. Different providers will have different processes and filenames. Typically, you will need to download or, otherwise, receive a private #key file from your provider, your signed domain certificate #crt file, and a general bundle #ca describing certificate chains:

```
var options = {
  key  : fs.readFileSync('mysite.key'),
  cert : fs.readFileSync('mysite.com.crt'),
  ca   : [ fs.readFileSync('gd_bundle.crt') ]
};
```

It is important to note that the #ca parameter must be sent as an *array* even if the bundle of certificates has been concatenated into one file.

Here are the key takeaways of this:

- HTTP sockets are abstracted into evented streams. This is true for all network interfaces provided by Node. These streams can easily be connected to one another.

- Because stream activity is evented, those events can be recorded. Very precise logging information on the behavior of a system can be recorded either in event handlers or by piping streams through a `PassThrough Stream` parameter that might listen for and record events.

- Node excels as an I/O service. Node servers can act as dispatchers solely interested in brokering communication between a client and any number of remote services or even specialized processes running on a local OS.

Now that you know how to set up an HTTP server and work with the protocol within Node, go ahead and experiment. Create a small application on your local machine that allows users to read a Twitter feed or connect to a public data API. Get used to authenticating remote services over the wire and interacting with them either through their API or by otherwise acting as a proxy for their data. Get used to composing network applications by integrating remote network services using Node as a broker.

Running your own servers in production can be expensive and time consuming, especially if you aren't familiar with systems administration. For this reason, a large number of cloud-hosting companies have sprung up and many are designed specifically for the Node developer.

Let's take a look at a few of them. By way of comparison, the same Node application will be deployed on each—an editable JSON document stored in **MongoDB** bound to a simple browser-based **User Interface (UI)**. You are encouraged to try these services out in order, which is not necessary though.

Installing applications on Heroku

Heroku is a mature PaaS cloud-hosting solution that supports the development of Node applications. To get started, visit `http://www.heroku.com` and submit an e-mail address. Heroku is free to start with. After you've confirmed your account, you can start deploying apps right away.

Scaling Heroku applications involves increasing the number of *dynos* that you are paying for. Each **dyno** is an isolated container running your application and you are able to increase or decrease the number of dynos your application uses with ease. In this way, there aren't any hosting *packages* to buy—you simply scale as needed by asking for more, or fewer, dynos.

Heroku allows you to deploy applications on many platforms and languages—it is not Node-centric. This is something to keep in mind should you anticipate the need to add services to your application not written in Node.

To control Heroku remote instances, you will use a local *utility belt* application. Once you've joined Heroku and confirmed your signup, log in and go to the **Apps** section of your dashboard. There should be instructions there on installing Heroku Toolbelt (`https://toolbelt.heroku.com/`).

 The `heroku` command-line client will be installed in `/usr/local/heroku` and `/usr/local/heroku/bin` will be added to your path.

Once you have Toolbelt installed, open a terminal and log in to Heroku with `heroku login`. Since this is your first time, you will most likely be asked to generate a public key. Once this key is generated and uploaded, you are secure, and, going forward, you can administer your Heroku deployments via Toolbelt and the command line.

Heroku recognizes your application as a Node application if it finds a `package.json` file in the root directory of your application folder. Our sample app already contains one, so there is no need to create another. However, as Heroku is not an exclusive Node host, it does not automatically find the start script for our -- `server.js` -- application at the `start` attribute of that package file:

```
"scripts": {
  "start": "node server.js"
}
```

Instead, Heroku requires what is called **Procfile**. Create a `Procfile` file in the root directory of our sample application and insert the following text into it:

```
web: node server.js
```

It's slightly different, but we can see that the effect is ultimately the same. Procfile declares that we want a "web" process—the process that will be spun up after the command `node server.js` is executed will expect to have HTTP traffic routed to it.

When you installed Heroku Toolbelt, another application was also installed: **Foreman**. Foreman helps you manage Procfile-based applications. Its primary importance for us is that it allows you to start Heroku applications locally. While you can simply update the `scripts` attribute of your Node package and run your application directly through Node, it does save a step. Try `foreman start` and visit `localhost:8080`.

In the following sections, we will look at how a repository is installed and managed on Heroku, and how to add to our applications on MongoDB, and we'll deploy a JSON editing application.

Add-ons

On Heroku, databases are understood as one of many add-ons. From logging tools, to caching layers, to databases, Heroku offers dozens of add-ons. Since we need a MongoDB instance to run our application, let's install one.

Note that, while a developer (sandbox) MongoDB instance from MongoLab is free, Heroku requires you to verify your account with a credit card. If you don't have a credit card, it is still possible to get a free MongoDB cloud account through other services and use those credentials for your Heroku application. In the end, we simply need a MongoDB endpoint somewhere to connect to.

To add a MongoDB account, run the `heroku addons:add mongolab` command:

```
Adding mongolab on mighty-hamlet-7855... done, v14 (free)
Welcome to MongoLab. Your new subscription is being created and will be
available shortly. Please consult the MongoLab Add-on Admin UI to check
on its progress.
```

Use `heroku addons:docs mongolab` to view documentation in your browser.

You just added a configuration option to your Heroku instance. Not surprisingly, you can view this information via `heroku config`, which will return you something like this:

```
MONGOLAB_URI: mongodb://heroku_app2485743:ie02k3nnic3l0tjfgi3135inq@
ds035488.mongolab.com:35488/heroku_app2487483
```

With our database established, let's now push our application into Heroku and get it running.

Git

Deploying applications on Heroku involves pushing your local version into the remote application repository you just provisioned. There is no `heroku deploy` command; what you do is push to **Git**, thus triggering post-receive hooks at Heroku's end. These deploy your app.

 If you're unfamiliar with Git, visit `http://git-scm.com/book/en/Getting-Started-Git-Basics`.

Let's try it out. Within your code bundle, there exists a `json-editor` folder. First, enter that folder and update the MongoDB connection and authentication code in `server.js` so that we can use the database connection defined earlier:

```
var mongodb = require('mongodb');
var db = new mongodb.Db('your_db_identifier',
  new mongodb.Server('dt019963.mongolab.com', 29960, {})
);
db.open(function (err, db_p) {
  if (err) { throw err; }
  db.authenticate('your_username', '6i490i5d3teoen62524vqkccgu',
    function (err, replies) {
    // You are now connected and authenticated.
  });
});
```

Next, run the following commands in your terminal:

```
git init
git add .
git commit -m "initial commit"
```

This initializes our application as a proper Git repository. Now, we need to inform Heroku of our new application and our new Git repository. Let's deploy.

From within the `json-editor` folder of your code bundle, use Heroku Toolbelt to create your first Heroku app:

```
heroku create
```

If all goes well, you should see something like this in your terminal:

```
Creating mighty-hamlet-7855... done, stack is cedar
http://mighty-hamlet-7855.herokuapp.com/ | git@heroku.com:mighty-
hamlet-7855.git
Git remote heroku added
```

If you visit that URL immediately, you will receive an error message. We haven't pushed our repository, so there is nothing deployed, which means there is nothing to show. To deploy an application to Heroku, push your local Git repo:

```
git push heroku master
```

This should result in a lot of build output, clearly informing you of what is happening:

```
-----> Node.js app detected
-----> Requested node range: 0.10.x
...
-----> Building runtime environment
-----> Discovering process types
       Procfile declares types -> web
...
-----> Launching... done, v3
       http://mighty-hamlet-7855.herokuapp.com/ deployed to Heroku
```

Deploying to Heroku, therefore, naturally combines the actual container deployment with the application version management via Git. What is more, pushing changes on your Git repository to Heroku will automatically update a running application, allowing "hot" code refreshes. Being able to continuously deploy your application can be of great benefit in some circumstances, as we'll see in later chapters.

Before we begin, take note that the URL of your deployed app has no port number. Heroku automatically assigns a port through which the web process communicates with your application—this is not in our control. However, it is made available to your Node process via `process.env.PORT`. For this reason, you will need to change the `}).listen(8081);` line in `server.js` to `}).listen(process.env.PORT || 8081);`.

We are now ready to start up our application. Remember that we are deploying a Procfile-based application—processes are defined as being of a certain type. In our case, that type is "web". We also need to assign dynos to our deployment—we need to requisition a process from Heroku to run our app within. The command to start up such an application is as follows:

```
heroku ps:scale web=1
```

This tells Heroku to give us one (1) dyno (also known as a process) of the *web type*. You could also ask for two, or more, depending on your needs.

Run that command. You should see something like the following:

```
Scaling dynos... done, now running web at 1:1X.
```

This tells us that everything is running fine and we have 1 dyno that is 1x in size handling our application. You can check that your process is running with the `heroku ps` command:

```
=== web (1X): `node server.js`
web.1: up 2014/04/04 17:40:34 (~ 27m ago)
```

Our application is running! Visit the Heroku URL you were given earlier. You should see a JSON editor and our MongoDB document:

This is a JSON editor reading the MongoDB document created on our server. It doesn't do much other than letting you change the value of the `for` attribute. If you look at the JavaScript code in `index.html`, you'll see that we've structured our client to send updates to the server via an `/update` path whenever values are changed in this document:

```
var editor = new jsoneditor.JSONEditor(container, {
  change : function() {
    var json = editor.get();

    var xhr = new XMLHttpRequest();
    xhr.open('POST', '/update', true);
    xhr.onload = function () {
      console.log("POST RESPONSE: ", this.responseText);
    };
    xhr.send('data=' + JSON.stringify(json));
  },
  mode : "form"
});
```

Try it out. Use the editor to change `Deploying NodeJS` to something else. If you open your browser's console, you should see **POST RESPONSE: OK** on each change you make to this value. After you've made a change, reload your browser. You'll see the new value—the changes you've made are being persisted on MongoDB via our Heroku instance.

Managing configuration variables

It is normal for certain aspects of an application to be configurable. For example, an application deployed for production will most likely be configured differently than one being built in a development environment. Also, authentication credentials (such as the one we are using for our MongoDB connection) will be included in environment variables.

As many configuration variables are sensitive, it is a bad idea to include them in an application repository or in a public file. How can variables be shared across multiple processes in a secure way? One solution is to pass environment variables when starting a Node process via the command line. If we wanted to inform a Node process that it should execute as a production server, for example, we can do something like this:

```
NODE_ENV=PRODUCTION node myprogram.js
```

Within that script, we can access the value via `process.env`:

```
console.log(process.env.NODE_ENV);
// production
```

While passing configuration variables in this way works very well in terms of privacy, it can be tedious to do this repeatedly for every process, especially if there are many variables.

Heroku provides an interface to help with managing environment variables. If you log in to your Heroku instance and visit the **Settings** section, you will see something like the following:

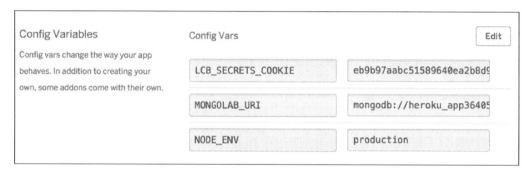

These environment variables will be passed to your application automatically when it is started and/or restarted. Using the **Edit** button, you can add or remove additional settings.

Managing your deployment

If your application crashes for any reason, `heroku ps` will indicate this. You also have access to your process logs via `heroku logs`. Just as when you are starting your process, stopping your process involves scaling your dynos down to zero:

```
heroku ps:scale web=0
```

Heroku allows you to very precisely scale and configure your process, scale to many dynos, add various workers, and change the size of the dynos themselves. In our example, we use the basic **1x** dyno, which has the smallest memory and compute power, and is the cheapest. For more information, visit `https://devcenter.heroku.com/articles/dyno-size` and `https://devcenter.heroku.com/articles/process-model`.

From time to time, you might commit a change that is incorrect or want to redeploy a previous release. Don't worry! Toolbelt allows you to manage your releases.

To list releases, use `heroku releases`:

```
v11 Deploy 310fe56  nataxia@gmail.com 2014/05/04 18:19:45 (~ 6m ago)
v10 Deploy a0c6005  nataxia@gmail.com 2014/05/04 18:15:17 (~ 10m ago)
...
```

You can get specific information on a release:

```
> heroku releases:info v11
=== Release v11
By:     spasquali@gmail.com
Change: Deploy 310fe56
When:   2014/04/04 18:19:45 (~ 8m ago)
```

Rolling back to the immediately previous version is accomplished with a simple Heroku rollback. You can also roll back to a specific release:

```
> heroku rollback v11
Rolling back mighty-hamlet-7855... done, v11
```

Just as when pushing changes, the version rolled back to will automatically "go live".

 You can open your application right from the command line with `heroku open`.

Installing applications on OpenShift

Red Hat, the enterprise Linux company, operates OpenShift, a cloud-hosting solution. OpenShift offers several options for how you want to deploy your apps—via a web-based interface, via the command line, or through an online IDE. As we've worked on the command line for our other deployment examples, we'll do the same with OpenShift.

Once you've joined and confirmed your account, you will need to install the OpenShift client tools—rhc. For the purposes of this section, I'll use the Mac OS X client. Regardless of which package you happen to choose, the command set remains the same:

```
sudo gem install rhc

gem update rhc
```

This will install the client and update it to the latest version.

Once installed, you will need to set up your SSH keys and authenticate with the system by running an rhc setup. Just enter your authentication information, confirm the installation of keys, and confirm the upload of credentials.

You will then be asked to enter a namespace. This will serve as your identifier in the system, among other things forming the subdomain of your deployed instance.

OpenShift works on the idea of **Gears** and **Cartridges**.

Gears are, roughly, containers with a certain allocation of compute units, memory, disk, bandwidth, and so on, with a given capacity of cartridges. Larger gears are more performant and (generally) can support a greater number of cartridges. You can think of your installation as a collection of managed runtimes (cartridges), fully isolated and deployed to one or more gears. As your application needs to grow, you will add gears and cartridges. When you add cartridges, the OpenShift system deploys your cartridge to the correct gear within your deployment—certain cartridges with access to only their own gear and others with access to all gears. Pricing depends on the number of gears used and, depending on the characteristic of those gears, the implied number of cartridge slots.

OpenShift supports many types of development environments, open source repositories, web frameworks, databases, and so on—a very rich ecosystem of tools, many more than are available in the providers we've looked at so far. You can even develop your own cartridges or use community cartridges.

The system makes it easy to dynamically scale your deployment in terms of gears, or cartridges, or both. The free tier we will use offers three small gears.

Installing a Node application and MongoDB

In the OpenShift ecosystem, Node is not a special citizen (as it is with NodeJitsu) or one of a fixed set of process types (as with Heroku). Because of the modularity that this concept of gears and cartridges offers, creating a sample Node application with access to a MongoDB instance can be accomplished in one line:

```
rhc app create MyApp nodejs-0.10 mongodb-2.4

Application Options

------------------

Domain:   <your namespace>

Cartridges: nodejs-0.10, mongodb-2.4

Gear Size: default

Scaling:  no


Creating application 'MyApp' ...

...

Your application 'myapp' is now available.


URL:     http://yoursub.rhcloud.com/

SSH to:   5366e4cc500446d15300022d@yoursub.rhcloud.com

Git remote: ssh://5366e4cc500446d15300022d@yoursub.rhcloud.com/~/git/
myapp.git/

Cloned to: /json_editor/myapp
```

As you can see, your deployment is powerfully configured, allowing SSH access and HTTP access, and is ready as a Git repo—if you look inside your json-editor folder, a new folder, `myapp/`, has been created. Go ahead and visit your URL. Full instructions on how to use Git are provided as well as how to access your application via other means.

We want to now replace this sample Node app with our own `json-editor` app.

Deploying your app

We, of course, do not want to use the sample app provided by OpenShift. Rather than reconfiguring, let's keep the `.git` remote configuration in `myapp/` and copy the following files and folders in our `json-editor/` folder into the `myapp` folder:

```
index.html
jsoneditor.css
jsoneditor.js
package.json
server.js
/img
```

These will overwrite any similar files that OpenShift created, while preserving the others. Make sure you have changed the directory to myapp/ as we'll be working from there from now on.

As we did when installing on Heroku, we will need to consult the `process.env` object when starting our Node server. Open `server.js` and go to this line:

```
}).listen(8081);
```

Now, change the line to the following:

```
}).listen(process.env.OPENSHIFT_NODEJS_PORT || 8081,
    process.env.OPENSHIFT_NODEJS_IP || "127.0.0.1");
```

We are now ready to deploy our app. Update Git with all local files, commit them, and push to OpenShift:

```
git add .

git commit -m "first"

git push
```

If all goes well, you should see the following at the tail end of the resulting output:

```
remote: Starting MongoDB cartridge

remote: Starting NodeJS cartridge

remote: Starting application 'myapp' ...

remote: -----------------------

remote: Git Post-Receive Result: success

remote: Activation status: success

remote: Deployment completed with status: success
```

We can see how both Node and MongoDB are cartridges (not special processes or add-ons) and how a successful post-receive hook will automatically deploy and activate our app (not unlike what we saw when deploying to Heroku).

Should anything go wrong, we have direct access to our deployment logs. To connect to your application (myapp) via SSH, use the rhc tool:

```
rhc ssh myapp
```

Once connected, jump to your log directory using cd $OPENSHIFT_LOG_DIR. You should see two logs:

```
mongodb.log
```
```
nodejs.log
```

These are standard Linux log files and you can read or otherwise manipulate them, for example, by tailing them.

You can also tail your logs via rhc:

```
rhc tail
```

 When you are remotely logged in to your virtual container, you can jump to the root directory of your app via cd $OPENSHIFT_REPO_DIR.

Controlling your application is easily done via rhc. Several commands are available via rhc app <command>. These are a few commonly used commands:

- **delete**: This deletes an application from the server
- **force-stop**: This stops all application processes
- **reload**: This reloads the application's configuration
- **restart**: This restarts the application
- **show**: This shows information about an application
- **start**: This starts the application
- **stop**: This stops the application
- **tidy**: This cleans out logs and tmp directories and tidies up the git repo on the server

OpenShift offers a flexible option for those who want a little more control over the application they are deploying—power tools for power users.

Using Docker to create lightweight virtual containers

This image from the Docker website (`http://www.docker.com/`) gives information on how and why the Docker team feels their technology fits into the future of application development:

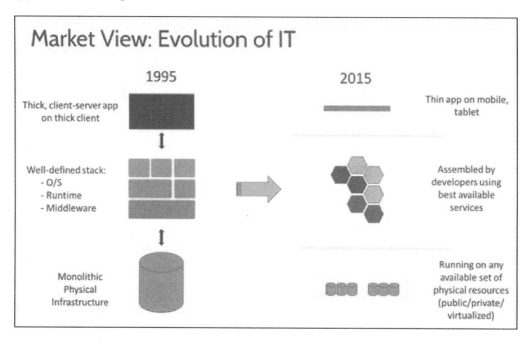

The preceding image, concisely describing the generational shift in application architecture we are now experiencing, can just as easily be used to describe the how and why of Node's design.

Docker, according to the website, ...*is an open source engine that automates the deployment of any application as a lightweight, portable, self-sufficient container that will run virtually anywhere.* Once you have created a Docker image of your application, a running instance of that image can be spun in milliseconds. Yes, that's right: a few milliseconds. Docker lets you create even hundreds of deployments of your application in a few seconds.

The Docker ecosystem has three main components. Here's some information about the components from the documentation:

- **Docker containers**: Docker containers are like directories. A Docker container holds everything that is needed for an application to run. Each container is created from a Docker image. Docker containers can be run, started, stopped, moved, and deleted. Each container is an isolated and secure application platform. You can consider Docker containers to be the `run` portion of the Docker framework.

- **Docker images**: The Docker image is a template, for example, an Ubuntu operating system with Apache and your web application installed. Docker containers are launched from images. Docker provides a simple way to build new images or update existing images. You can consider Docker images to be the `build` portion of the Docker framework.

- **Docker registries**: Docker registries hold images. These are public (or private) stores that you can upload or download images to and from. These images can be images you create yourself, or you can make use of images that others have previously created. Docker registries allow you to build simple and powerful development and deployment workflows. You can consider Docker registries to be the `share` portion of the Docker framework.

You can create images of applications to be run in any number of isolated containers, sharing those images with others if you'd like. The concept of composing Node applications out of many independent processes naturally aligns with the philosophy behind Docker. Docker containers are sandboxed, with their own filesystems, and so on, and are unable to execute instructions on their host without your knowledge. They can expose a port to their host OS, however, and later in this chapter, we'll learn how to use Node to link together many independent virtual containers into a larger application.

First, some Unix

Docker is a new technology, and at the time of this writing, it is not yet available on all flavors of Unix (although the team is working hard to make that a reality in the near future). I will install Docker on CentOS. The Docker website (`https://www.docker.io/`) is regularly updated with information on how to install on your favorite flavor of Unix.

Knowing the details of your OS is important. To find out your OS distribution name and version, use `cat /etc/*-release`, which should return something like this:

```
CentOS release 6.5 (Final)
```

Or you can try `cat /proc/version`:

```
Linux version 2.6.32-279.14.1.el6.x86_64 (mockbuild@cb79.bsys.dev.centos.
org) (gcc version 4.4.6 20120305 (Red Hat 4.4.6-4) (GCC) ) #1 SMP Tue Nov
6 23:43:09 UTC 2012
```

When you begin to create virtual machines and bind to ports, it will be necessary to check the status of your network on occasion. You should definitely install a good process viewer, such as **HTOP** (`http://hisham.hm/htop/`), as this will let you quickly scan/search through your open process list.

To get a quick list of stats on the network connections for your box, use `netstat`, which will return a list somewhat like this:

```
> netstat -tulpn
Active Internet connections (only servers)
Proto Recv-Q Send-Q Local Address          Foreign Address       State     PID/Program name
tcp        0      0 127.0.0.1:6379         0.0.0.0:*             LISTEN    4189/redis-server 1
tcp        0      0 0.0.0.0:80             0.0.0.0:*             LISTEN    27536/node
tcp        0      0 0.0.0.0:8080           0.0.0.0:*             LISTEN    31878/node
tcp        0      0 0.0.0.0:22             0.0.0.0:*             LISTEN    4076/sshd
```

You can see that port `8080` is bound to the Node process `31878`. You can also directly ask for the process ID associated with a port:

```
> fuser 8080/tcp
```

```
8080/tcp:       31878
```

To get more information on a process, type `ls -l /proc/31878/exe`:

```
lrwxrwxrwx 1 root root 0 Oct 9 2013 /proc/31878/exe -> /root/nvm/
v0.10.20/bin/node
```

To get more information on a port user, try `lsof`:

```
> lsof -i :8080
```

```
COMMAND  PID USER  FD   TYPE  DEVICE NODE NAME
```

```
node   31878 root   10u IPv4 22570201 TCP *:webcache (LISTEN)
```

Keeping on top of who is listening where, and to what, will serve you well as you move through this book.

Getting started with Docker

First, you will need to install Docker. Installation instructions for all supported Linux distributions can be found at `http://docs.docker.io/installation/`.

Once you have the Docker service installed, you will need to start it:

```
service docker start
```

Then, stop the Docker service:

```
service docker stop
```

If everything is working, this command should tell you something about your Docker installation:

```
docker info
```

A Docker container runs an image of your application. You can create these images yourself, of course, but there does exist a large ecosystem of existing images. Let's create our own image of a Node server running Express.

 To search the Docker image repository, visit `https://index.docker.io/`.

First, we'll need to build an application to run. Create a folder to put your application files into. Just as with all Node applications, we'll need to create a `package.json` file for npm to parse:

```
{
  "name": "docker-example",
  "private": true,
  "version": "0.0.0",
  "description": "Example of running a Node app within a CENTOS
    container",
  "author": "Sandro Pasquali <spasquali@gmail.com>",
  "dependencies": {
    "express": "4.1.1"
  }
}
```

Next, we need a program that will start an Express HTTP server. Create the following file and name it `server.js`:

```
var express = require('express');

var port = 8087;

var app = express();
app.get('/', function (req, res) {
  res.send('You just deployed some Node!\n');
});

app.listen(port);
console.log('Running on http://localhost:' + port);
```

Now, install and start your application:

```
npm install;
node app.js
// Running on http://localhost:8087
```

You can now point your browser to your host on port `8087` and see **You just deployed some Node!** displayed.

Now, we will look at how we can build these files into a virtual container using Docker.

Creating a Dockerfile

Our goal is to describe the environment this application executes within such that Docker can reproduce that environment in a container. Also, we want to add the source files of our application to run in this newly virtualized environment. Docker can act as a builder that follows the instructions you provide on how to build an image of your application.

To begin with, you should have a folder containing your application files. This is your source code repository. Within this repository, create a `./src` folder. We will shortly learn why this folder is created. If this folder is the one where your test application was built, remove the `node_modules` folder.

A Dockerfile is a list of instructions to build an application. You can build Docker images manually, of course, but it is likely that you will want to repeat those actions many times. A Dockerfile describes a build process. What you will normally declare in a Dockerfile is the Linux version that the container will run and any OS installations you might need to do—such as Node and npm. Additionally, you will indicate where the source code for your application resides: within the ./src folder created earlier.

A Dockerfile is always built upon another Docker image. Normally, you will build upon an OS image. We'll use CentOS 6.4 for this example. My Dockerfile starts with a comment about the version of Docker I am building on and the name of the image this image will be built from:

```
# DOCKER-VERSION 0.9.0
FROM   centos:6.4
```

We have now established an OS to run in the container. Now we will simply list typical Unix commands to set up a build environment. First, we'll need Node and npm:

```
# Enable EPEL for Node.js
RUN   rpm -Uvh http://download.fedoraproject.org/pub/epel/6/i386/epel-
release-6-8.noarch.rpm
# Install Node.js and npm
RUN   yum install -y npm
```

Great! Now our container knows how to build Node and npm. Now let's bundle our application into the ./src directory of our container using the ADD directive:

```
# Bundle app source
ADD . /src
```

Now that our application files are bundled into ./src, let's enter that directory and install the application package:

```
# Install app
RUN cd /src; npm install
```

Our app is now installed. Note that in app.js we are exposing an Express server on port 8087. A container can't know this, so we have to tell the container to set up the port redirection on the host system:

```
EXPOSE 8087
```

Finally, the container is told to start the Node application:

```
CMD ["node", "/src/app.js"]
```

That's it. Now, create a file named (exactly) `Dockerfile`, containing the preceding instructions. We can now use this Dockerfile to build a Docker image.

Building and running a Docker image

The command to build a Docker image is `docker build`. Docker will look in the current folder for a Dockerfile and build an image based on the instructions contained therein. Since we will most likely reuse this image, it is a good idea to tag it with a special name. To give an image a name, use the `-t` directive, followed by the tag of your choice, followed by a path to the Dockerfile (here, the current directory):

```
docker build -t docker/example .
```

When you run that command, you will see a lot of output to your terminal as the requested packages are downloaded and installed. This may take some time. Thankfully, Docker caches these installs—the next build using this Dockerfile, or others containing identical install instructions, will be much faster.

If the build went well, your image can be listed, with the `docker images` command outputting something like this:

```
REPOSITORY    TAG    IMAGE ID    CREATED    VIRTUAL SIZE
docker/example latest d8bb295407f1 20 minutes ago   667.8 MB
centos    6.4  539c0211cd76 2 months ago   300.6 MB
```

To remove an image, use `docker rmi <image id>`.

Our application is now containerized. We can run it using the following command:

```
docker run -p 49001:8087 -d docker/example
```

The `-d` directive instructs Docker to run this image in detached mode—to run it in the background. The `49001:8087` segment is necessary to map the *virtual* port that our Express server is listening to *within the container* (`8087`) to an actual port on our host machine.

Open your browser and point it to the host machine at port `49001`. You should see **You just deployed some Node!** displayed. The Node application we created earlier is now running in a container.

To demonstrate the point of Docker, execute the same `run` instruction given earlier, but change the port mapping to something like `49002:8087`. Open a different browser window on your application by changing the port accordingly. You now have two identical copies of your application running on the same host in isolated containers.

> More details on run directives can be found at `http://docs.docker.io/reference/run/`.
>
> To learn more about port redirection, visit `http://docs.docker.io/use/port_redirection/#port-redirection`.

You will want to be able to check for the running Docker instances. The command to do this is `docker ps`, which will display information similar to the following:

```
CONTAINER ID   IMAGE                   COMMAND          PORTS
4347e7d03153   docker/example:latest   node /src/app.js  0.0.0.0:49002->8087/tcp
7cd7218c39a1   docker/example:latest   node /src/app.js  0.0.0.0:49001->8087/tcp
```

Here we see our two running containers, including information about what they are running and how they are mapped. To stop a running container, use `docker stop <container id>`. You can use `docker start <container id>` to either restart a stopped container or, of course, start a new one. This implies that stopping a container does not destroy the container. To do that, use `docker rm <container id>`.

> For a full list of Docker commands, simply type `docker` in your terminal.

Summary

In this chapter, you learned how to create Node servers and applications, both locally and *in the cloud*. Having deployed a simple document-editing application using Node and MongoDB across three different PaaS providers, you have an early sense of what is available to the Node developer who is looking to scale their application. You were introduced to Docker, which offers a powerful new containerization technology, allowing us to make many cheap clones of our applications; wherever there is Linux, there exists a deploy target for Docker.

In the next chapter, we will take these simple ideas about scaling farther and deeper by exploring in more detail how Node can be scaled both vertically and horizontally—across cores and across many machines.

3
Scaling Node

Like *concurrency* and *parallelism*, *scalability* and *performance* are not the same thing.

> *"The terms "performance" and "scalability" are commonly used interchangeably, but the two are distinct: performance measures the speed with which a single request can be executed, while scalability measures the ability of a request to maintain its performance under increasing load. For example, the performance of a request may be reported as generating a valid response within three seconds, but the scalability of the request measures the request's ability to maintain that three-second response time as the user load increases."*
>
> – *Pro Java EE 5, Steve Haines*

It is not unusual for a reviewer to assert that Node cannot scale across cores and is, therefore, unable to optimize performance on a given machine. This belief is based on two false impressions—that Node is "not good at" CPU-intensive tasks and that it *cannot scale* because its process can only leverage a single core. These claims are often stretched further into assertions about how Node's claim of being nonblocking is false, primarily by imagining locked threads and underutilized hardware.

Scalable applications remain responsive under increasing load. Scalable applications imply that more nodes can be added to, and removed from, a system depending on fluctuations in both client connections and resource needs (such as more memory or storage space). Node aims to make it easy to conceptualize, describe, and implement scalable networked applications. The primary focus is on creating a toolkit to build structures out of many nodes connected through evented network streams communicating through standard protocols. Distributed systems are concerned with failure more than with performance and the question that arises is: how can we swap, add, and remove nodes intelligently within a running system?

 Solving the **C10K problem**, which is *the problem of optimizing network sockets to handle a large number of clients at the same time* (https:// en.wikipedia.org/wiki/C10k_problem) is a key design goal for many modern application tools and environments, including Node.

We will look at two common scaling strategies—vertical and horizontal scaling. Vertical scaling (*scaling up*) involves increasing the ability of a single server to handle increasing load, usually by increasing the number of CPUs, memory, storage space, and so on, on a single box. Horizontally scaling systems (*scaling out*) respond to a load by adding or subtracting servers or other network resources. Deploying a scalable Node solution can be done by utilizing both of these techniques either individually or in tandem.

Scaling vertically across multiple cores

As we discussed in *Chapter 1, Appreciating Node*, libuv is used within the Node environment to manage multiple I/O threads. The OS itself also schedules threads, distributing the work required by various processes. Node provides a way for a developer to take advantage of this OS-level scheduling by spawning and forking many processes. In this section, we will learn how to distribute your program's tasks across independent processes generally and how to distribute a Node server's load across multiple cooperating server processes.

Modern software development is no longer the realm of monolithic programs. Modern applications are distributed and decoupled. We now build applications that connect users with resources distributed across the Internet. Many users are accessing shared resources simultaneously. A complex system is easier to understand if the whole is understood as a collection of interfaces to programs that solve one or a few clearly defined, related problems. In such a system, it is expected (and desirable) that processes should not sit idle.

While a single Node process runs on a single core, any number of Node processes can be "spun up" through the use of the `child_process` module. Basic usage of this module is straightforward: we fetch a `ChildProcess` object and listen for data events. This example will call the Unix command `ls`, listing the current directory:

```
var spawn = require('child_process').spawn;
var ls  = spawn('ls', ['-lh', '.']);
ls.stdout.on('readable', function() {
 var d = this.read();
 d && console.log(d.toString());
});
ls.on('close', function(code) {
 console.log('child process exited with code ' + code);
});
```

Here, we use `spawn` on the `ls` process (list directory) and read from the resulting readable stream, receiving something like this:

```
-rw-r--r-- 1 root root  43 Jul 9 19:44 index.html

-rw-rw-r-- 1 root root 278 Jul 15 16:36 child_example.js

-rw-r--r-- 1 root root 1.2K Jul 14 19:08 server.js


child process exited with code 0
```

Any number of child processes can be spawned in this way. It is important to note here that when a child process is spawned or otherwise created, the OS itself assigns the responsibility for that process to a given CPU. Node is not responsible for how an OS allocates resources. The upshot is that on a machine with eight cores, it is likely that spawning eight processes will result in each being allocated to independent processors. In other words, child processes are automatically spread by the OS across CPUs, putting the lie to claims that Node cannot take full advantage of multicore environments.

Each new Node process (child) is allocated 10 MB of memory and represents a new V8 instance that will take at least 30 milliseconds to start up. While it is unlikely that you will spawn many thousands of these processes, understanding how to query and set OS limits on user-created processes is beneficial. You can use `htop` or `top` to report the number of processes currently running, or you can use `ps  aux  |  wc -l` from the command line. The Unix command `ulimit` (`http://ss64.com/bash/ulimit.html`) provides important information on user limits on an OS. Passing `ulimit` the `-u` argument will show the maximum number of user processes that can be spawned. Changing the limit is accomplished by passing it as an argument—`ulimit  -u  8192`.

The `child_process` module represents a class exposing four main methods: `spawn`, `fork`, `exec`, and `execFile`. These methods return a `ChildProcess` object that extends `EventEmitter`, exposing an interface to child events, and a few functions helpful to manage child processes. We'll take a look at its main methods and follow up with a discussion of the common `ChildProcess` interface.

spawn(command, [arguments], [options])

This powerful command allows a Node program to start and interact with processes spawned via system commands. In the preceding example, we used `spawn` to call a native OS process, `ls`, passing that command the arguments `'-lh'` and `'.'`. In this way, any process can be started just as one might start it via a command line. The method takes three arguments:

- **command**: This is a command to be executed by the OS shell

- **arguments**: These are optional command-line arguments sent as an array

- **options**: This is an optional map of settings for `spawn`

The options for `spawn` allow its behavior to be carefully customized:

- **cwd** (string): By default, this command will understand its current working directory to be the same as that of the Node process calling `spawn`. Change that setting using this directive.

- **env** (object): This is used to pass environment variables to a child process, for instance, we spawn a child process with an environment object, such as:

  ```
  {
    name : "Sandro",
    role : "admin"
  }
  ```

  The child process environment will have access to the values specified in the preceding code.

- **detached** (Boolean): When a parent process spawns a child process, both processes form a group, and the parent process is normally the leader of that group. To make a child process the group leader, use `detached`. This allows the child process to continue running even after the parent process exits. Because the parent process waits for the child process to exit by default, you can call `child.unref()` to tell the parent process's event loop that it should not count the child reference and exit if no other work exists.

- **uid** (number): Set the uid (user identity) for the child process in terms of standard system permissions, such as a uid that has privileges to execute on the child process.

- **gid** (number): Set the gid (group identity) for the child process in terms of standard system permissions, such as a gid that has execute privileges on the child process.

- **stdio** (string or array): Child processes have file descriptors, the first three being `process.stdin`, `process.stdout`, and `process.stderr` standard I/O descriptors in that order (fds = 0,1,2). This directive allows those descriptors to be redefined, inherited, and so on.

Normally, to read the output of the following child process program, a parent process would listen on `child.stdout`:

```
process.stdout.write(new Buffer("Hello!"));
```

If, instead, we wanted a child to inherit its parent's `stdio` such that when the child writes to `process.stdout`, what is emitted is piped through to the parent process's `process.stdout` stream, we would pass the relevant parent file descriptors to the child, overriding its own:

```
spawn("node", ['./reader.js', './afile.txt'], {
  stdio: [process.stdin, process.stdout, process.stderr]
});
```

In this case, the child's output will pipe straight through to the parent process's standard output channel. Also, see `fork`, in the upcoming paragraphs, for more information on this kind of pattern.

Each of the three (or more) file descriptors can take one of six values:

- **'pipe'**: This creates a pipe between the child process and the parent process. As the first three child file descriptors are already exposed to the parent process (`child.stdin`, `child.stdout`, `child.stderr`), this is only necessary in more complex child implementations.

- **'ipc'**: Create an IPC channel to pass messages between a child process and a parent process. A child process can have a maximum of one IPC file descriptor. Once this connection is established, the parent process can communicate with the child process via `child.send`. If the child sends JSON messages through this file descriptor, those emissions can be caught using `child.on("message")`. If you are running a Node program as a child, it is likely a better choice to use `ChildProcess.fork`, which has this messaging channel built in.

- **'ignore'**: The file descriptors 0–2 will have `/dev/null` attached to them. For others, the referenced file descriptor will not be set on the child.

- **A stream object**: This allows the parent to share a stream with the child. For demonstration purposes, given a child that will write the same content to any provided `Writable` stream, we could do something like this:

```
var writer = fs.createWriteStream("./a.out");
writer.on('open', function() {
  var cp = spawn("node", ['./reader.js'], {
    stdio: [null, writer, null]
  });
});
```

    The child will now fetch its content and pipe it to whichever output stream it has been sent to:

```
fs.createReadStream('cached.data').pipe(process.stdout);
```

- **An integer**: This is a file descriptor ID.
- **null, undefined**: These are the default values. For file descriptors 0–2 (`stdin`, `stdout`, `stderr`), a pipe is created. Others default to *ignore*.

In addition to passing `stdio` settings as an array, certain common groupings can be implemented by passing a shortcut string value:

- `'ignore'` = `['ignore', 'ignore', 'ignore']`
- `'pipe'` = `['pipe', 'pipe', 'pipe']`
- `'inherit'` = `[process.stdin, process.stdout, process.stderr]` or `[0,1,2]`

It should be noted that the ability to spawn any system process means that one can use Node to run other application environments installed on the OS. If we had the popular PHP language installed, the following would be possible:

```
var spawn = require('child_process').spawn;

var php = spawn("php", ['-r', 'print "Hello from PHP!";']);

php.stdout.on('readable', function() {
  var d;
  while(d = this.read()) {
    console.log(d.toString());
  }
});

// Hello from PHP!
```

Running a more interesting, larger program would be just as easy.

Apart from the ease with which one can run Java, Ruby, or other programs through Node using this technique, asynchronously, we also have here a good answer to a persistent criticism of Node: JavaScript is not as fast as other languages for crunching numbers or doing other CPU-heavy tasks. This is true in the sense that Node is primarily optimized for I/O efficiency and helping with the management of high-concurrency applications, and JavaScript is an interpreted language without a strong focus on heavy computation.

However, using `spawn`, one can very easily pass massive computations and long-running routines on analytic engines or calculation engines to separate processes in other environments. Node's simple event loop will notify the main application when those operations are done, seamlessly integrating the resultant data. Meantime, the main application is free to keep serving clients.

fork(modulePath, [arguments], [options])

Just like `spawn`, `fork` starts a child process but is designed to run Node programs with the added benefit of having a communication built in. Rather than passing a system command to `fork` as its first argument, we pass the path to a Node program. As with `spawn`, command-line options can be sent as a second argument, accessible via `process.argv` in the forked child process.

An optional object can be passed as its third argument, with the following parameters:

- **cwd** (string): By default, this command will understand its current working directory to be the same as that of the Node process calling `fork`. Change that setting using this directive.

- **env** (object): This is used to pass environment variables to a child process. See `spawn`.

- **encoding** (string): This sets the encoding of the communication channel.

- **execPath** (string): This is the executable used to create the child process.

- **silent** (Boolean): By default, a child process for which `fork` has been used will have `stdio` associated with that of the parent process (`child.stdout` is identical to `parent.stdout`, for example). Setting this option to 'true' disables this behavior.

An important difference between `fork` and `spawn` is that the former's child process *does not automatically exit* when it is finished. Such a child process must explicitly exit when it is done, which is easily accomplished via `process.exit()`.

In the following example, we will create a child process that emits an incrementing number every tenth of a second, which its parent process then dumps to the system console. First, let's look at the child program:

```
var cnt = 0;

setInterval(function() {
  process.stdout.write(" -> " + cnt++);
}, 100);
```

Again, this will simply write a steadily increasing number. When forked a child process, a child process will inherit the `stdio` stream of its parent, so we only need to create the child process in order to get the output in a terminal running the parent process:

```
var fork = require('child_process').fork;
fork('./emitter.js');

// -> 0 -> 1 -> 2 -> 3 -> 4 -> 5 -> 6 -> 7 -> 8 -> 9 -> 10 ...
```

 The silent option can be demonstrated here. The following code turns off any output to the terminal:

```
fork('./emitter.js', [], { silent: true });
```

Creating multiple, parallel processes is easy. Let's multiply the number of children created:

```
fork('./emitter.js');
fork('./emitter.js');
fork('./emitter.js');

-> 0 -> 0 -> 0 -> 1 -> 1 -> 1 -> 2 -> 2 -> 2 -> 3 -> 3 -> 3 -> 4
  ...
```

It should be clear at this point that using `fork`, we are creating many parallel execution contexts spread across all machine cores.

This is straightforward enough, but the built-in communication channel that `fork` provides makes communicating with child processes for which `fork` has been used even easier and cleaner. Consider the following two code snippets:

Parent:

```
var fork = require('child_process').fork;
var cp = fork('./child.js');
cp.on('message', function(msgobj) {
  console.log('Parent got message:', msgobj.text);
});

cp.send({
  text: "I love you"
});
```

Child:

```
process.on('message', function(msgobj) {
  console.log('Child got message:', msgobj.text);
  process.send({
    text: msgobj.text + ' too'
  });
});
```

By executing the parent script, we will see the following in our console:

```
Child got message: I love you
Parent got message: I love you too
```

exec(command, [options], callback)

In cases where the complete buffered output of a child process is sufficient, with no need to manage data through events, `child_process` offers the `exec` method. The method takes three arguments:

command: This is a command-line string. Unlike `spawn` and `fork`, which pass arguments to a command via an array, this first argument accepts a full command string, such as `ps aux | grep node`.

- **options**: This is optional.
- **cwd**: This is a string. Set the working directory for the command process.
- **env**: This is an object. It's a map of key-value pairs that will be exposed to the child process.
- **encoding**: This is a string. It is the encoding of the child process's data stream. The default value is `'utf8'`.

- **timeout**: This is a number. It is the number of milliseconds that we need to wait for the process to complete, at which point the child process will be sent the **killSignal** signal.

- **maxBuffer**: This is a number. It is the maximum number of bytes allowed on stdout or stderr. When this number is exceeded, the process is killed. The default value is 200 KB.

- **killSignal**: This is a string. The child process receives this signal after a **timeout**. The default value is SIGTERM.

- **callback**: This receives three arguments: an Error object, if any; stdout (a Buffer containing the result); and stderr (a Buffer containing error data, if any). If the process was killed, Error.signal will contain the kill signal.

execFile

Use this method when you want the functionality of exec but are targeting a Node file. Importantly, execFile does not spawn a new subshell, which makes it slightly less expensive to run.

Communicating with your child process

All instances of the ChildProcess object extend EventEmitter, exposing events which are useful to manage child data connections. Additionally, ChildProcess objects expose useful methods of interacting with child processes directly. Let's go through these now, beginning with attributes and methods.

child.connected

When a child process is disconnected from its parent process via child.disconnect(), this flag will be set to false.

child.stdin

This is a Writable stream corresponding to the child process's standard in.

child.stdout

This is a Readable stream corresponding to the child process's standard out.

child.stderr

This is a Readable stream corresponding to the child process's standard error.

child.pid

This is an integer representing the **process ID (PID)** assigned to the child process.

child.kill([signal])

Try to terminate a child process, sending it an optional signal. If no signal is specified, the default is SIGTERM (for more about signals, see http://unixhelp. ed.ac.uk/CGI/man-cgi?signal+7). While the method name sounds terminal, it is not guaranteed to kill a process—it only sends a signal to a process. Dangerously, if kill is attempted on a process that has already exited, it is possible that another process, which has been newly assigned the PID of the dead process, will receive the signal, with indeterminable consequences. You should fire a close event, which will receive the signal used to close the process.

child.disconnect()

When child.disconnect() is triggered on a child process belonging to a process group that it does not lead, the IPC connection between the child and its parent will be severed, resulting in the child dying gracefully as it has no IPC channel to keep it alive. You can also call process.disconnect() from within the child process itself. Once a child process has disconnected, the connected flag on that child reference will be set to false.

child.send(message, [sendHandle])

As we saw in our discussion of fork, and when using the ipc option on spawn, child processes can be sent messages via this method. A TCP server or socket object can be passed along with the message as a second argument. In this way, a TCP server can spread requests across multiple child processes. For example, the following server distributes socket handling across a number of child processes equaling the total number of CPUs available. Each forked child is given a unique ID, which it reports when started. Whenever the TCP server receives a socket, that socket is passed as a handle to a random child process. That child process then sends a unique response, demonstrating that socket handling is being distributed. The following code snippets show this:

Parent:

```
var fork = require('child_process').fork;
var net = require('net');

var children = [];
```

```
require('os').cpus().forEach(function(f, idx) {
  children.push(fork("./child.js", [idx]));
});

net.createServer(function(socket) {
  var rand = Math.floor(Math.random() * children.length);
  children[rand].send(null, socket);
}).listen(8080);
```

Child:

```
var id = process.argv[2];
process.on('message', function(n, socket) {
  socket.write('child ' + id + ' was your server today.\r\n');
  socket.end();
});
```

Start the parent server in a terminal window. In another window, run `telnet` `127.0.0.1 8080`. You should see something similar to the following, with a random child ID being displayed on each connection (assuming there exist multiple cores):

Trying 127.0.0.1...

...

child 3 was your server today.

Connection closed by foreign host.

The cluster module

We saw how spreading work across multiple cores by spawning independent processes helps to vertically scale Node applications. The Node API has been further augmented with a `cluster` module that formalizes this pattern and extends it. Continuing with Node's core purpose of helping to make scalable network software easier to build, the particular goal of the `cluster` module is to facilitate the sharing of network sockets among many child workers.

For example, the following code creates a cluster of worker processes, all sharing the same HTTP connection:

```
var cluster = require('cluster');
var http = require('http');
var numCPUs = require('os').cpus().length;

if(cluster.isMaster) {
  for(var i = 0; i < numCPUs; i++) {
```

```
      cluster.fork();
    }
  }

  if(cluster.isWorker) {
    http.createServer(function(req, res) {
      res.writeHead(200);
      res.end("Hello from " + cluster.worker.id);
    }).listen(8080);
  }
```

We'll dig into the details shortly. The important thing to note is how this program does different things depending on whether it is running as a master process or as a child process. On its first execution, it is the master, indicated by `cluster.isMaster`. When a master process calls `cluster.fork`, this same program is forked as a child process, in this case one child for each CPU. When this program is re-executed, in a forking context, `cluster.isWorker` will be `true`, and a new HTTP server *running on a shared port* is started. Multiple processes are sharing the load for a single server.

Connect to this server with a browser. You will see something like **Hello from 8**, the integer corresponding to the unique `cluster.worker.id` ID of the worker that is assigned the responsibility of handling your request. Balancing across all workers is handled automatically such that refreshing your browser a few times will result in different worker IDs being displayed.

The `cluster` API breaks down into two sections: the methods, attributes, and events available to the cluster master and those available to the child process. As workers in this context are defined using `fork`, the documentation for that method of `child_process` can be applied here as well.

cluster.isMaster

This is a Boolean value indicating whether the process is a master.

cluster.isWorker

This is a Boolean value indicating whether the process was forked from a master.

cluster.worker

This is a reference to the current worker object and is only available to a child process.

cluster.workers

This is a hash containing references to all active worker objects, keyed by the worker ID. Use this to loop through all worker objects. This only exists within the master process.

cluster.setupMaster([settings])

This is a convenient way of passing a map of default arguments when a child is forked. If all child processes are going to use fork on the same file (as is often the case), you will save time by setting it here. The available defaults are as follows:

- **exec**: This is a string. The file path to the process file defaults to __filename.
- **args**: This is an array. Strings are sent as arguments to the child process.
- **silent**: This is a Boolean value that determines whether or not to send output to the master's stdio.

cluster.fork([env])

This creates a new worker process. Only the master process can call this method. To expose a map of key-value pairs to the child's process environment, send an object to env.

cluster.disconnect([callback])

This is used to terminate all workers in a cluster. Once all the workers have died gracefully, the cluster process will itself terminate if it has no further events to wait on. To be notified when all child processes have expired, pass callback.

cluster events

This cluster object emits several events:

- **fork**: This is fired when the master tries to use fork on a new child. This is not the same as online. This receives a worker object.
- **online**: This is fired when the master receives notification that a child is fully bound. This differs from the fork event. This receives a worker object.
- **listening**: When the worker performs an action that requires a listen() call (such as starting an HTTP server), this event will be fired in the master. The event emits two arguments: a worker object and the address object containing the address, port, and addressType of the connection.

- **disconnect**: This is called whenever a child disconnects, which can happen either through process exit events or after calling `child.kill()`. This will fire prior to the `exit` event—they are not the same. This receives a worker object.
- **exit**: Whenever a child dies, this event is emitted. It receives three arguments: a worker object, the exit code number, and the signal string, such as SIGHUP, that caused the process to be killed.
- **setup**: This is called after `cluster.setupMaster` has executed.

worker.id

This is the unique ID assigned to a worker, which also represents the worker's key in the `cluster.workers` index.

worker.process

This is a `ChildProcess` object referencing a worker.

worker.suicide

These workers, that have recently had `kill` or `disconnect` called on them, will have their `suicide` attribute set to true.

worker.send(message, [sendHandle])

See `child_process.fork()` in the *Scaling vertically across multiple cores* section where I describe the `#fork` method.

worker.kill([signal])

This kills a worker. The master can check this worker's `suicide` property in order to determine whether the death was intentional or accidental. The default signal sent is SIGTERM.

worker.disconnect()

This instructs a worker to disconnect. Importantly, existing connections to the worker are not immediately terminated (as with `kill`) but are allowed to exit normally prior to the worker fully disconnecting. Because existing connections can stay in existence for a very long time, it is a good habit to regularly check whether the worker has actually disconnected, perhaps using timeouts.

Workers also emit events:

- **message**: See `child_process.fork` in the *Scaling vertically across multiple cores* section where I describe the `#fork` method

- **online**: This is identical to `cluster.online` except that the check is against only the specified worker

- **listening**: This is identical to `cluster.listening` except that the check is against only the specified worker

- **disconnect**: This is identical to `cluster.disconnect` except that the check is against only the specified worker

- **exit**: See the `exit` event for `child_process`

- **setup**: This is called after `cluster.setupMaster` has executed

Now that we have a good understanding of how to accomplish vertical scaling with Node, let's take a look at some ways to handle horizontal scaling

Scaling horizontally across different machines

Because Node is so efficient, most websites or applications can accommodate all of their scaling needs in the vertical dimension. As we learned from Eran Hammer's experiences at Walmart, Node can handle enormous levels of traffic using only a few CPUs and an unexceptional volume of memory.

Nevertheless, horizontal scaling can still be the right choice, even if only for architectural reasons. Having one point of failure, no matter how robust, still entails some risk. The *parking lot problem* is another consideration that Walmart likely faces—during shopping holidays, you will need many thousands of parking spots, but during the rest of the year this investment in empty space is hard to justify. In terms of servers, the ability to dynamically scale both up and down argues against building fixed vertical silos. Adding hardware to a running server is also a more complicated process than spinning up and seamlessly linking another virtual machine to your application.

In this section, we'll look at a few techniques for horizontal scaling, considering load balancing using native Node techniques, third-party solutions, and some ideas for cross-server communication.

Using Nginx

Nginx (pronounced **Engine X**) remains a popular choice for those whose architecture benefits from hiding Node servers behind a proxy. Nginx is a very popular high-performance web server that is often used as a proxy server. Given its design, Nginx is a popular choice with Node developers. According to `http://www.linuxjournal.com/magazine/nginx-high-performance-web-server-and-reverse-proxy`:

> *"Nginx is able to serve more requests per second with less resources because of its architecture. It consists of a master process, which delegates work to one or more worker processes. Each worker handles multiple requests in an event-driven or asynchronous manner using special functionality from the Linux kernel (epoll/ select/poll). This allows Nginx to handle a large number of concurrent requests quickly with very little overhead."*

Its similarity in design to Node is striking: event delegation across processes and an evented, asynchronous environment coordinated by the OS delivering high concurrency.

A **proxy** is someone or something acting on behalf of another.

A *forward* proxy normally works on behalf of clients in a private network, brokering requests to an outside network, such as retrieving data from the Internet. Early *web providers*, such as AOL, functioned in this way:

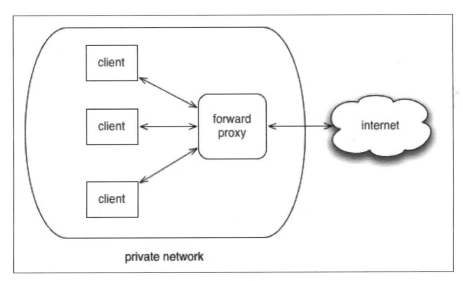

Network administrators often use forward proxies when restrictions on access to the outside world (that is, the Internet) are needed. If malware is downloaded from a bad website via an e-mail attachment, the administrator might block access to that location. Restrictions on access to social networking sites might be imposed on an office network. Some countries even restrict access to the general Internet in this way.

A *reverse* proxy, not surprisingly, works in the opposite manner, accepting requests from a public network and servicing those requests within a private network that the client might not have much visibility into. Direct access to servers by clients is first delegated to a reverse proxy. This can be shown with the help of the following diagram:

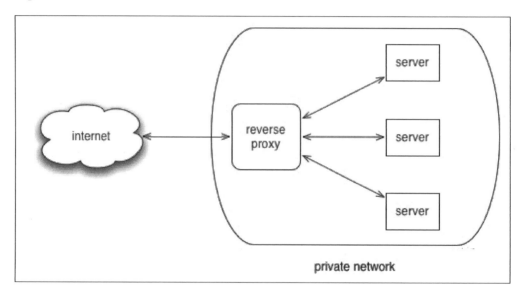

This is the type of proxy we can use to balance requests from clients across many Node servers. Client X does not communicate with any given server directly. A broker Y is the first point of contact that is able to direct X to a server under less load, is located closer to X, or is, in some other way, the best server for X to access at the time.

Let's take a look at how Nginx can be used as a proxy, in particular, as a load balancer, by deploying such a system on the cloud hosting service **Digital Cloud**.

Deploying an Nginx load balancer on DigitalOcean

DigitalOcean is a cloud hosting provider that is inexpensive and easy to set up. We will build an Nginx load balancer on this service.

To sign up, visit `http://www.digitalocean.com`. The basic package (at the time of writing this) incurs a $5 fee, but promotion codes are regularly made available—a simple web search should result in a usable code. Create and verify an account to get started.

DigitalOcean packages are described as droplets with certain characteristics—the amount of storage space, transfer limits, and so on. A basic package is sufficient for our needs. Also, you will indicate a hosting region and the OS to install in your droplet (in this example, we'll use the latest version of Ubuntu). Create a droplet and check your e-mail for login instructions. You're done!

You will receive full login information for your instance. You can now open a terminal and SSH into your box using those login credentials.

 On your initial login, you might want to update your packages. For Ubuntu, you would run `apt-get update` and `apt-get upgrade`. Other package managers have similar commands (such as `yum update` for RHEL/CentOS).

Before we begin to install, let's change our root password and create a nonroot user (it is unsafe to expose the root to external logins and software installs). To change your root password, type `passwd` and follow the instructions in your terminal. To create a new user, enter `adduser <new user name>` (for example, `adduser john`). Follow the instructions mentioned in the upcoming paragraphs.

One more step: we want to give some administrative privileges to our new user as we'll install software as that user. In Unix parlance, you want to give `sudo` access to this new user. Instructions on how to do this are easy to find for whichever OS you've chosen. Essentially, you will want to change the `/etc/sudoers` file. Remember to do this using a command such as `visudo`—do not edit the `sudoers` file by hand! You may also want to restrict root logins and do other SSH access management at this point.

 After successfully executing `sudo -i` in your terminal, you will be able to enter commands without prefixing each one with `sudo`. The following examples assume that you've done this.

We'll now create an Nginx load balancer frontend for two Node servers. This means that we will create three droplets—one for the balancer and two added droplets as Node servers. In the end, we will end up with an architecture that looks something like this:

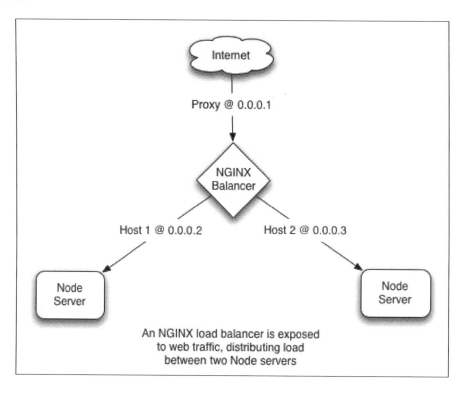

An NGINX load balancer is exposed
to web traffic, distributing load
between two Node servers

Installing and configuring Nginx

Let's install Nginx and Node/npm. If you're still logged in as root, log out and reauthenticate as the new user you've just created. To install Nginx (on Ubuntu), simply type:

```
apt-get install nginx
```

Most other Unix package managers will have Nginx installers. To start Nginx, use:

```
service nginx start
```

 Full documentation for Nginx can be found at `http://wiki.nginx.org/Configuration`.

You should now be able to point your browser to the IP you were assigned (check your inbox if you've forgotten) and see something like this:

Welcome to nginx!

If you see this page, the nginx web server is successfully installed and working. Further configuration is required.

For online documentation and support please refer to nginx.org. Commercial support is available at nginx.com.

Thank you for using nginx.

Now, let's set up the two servers that Nginx will balance.

Create an additional two droplets in DigitalOcean. You must *not* install Nginx on these servers. Configure permissions on these servers as we did earlier. Now, install Node in both droplets. An easy way to manage your Node installation is using Tim Caswell's **Node Version Manager** (**NVM**). NVM is essentially a bash script that provides a set of command-line tools facilitating Node version management and allowing you to easily switch between versions. To install it, use the following command:

```
curl -o- https://raw.githubusercontent.com/creationix/nvm/v0.25.4/
install.sh | bash
```

Now, install your preferred Node version (here we ask for the latest release of the 0.12 version):

```
nvm install 0.12
```

You might want to add a command to your `.bashrc` or `.profile` file to ensure that a certain node version is used each time you start a shell:

```
# start with node 0.12
```

```
nvm use 0.12
```

To test our system, we need to set up Node servers on both of these machines. Create the following program file on each server, changing '**' to something unique on each (such as *one* and *two*):

```
var http = require('http');

http.createServer(function(req, res) {
    res.writeHead(200, {
      "Content-Type" : "text/html"
    });
```

```
    res.write('HOST **');
    res.end();
}).listen(8080)
```

Start this file on each server (`node serverfile.js`). Each server will now answer on port `8080`.

You should now be able to reach this server by pointing a browser to each droplet's IP:8080. Once you have two servers responding with distinct messages, we can set up the Nginx load balancer.

Load balancing across servers is straightforward with Nginx. You need to simply indicate in the Nginx configuration script which **upstream** servers should be balanced. The two Node servers we've just created are the upstream servers. The following diagram describes how Nginx evenly distributes requests across upstream servers:

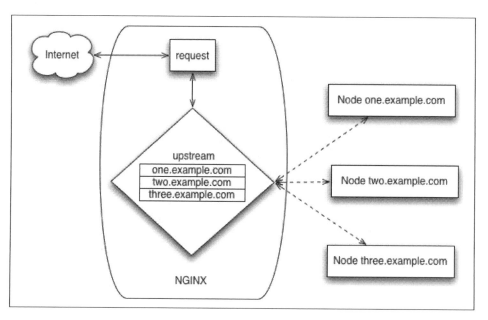

Each request will be handled first by Nginx, which will check its *upstream* configuration and, based on how it is configured, will (reverse) proxy requests to upstream servers that will actually handle the request.

You will find the default Nginx server configuration file on your balancer droplet at `/etc/nginx/sites-available/default`. In production, you'll most likely want to create a custom directory and configuration file, but for our purposes, we'll simply modify the default configuration file (you might want to make a backup before you start modifying it).

At the top of the Nginx configuration file, we want to define *upstream* servers that will be candidates for redirection. This is simply a map with the arbitrary key `lb-servers` to be referenced in the server definition that follows:

```
upstream lb_servers {
  server first.node.server.ip;
  server second.node.server.ip;
}
```

Now that we've established the candidate map, we need to configure Nginx such that it forwards requests in a balanced way to each of the members of `lb-servers`:

```
server {
  listen 80 default_server;
  listen [::]:80 default_server ipv6only=on;

  #root /usr/share/nginx/html;
  #index index.html index.htm;

  # Make site accessible from http://localhost/
  server_name localhost;

  location / {
    proxy_pass http://lb-servers; # Load balance mapped servers
    proxy_http_version 1.1;
    proxy_set_header Upgrade $http_upgrade;
    proxy_set_header Connection 'upgrade';
    proxy_set_header Host $host;
    proxy_cache_bypass $http_upgrade;
  }

  ... more configuration options not specifically relevant to our
  purposes
}
```

The key line is this one:

```
proxy_pass http://lb-servers
```

Note how the name `lb-servers` matches the name of our upstream definition. This should make what is happening clear: an Nginx server listening on port 80 will pass the request on to a server definition contained in `lb-servers`. If the upstream definition has only one server in it, that server gets all the traffic. If several servers are defined, Nginx attempts to distribute traffic evenly among them.

It is also possible to balance load across several *local servers* using the same technique. One would simply run different Node servers on different ports, such as `server 127.0.0.1:8001; server 127.0.0.1:8002; ....`

Go ahead and change the Nginx configuration (consult the `nginx.config` file in the code bundle for this book if you get stuck). Once you've changed it, restart Nginx with the following command:

```
service nginx restart
```

Or, you can use this command:

```
service nginx stop
service nginx start
```

Assuming that the other two droplets running Node servers are active, you should now be able to point your browser to your Nginx-enabled droplet and see messages from those servers!

Because we will likely want more precise control over how traffic is distributed across our upstream servers, there are further directives that can be applied to upstream server definitions.

Nginx balances load using a weighted round-robin algorithm. In order to control the relative weighting of traffic distribution, we use the **weight** directive:

```
upstream lb-servers {
   server first.node.server.ip weight=10;
   server second.node.server.ip weight=20;
}
```

This definition tells Nginx to distribute twice as much load to the second server as to the first. Servers with more memory or CPUs might be favored, for example. Another way to use this system is to create an A/B testing scenario, where one server containing a proposed new design receives a small fraction of the total traffic such that metrics on the testing server (sales, downloads, engagement length, and so on) can be compared against the wider average.

Three other useful directives are available, which work together to manage connection failures:

- **max_fails**: This is the number of times communication with a server fails prior to marking that server as inoperative. The period of time within which these failures must occur is defined by **fail_timeout**.

- **fail_timeout**: This is the time slice during which **max_fails** must occur, indicating that a server is inoperative. This number also indicates the amount of time after a server is marked inoperative that Nginx will again attempt to reach the flagged server. Here's an example:

```
upstream lb-servers {
    server first.node.server.ip weight=10 max_fails=2
        fail_timeout=20s;
    server second.node.server.ip weight=20 max_fails=10
        fail_timeout=5m;
}
```

- **backup**: A server marked with this directive will only be called when and if *all* of the other listed servers are unavailable.

Additionally, there are some directives for the upstream definition that add some control over how clients are directed to upstream servers:

- **least_conn**: This passes a request to the server with the least connections. This provides a slightly smarter balancing, taking into consideration server load as well as weighting.
- **ip_hash**: The idea here is to create a hash of each connecting IP and to ensure that requests from a given client are always passed to the same server.

 Another commonly used tool for balancing Node servers is the dedicated load balancer **HAProxy**, which is available at `http://haproxy.1wt.eu/`.

Load balancing with Node

For many years, it was recommended that a web server (such as Nginx) be placed in front of Node servers. The claim was that mature web servers handle static file transfers more efficiently. While this may have been true for earlier Node versions (which did suffer from the bugs that new technologies face), it is no longer necessarily true in terms of pure speed. Some recent benchmarks bear this out: `http://centminmod.com/siegebenchmarks/2013/020313/index.html`.

File serving speeds are, of course, not the only reason you might use a proxy such as Nginx. It is often true that network topology characteristics make a reverse proxy the better choice, especially when the centralization of common services, such as compression, makes sense. The point is simply that Node should not be excluded solely due to outdated biases about its ability to efficiently serve files. Let's look at one example of a purely Node-based proxying and balancing solution, `node-http-proxy`.

Using node-http-proxy

Node is designed to facilitate the creation of network software, so it comes as no surprise that several proxying modules have been developed. The team at NodeJitsu has released the proxy they use in production—http-proxy. Let's take a look at how we would use it to route requests to different Node servers.

Unlike with Nginx, the entirety of our routing stack will exist in Node. Listening on port 80, one Node server will run our proxy. Three scenarios will be covered: using a single box to run multiple Node servers on separate ports on the same machine; using one box as a pure router proxying to external URLs; and creating a basic round-robin load balancer.

As an initial example, let's look at how to use this module to redirect requests:

```
var httpProxy = require('http-proxy');

var proxy = httpProxy.createServer({
  target: {
    host: 'www.example.com',
    port: 80
  }
}).listen(80);
```

By starting this server on port 80 of our local machine, we are able to redirect the user to another URL.

To run several distinct Node servers, each responding to a different URL, on a single machine, you simply have to define a router:

```
var httpProxy = httpProxy.createServer({
  router: {
    'www.mywebsite.com'    : '127.0.0.1:8001',
    'www.myothersite.com'  : '127.0.0.1:8002',
  }
});
httpProxy.listen(80);
```

For each of your distinct websites, you can now point your DNS name servers (via ANAME or CNAME) to the same endpoint (wherever this Node program is running), and they will resolve to different Node servers. This is handy when you want to run several websites but don't want to create a new physical server for each one. Another strategy is to handle different paths within the same website on different Node servers:

```
var httpProxy = httpProxy.createServer({
  router: {
    'www.mywebsite.com/friends'  : '127.0.0.1:8001',
    'www.mywebsite.com/foes'  : '127.0.0.1:8002',
  }
});
httpProxy.listen(80);
```

This allows specialized functionality in your application to be handled by uniquely configured servers.

Setting up a load balancer is also straightforward. As with Nginx's `upstream` directive, we simply list the servers to be balanced and cycle through them:

```
var httpProxy = require('http-proxy');
var addresses = [
  {
    host: 'one.example.com',
    port: 80
  },
  {
    host: 'two.example.com',
    port: 80
  }
];

httpProxy.createServer(function(req, res, proxy) {
  var target = addresses.shift();
  proxy.proxyRequest(req, res, target);
  addresses.push(target);
}).listen(80);
```

Unlike with Nginx, we are responsible for doing the actual balancing. In this example, we treat servers equally, cycling through them in order. After the selected server is proxied, it is returned to the *rear* of the list.

It should be clear that this example could be easily extended to accommodate other directives, such as Nginx's `weight`.

Another good option for proxying Node is James Halliday's `bouncy` module available at `https://github.com/substack/bouncy`.

Using message queues

One of the best ways to ensure that distributed servers maintain a dependable communication channel is to bundle the complexity of remote procedure calls into a messaging queue. When one server wishes to send a message to another server, the message can simply be placed on this queue—like a "to-do" list for your application—with the queue service doing the work of ensuring that messages get delivered as well as delivering any important replies back to the original sender.

There are a few enterprise-grade message queues available, many of which deploy the **Advanced Message Queuing Protocol (AMQP)**. We will focus on a very stable and well-known implementation: RabbitMQ.

 To install RabbitMQ in your environment, follow the instructions found at http://www.rabbitmq.com/download.html. Note that you will also need to install Erlang (the instructions for which can be found at the same link).

After installing it, you can start the RabbitMQ server with this command:

```
service rabbitmq-server start
```

To interact with RabbitMQ using Node, we will use Theo Schlossnagle's node-amqp module:

```
npm install amqp
```

To use a message queue, one must first create a consumer bound to RabbitMQ that will listen for messages published to the queue. The most basic consumer will listen for all messages:

```
var amqp = require('amqp');

var consumer = amqp.createConnection({ host: 'localhost', port: 5672
});
var exchange;

consumer.on('ready', function() {
  exchange = consumer.exchange('node-topic-exchange', {type:
    "topic"});
  consumer.queue('node-topic-queue', function(q) {

    q.bind(exchange, '#');
```

```
    q.subscribe(function(message) {
      // Messages are buffers
      //
      console.log(message.data.toString('utf8'));
    });
  });
});
```

We are now listening for messages from the RabbitMQ server bound to port 5672. It should be obvious that the *localhost* can be replaced with a proper server address and bound to any number of distributed servers.

Once this consumer establishes a connection, it will establish the name of the queue it will listen to and should `bind` to an **exchange**. In this example, we create a topic `exchange` (the default), giving it a unique name. We also indicate that we would like to listen for *all* messages via #. All that is left to do is subscribe to the queue, receiving a message object. We will learn more about the message object as we progress. For now, note the important `data` property containing the sent messages.

Now that we have established a consumer, let's publish a message to the exchange. If all goes well, we will see the sent message appear in our console:

```
consumer.on('ready', function() {

  ...

  exchange.publish("some-topic", "Hello!");
});
```

```
// Hello!
```

We have already learned enough to implement useful scaling tools. If we have a number of distributed Node processes, even on different physical servers, each can reliably send messages to the others via RabbitMQ. Each process needs to simply implement an exchange queue subscriber to receive messages and an exchange publisher when messages need to be sent.

Three types of exchanges exist: **direct**, **fanout**, and **topic**. The differences appear in the way each type of exchange processes **routing keys**—the first argument sent to `exchange.publish`.

A direct exchange matches routing keys directly. Here's an example of a queue binding:

```
queue.bind(exchange, 'room-1');
```

The preceding queue binding will match *only* messages sent to room-1. Because no parsing is necessary, direct exchanges are able to process more messages than topic exchanges in a set period of time.

A fanout exchange is indiscriminate: it routes messages to all of the queues bound to it, ignoring routing keys. This type of exchange is used for wide broadcasts.

A topic exchange matches routing keys based on the wildcards # and *. Unlike other types, routing keys for topic exchanges *must* be composed of words separated by dots—*animals.dogs.poodle*, for example. A # matches *zero or more* words—it will match every message (as we saw in the previous example) just like a fanout exchange. The other wildcard is *, and this matches *exactly one* word.

Direct and fanout exchanges can be implemented using nearly the same code as the given topic exchange example, requiring only that the exchange type be changed, and that bind operations be aware of how they will be associated with routing keys (fanout subscribers receive all messages, regardless of the key; for a direct exchange, the routing key must match directly).

This last example should drive home how topic exchanges work. We will create three queues with different matching rules, filtering the messages each queue receives from the exchange:

```
consumer.on('ready', function() {

  // When all 3 queues are ready, publish.
  //
  var cnt = 3;
  var queueReady = function() {
    if(--cnt > 0) {
      return;
    }
    exchange.publish('animals.dogs.poodles', 'Poodle!');
    exchange.publish('animals.dogs.dachshund', 'Dachshund!');
    exchange.publish('animals.cats.shorthaired', 'Shorthaired
      Cat!');
    exchange.publish('animals.dogs.shorthaired', 'Shorthaired
      Dog!');
    exchange.publish('animals.misc', 'Misc!');
  }

  var exchange = consumer.exchange('topical', {type: "topic"});
```

```
consumer.queue('queue-1', function(q) {

    q.bind(exchange, 'animals.*.shorthaired');
    q.subscribe(function(message) {
      console.log('animals.*.shorthaired -> ' +
        message.data.toString('utf8'));
    });

    queueReady();
  });

  consumer.queue('queue-2', function(q) {
    q.bind(exchange, '#');
    q.subscribe(function(message) {
      console.log('# -> ' + message.data.toString('utf8'));
    });

    queueReady();
  });

  consumer.queue('queue-3', function(q) {
    q.bind(exchange, '*.cats.*');
    q.subscribe(function(message) {
      console.log('*.cats.* -> ' + message.data.toString('utf8'));
    });

    queueReady();
  });
});

//  # -> Poodle!
//  animals.*.shorthaired -> Shorthaired Cat!
//  *.cats.* -> Shorthaired Cat!
//  # -> Dachshund!
//  # -> Shorthaired Cat!
//  animals.*.shorthaired -> Shorthaired Dog!
//  # -> Shorthaired Dog!
//  # -> Misc!
```

The node-amqp module contains further methods to control connections, queues, and exchanges, in particular methods of removing queues from exchanges and subscribers from queues. Generally, changing the makeup of a running queue on the fly can lead to unexpected errors, so use these with caution.

To learn more about the AMQP (and the options available when setting up with node-amqp), visit http://www.rabbitmq.com/ tutorials/amqp-concepts.html.

Using Node's UDP Module

User Datagram Protocol (UDP) is a lightweight core Internet messaging protocol, enabling servers to pass around concise *datagrams*. UDP was designed with a minimum of protocol overhead, forgoing delivery, ordering, and duplication prevention mechanisms in favor of ensuring high performance. UDP is a good choice when perfect reliability is not required and high-speed transmission is, as found in networked video games and videoconferencing applications. Logging is another popular use for UDP.

This is not to say that UDP is *normally* unreliable. In most applications, it delivers messages with high probability. It is simply not suitable when *perfect* reliability is needed, such as in a banking application. It is an excellent candidate for monitoring and logging applications and for noncritical messaging services.

Creating a UDP server with Node is straightforward:

```
var dgram = require('dgram');
var socket = dgram.createSocket('udp4');

socket.on('message', function(msg, info) {
  console.log('socket got: ' + msg + ' from ' +
  info.address + ':' + info.port);
});

socket.bind(41234);

socket.on('listening', function() {
  console.log('Listening for datagrams.');
});
```

The bind command takes three arguments:

- **port**: This is the integer port number.
- **address**: This is an optional address. If this is not specified, the OS will try to listen on all addresses (which is often what you want). You might also try using 0.0.0.0 explicitly.
- **callback**: This is an optional callback, which receives no arguments.

This socket will now emit a **message** event whenever it receives a datagram via port 41234. The event callback receives the message itself as the first parameter and a map of packet information as the second:

- **address**: This is the originating IP
- **family**: This is one of IPv4 or IPv6
- **port**: This is the originating port
- **size**: This is the size of the message in bytes

This map is similar to the map returned when calling socket.address().

In addition to the message and listening events, a UDP socket also emits a close event and an error event, with the latter receiving an Error object whenever an error occurs. To close a UDP socket (and trigger the close event), use server.close().

Sending a message is even easier:

```
var client = dgram.createSocket('udp4');
var message = new Buffer('UDP says Hello!');
client.send(message, 0, message.length, 41234, 'localhost',
  function(err, bytes) {
  client.close();
});
```

The send method takes the form client.send(buffer, offset, length, port, host, callback):

- **buffer**: This is a buffer containing the datagram to be sent
- **offset**: This is an integer indicating the position in the **buffer** where the datagram begins
- **length**: This is the number of bytes in a datagram. In combination with **offset**, this value identifies the full datagram within the **buffer**
- **port**: This is an integer identifying the destination port
- **address**: This is a string indicating the destination IP for the datagram
- **callback**: This is an optional callback function called after the send has taken place.

 The size of a datagram cannot exceed 65,507 bytes, which is equal to $2^{16}-1$ (65,535) bytes minus the 8 bytes used by the UDP header minus the 20 bytes used by the IP header.

We now have another candidate for interprocess messaging. It would be rather easy to set up a monitoring server for our Node application that listens on a UDP socket for program updates and statistics sent from other processes. The protocol speed is fast enough for real-time systems, and any packet loss or other UDP hiccups would be insignificant taken as a percentage of total volume over time.

Taking the idea of broadcasting further, we can also use the `dgram` module to create a multicast server. A "multicast" is simply a one-to-many server broadcast. We can broadcast to a range of IPs that have been permanently reserved as multicast addresses. The website `http://www.iana.org/assignments/multicast-addresses/multicast-addresses.xhtml` has this to say:

> *"Host Extensions for IP Multicasting [RFC1112] specifies the extensions required of a host implementation of the Internet Protocol (IP) to support multicasting. The multicast addresses are in the range 224.0.0.0 through 239.255.255.255."*

Additionally, the range between 224.0.0.0 and 224.0.0.255 is further reserved for special routing protocols.

Also, certain port numbers are allocated for use by UDP (and TCP), a list of which can be found at `https://en.wikipedia.org/wiki/List_of_TCP_and_UDP_port_numbers`.

The upshot of all this fascinating information is the knowledge that there is a block of IPs and ports reserved for UDP and/or multicasting, and we are now going to use some of them to implement multicasting over UDP with Node.

The only difference between setting up a multicasting UDP server and a "standard" one is the binding of the multicasting server to a special UDP port to indicate that we'd like to listen to *all* available network adapters. Our multicasting server initialization looks like this:

```
var socket = dgram.createSocket('udp4');

var multicastAddress   = '230.1.2.3';
var multicastPort   = 5554;

socket.bind(multicastPort);

socket.on('listening', function() {
  this.setMulticastTTL(64);
  this.addMembership(multicastAddress);
});
```

After requesting a multicast port binding, we wait for the socket listen event, at which point we can configure our server.

The most important command is `socket.addMembership`, which tells the kernel to join the multicast group at `multicastAddress`. Other UDP sockets can now subscribe to the multicast group at this address.

Datagrams hop through networks just like any network packet. The `setMulticastTTL` method is used to set the maximum number of hops ("time to live") a datagram is allowed to make before it is abandoned and not delivered. The acceptable range is 0–255, with the default being one (1) on most systems. This is not usually a setting one must worry about, but it is available if deep visibility into network topology lends relevance to this aspect of packet delivery.

 If you'd also like to allow listening on the *local* interface, use `socket.setBroadcast(true)` and `socket.setMulticastLoopback(true)`. This is normally not necessary.

We are eventually going to use this server to broadcast messages to all UDP listeners on `multicastAddress`. For now, let's create two clients that will listen for multicasts:

```
dgram.createSocket('udp4')
.on('message', function(message, remote) {
  console.log('Client1 received message ' + message + ' from ' +
    remote.address + ':' + remote.port);
})
.bind(multicastPort, multicastAddress);

dgram.createSocket('udp4')
.on('message', function(message, remote) {
  console.log('Client2 received message ' + message + ' from ' +
    remote.address + ':' + remote.port);
})
.bind(multicastPort, multicastAddress);
```

We now have two clients listening to the same multicast port. All that is left to do is the multicasting. In this example, we will use `setTimeout` to send a counter value every second:

```
var cnt = 1;
var sender;
```

```
(sender = function() {
  var msg = new Buffer("This is message #" + cnt);
  socket.send(
    msg,
    0,
    msg.length,
    multicastPort,
    multicastAddress
  );

  ++cnt;

  setTimeout(sender, 1000);

})();
```

The preceding code will produce something like the following:

```
Client2 received message This is message #1 from 67.40.141.16:5554
Client1 received message This is message #1 from 67.40.141.16:5554
Client2 received message This is message #2 from 67.40.141.16:5554
Client1 received message This is message #2 from 67.40.141.16:5554
Client2 received message This is message #3 from 67.40.141.16:5554
...
```

We have two clients listening to broadcasts from a specific group. Let's add another client, listening on a different group—let's say at the multicast address 230.3.2.1:

```
dgram.createSocket('udp4')
.on('message', function(message, remote) {
  console.log('Client3 received message ' + message + ' from ' +
    remote.address + ':' + remote.port);
})
.bind(multicastPort, '230.3.2.1');
```

Because our server currently broadcasts messages to a different address, we will need to change our server configuration and add this new address with another addMembership call:

```
socket.on("listening", function() {
  this.addMembership(multicastAddress);
  this.addMembership('230.3.2.1');
});
```

We can now send messages to *both* addresses:

```
(sender = function() {
  socket.send(

    ...

    multicastAddress
  );

  socket.send(

    ...

    '230.3.2.1'
  );


  ...
})();
```

Of course, nothing stops the client from broadcasting to others in its group or even members of *another* group:

```
dgram.createSocket('udp4')
.on('message', function(message, remote) {
  var msg = new Buffer("Calling original group!");
  socket.send(
    msg,
    0,
    msg.length,
    multicastPort,
    '230.1.2.3' // multicastAddress
  );
})
.bind(multicastPort, '230.3.2.1');
```

Any Node process that has an address on our network interface can now listen on a UDP multicast address for messages, providing a fast and elegant interprocess communication system.

Summary

In this chapter, we looked at ways in which Node applications can be scaled both vertically and horizontally. We learned how to use `spawn` on OS processes and to use `fork` on new Node processes. The overview of the `cluster` module demonstrated how easy it is to scale across cores using Node and efficiently and easily distribute client connections across workers with built-in messaging channels to the central (master) hub. We also looked at how horizontally distributed processes and servers can communicate using message queues and UDP servers and how these servers can be load balanced and proxied using Nginx or using Node modules designed for that purpose.

Scaling is not only about servers and load balancing. In the next chapter, we'll look at how to scale and manage resources, learn about memory management techniques, synchronize data across distributed services, synchronize data-caching strategies, and look at how to deal with massive numbers of simultaneous connections.

4
Managing Memory and Space

Today's developer has easy access to surprisingly inexpensive storage solutions. The movement away from monolithic systems toward composed and distributed ones has certain advantages, yet inevitably introduces a few new problems. The availability of cheap storage should not be an excuse to push everything you can into memory or onto a disk without any limit, for instance. Also, where does the state reside in such a system? Does a cluster of servers share a common database connection? How is data synchronized in such a setup? If you are using a *shared-nothing noSQL* architecture, how are state changes communicated across all actors?

There are many considerations. Always seeking to use a minimum of resources is a good guiding principle. In this chapter, we will look at ways to reduce the cost of data storage in your Node programs, including tips on writing efficient, optimized code. Certain strategies for efficiently sharing data across distributed servers will be discussed, including caching strategies, microservices, interprocess messaging, and other techniques to keep your systems fast, light, and scalable. Examples demonstrating how to use tokens to manage user session data efficiently at scale and storing extensive user activity data compactly using Redis will help you put these ideas into practice.

Dealing with large crowds

Because Node is designed to make the writing of networked applications easier, those using Node are often building applications composed of many isolated services that are connected via message queues, sockets, REST APIs, and so on. I will describe these as distributed applications composed of isolated services coupled and coordinated through a network into systems that appear integrated to clients. In this section and the sections that follow, we will consider how isolated services can be designed to be memory efficient with a small footprint.

For the purposes of this section and what follows, the word **microservice** will be used when referring to application architectures composed of many small cooperating services. Generally, we'll explore ideas around how well-designed modularization can often help keep a system from becoming inscrutable by helping maintain expressive, scalable, testable systems that maintain production readiness.

Then, we'll put the microservice theory into practice by using Richard Rogers' microservice toolkit for Node, **Seneca** (`https://github.com/rjrodger/seneca`). Finally, we'll take a look at how to use Redis pub/sub as a cross-process communication system, thus demonstrating another way to compose your own microservice clusters.

Microservices

Any nontrivial, network-based application is composed of several independent subsystems that must cooperate to fulfill the business or other requirements of the larger system. For example, many web applications present browser-based interfaces composed of one or several libraries and/or UI frameworks translating user actions against JavaScript controllers into formalized network requests issued across several web protocols. These ultimately communicate with any number of servers running programs that implement various sorts of business logic—all sharing one or several databases, perhaps across several data centers. These initiate and coordinate even longer chains of requests.

Because there is no absolute *right way* to build software, every design is biased toward one or a few key principles, in particular, principles guiding how a system should scale, which normally affects how it is deployed. A few of the key principles informing the Node community—modular systems composed of small programs that do one thing well and are event-driven, I/O focused, and network focused—align closely with those underpinning microservices.

Microservice architecture designs typically respect the following principles:

- A system should be broken down into many small services that each do one thing and no more. This helps with clarity.

- The code-powering services should be short and simple. A common guideline in the Node community is to limit programs to somewhere near 100 lines of code. This helps with maintainability.

- No service should depend on the existence of another service or even know of the existence of other services. Services are decoupled. This helps with scalability, clarity, and maintainability.

- Data models should be decentralized, with a common (but not required) microservice pattern—that each service maintains its own database or a similar model. Services are stateless (this reinforces the previous point).

- Independent services are easy to replicate (or cull). Scaling (in both directions) is a natural feature of microservice architectures as new *nodes* can be added or removed as necessary. This also enables easy experimentation, where prototype services can be tested, new features can be tested or deployed temporarily, and so on.

- Independent, stateless services can be replaced or upgraded (or downgraded) independently regardless of the state of any system they form a part of. This opens the possibility of more focused, discrete deployments and refactors.

- Failure is unavoidable, so systems should be designed to fail gracefully. Localize points of failure (the first and second points of this list), isolate failure (the third and fourth points of this list), and implement recovery mechanisms (easier when error boundaries are clearly defined, small, and noncritical). Promote robustness by reducing the scope of unreliability.

- Testing is essential to any nontrivial system. Unambiguous and simple stateless services are easy to test. A key aspect of testing is simulation—the *stubbing* or *mocking* of services in order to test service interoperability. Clearly delineated services are also easy to simulate and can, therefore, be intelligently composed into testable systems.

The idea is simple: smaller services are easy to reason about individually, encouraging correctness of specifications (little or no gray area) and clarity of APIs (constrained sets of output follow constrained sets of input). Being stateless and decoupled, services promote system composability, help with scaling and maintainability, and are easier to deploy. Also, very precise, discrete monitoring of these sorts of systems is possible.

Redis pub/sub

In the previous chapter, we discussed the use of message queues, an excellent technique for rapid cross-process communication. Redis offers an interface allowing connected clients to subscribe to a particular channel and broadcast messages to that channel. This is generally described as a publish/subscribe paradigm. When you do not need more complex message exchanges and brokers but a simple and fast notification network, pub/sub works well.

Let's set up a basic pub/sub example and then move on to an example of using pub/sub to create a microservice architecture where many components doing a particular job are passed requests for their services and pass back results—all coordinated via Redis.

First, let's look at the most basic example of pub/sub—a script that demonstrates how to subscribe to a channel and how to publish to that channel:

```
var redis = require("redis");

var publisher = redis.createClient();
var subscriber = redis.createClient();

subscriber.subscribe('channel5');

subscriber.on('message', function(channel, message) {
  console.log('channel: ', channel)
  console.log('message: ', message)
})

subscriber.on('subscribe', function() {
  publisher.publish('channel5', 'This is a message')
})
```

 We are using Matt Ranney's **Redis** npm module. Find out more at https://github.com/mranney/node_redis.

To create both a publisher and a subscriber, we create two Redis clients. Note that, once a subscribe or psubscribe (more on psubscribe later) command is issued to a client, that client will enter *subscriber mode*, no longer accepting standard Redis commands. Typically, you will create two clients: one listening for messages on subscribed channels and the other a standard Redis client used for all other commands.

Also note that we must wait for the `subscribe` event to be fired on the `subscriber` client prior to publishing any messages. Redis does not hold a queue of published messages, which involves waiting for subscribers. A message for which there are no subscribers is simply dropped. The following is based on the Redis documentation:

> *"...published messages are characterized into channels, without knowledge of what (if any) subscribers there may be. Subscribers express interest in one or more channels, and only receive messages that are of interest, without knowledge of what (if any) publishers there are. This decoupling of publishers and subscribers can allow for greater scalability and a more dynamic network topology."*

So, we must wait for a subscriber prior to publishing. Once that subscription is made, we can publish to the `channel5` channel, and the `subscriber` handle listening on that channel receives our message:

```
channel: channel5

message: This is a message
```

Let's take this a little further by creating two distinct Node processes, each performing a simple (micro) service. We'll build a calculator service with two operations—add and subtract. A separate, dedicated process will perform each operation, and the two-way communication between the calculator service and its helper services will be managed by Redis pub/sub.

First, we design two Node programs, one that adds and one that subtracts. We'll only show the adder here:

```
var redis = require("redis");
var publisher = redis.createClient();
var subscriber = redis.createClient();

subscriber.subscribe('service:add');
subscriber.on('message', function(channel, operands) {
  var result = JSON.parse(operands).reduce(function(a, b) {
    return a + b;
  })
  publisher.publish('added', result);
})
subscriber.on('subscribe', function() {
  process.send('ok')
})
```

The subtraction program is nearly identical, differing only in the channel it listens on and the calculation it performs. These two services exist in the `add.js` and `subtract.js` files.

We can see what this service does. When it receives a message on the `service:add` channel, it will fetch the two operands passed to it, add them, and publish the result to the `added` channel. As we'll soon see, the calculator service will listen for results on the `added` channel. Also, you will notice a call to `process.send`—this is used to notify the calculator service that the add service is ready. This will make more sense shortly.

Now, let's build the `calculator.js` service itself:

```
var redis = require("redis");
var publisher = redis.createClient();
var subscriber = redis.createClient();

var child_process = require('child_process');
var add = child_process.fork('add.js');
var subtract = child_process.fork('subtract.js');

add.on('message', function() {
  publisher.publish('service:add', JSON.stringify([7,3]))
})
subtract.on('message', function() {
  publisher.publish('service:subtract', JSON.stringify([7,3]))
})
subscriber.subscribe('result:added')
subscriber.subscribe('result:subtracted')
subscriber.on('message', function(operation, result) {
  console.log(operation + ' = ', result);
});
```

The main calculator service forks two new processes running the `add.js` and `subtract.js` microservices. Typically, in a real system, the creation of these other services would be done independently, perhaps even on completely separate machines. This simplification is useful for our example, but it does demonstrate a simple way to create vertical scaling across cores. Clearly, each child process in Node on which `fork` has been used comes with a communication channel built in, allowing child processes to communicate with their parents as seen in the calculator service's use of `add.on(...)` and `substract.on(...)` and in our calculation services with `process.send(...)`.

Once the calculator service receives notice that its dependent services are ready, it publishes a request for work to be done on the `service:add` and `service:subtract` channels by passing operands. As we saw earlier, each service listens on its own channel and performs the work requested, publishing a result that this calculator service can then receive and use. When `calculator.js` is executed, the following will be displayed in your terminal:

```
result:subtracted = 4

result:added = 10
```

Earlier, we mentioned the `psubscribe` method. The p prefix signifies *pattern* and is useful when you want to subscribe to channels using a typical glob pattern. For example, rather than the calculator service subscribing to two channels with the common `result:` prefix, we can simplify it as follows:

```
subscriber.psubscribe('result:*')
subscriber.on('pmessage', function(operation, result) {
  console.log(operation + ' = ', result);
})
```

Now, any additional service can publish results with the `result:` prefix and can be picked up by our calculator. Note that the p prefix must also be reflected in the `pmessage` event listener.

Microservices with Seneca

Seneca is a Node-based microservice construction kit that helps you organize your code into distinct **actions** triggered by **patterns**. Seneca applications are composed of services that can accept JSON messages and, optionally, return some JSON. Services register an interest in messages with certain characteristics. For example, a service might run whenever a JSON message displaying { `cmd: "doSomething"` } is broadcast.

To start, let's create a service that responds to two patterns, one pattern returning `"Hello!"` and the other returning `"Goodbye!"`. Create a `hellogoodbye.js` file containing the following code:

```
var seneca = require('seneca')();
var client = seneca.client(8080);

require('seneca')()
.add({
  operation:'sayHello'
},
function(args, done) {
```

```
    done(null, {message: "Hello!"})
  })
  .add({
    operation:'sayGoodbye'
  },
  function(args, done) {
    done(null, {message: "Goodbye!"})
  })
  .listen(8080);

  client.act({ operation: "sayHello" }, function(err, result) {
    console.log(result.message);
  })

  client.act({ operation: "sayGoodbye" }, function(err, result) {
    console.log(result.message);
  })
```

The call to `seneca()` starts up a service that will listen on port `8080` on `localhost` for patterns rendered in the JSON format—one of either `{ operation: "sayHello" }` or `{ operation: "sayGoodbye" }`. We also create a `client` object connected to the Seneca service on `8080` and have that client act against those patterns. When this program is executed, you will see `Hello!` and `Goodbye!` displayed in your terminal.

Because the Seneca service is listening on HTTP by default, you can achieve the same result by making a direct call over HTTP, operating against the `/act` route:

```
curl -d '{"operation":"sayHello"}' http://localhost:8080/act
// {"message":"Hello!"}
```

Now, let's replicate the calculator application developed earlier, this time using Seneca. We're going to create two services, each listening on a distinct port, with one performing addition and the other performing subtraction. As in the previous calculator example, each will be started as an individual process and called remotely.

Create an `add.js` file as follows:

```
  require('seneca')()
  .add({
    operation:'add'
  },
  function(args, done) {
    var result = args.operands[0] + args.operands[1];
    done(null, {
      result : result
```

```
    })
  })
  .listen({
    host:'127.0.0.1',
    port:8081
  })
```

Next, create a `subtract.js` file identical to `add.js`, changing only its operation parameter and, of course, its algorithm:

```
  ...
  .add({
    operation:'subtract'
  },
  ...
    var result = args.operands[0] - args.operands[1];
  ...
```

Open two terminals, and start both services:

node add.js

...

node subtract.js

To demonstrate the usage of these services, create a `calculator.js` file that binds a client to each service on its unique port and acts against them. Note that you must create distinct Seneca clients:

```
  var add = require('seneca')().client({
    host:'127.0.0.1',
    port:8081
  })
  var subtract = require('seneca')().client({
    host:'127.0.0.1',
    port:8082
  })
  add.act({
    operation:'add',
    operands: [7,3]
  },
  function(err, op) {
    console.log(op.result)
  })
  subtract.act({
    operation:'subtract',
    operands: [7,3]
```

```
  },
  function(err, op) {
    console.log(op.result)
  })
```

Executing this program will result in the following:

```
10 // adding
```

```
4 // subtracting
```

Just as with the previous example, we can make a direct HTTP call:

```
curl -d '{"operation":"add","operands":[7,3]}' http://127.0.0.1:8081/act
// {"result":10}
```

By building out your calculator in this way, each operation can be isolated into its own service, and you can add or remove functionality as needed without affecting the overall program. Should a service develop bugs, you can fix and replace it without stopping the general calculator application. If one operation requires more powerful hardware or more memory, you can shift it to its own server without stopping the calculator application or altering your application logic—you only need to change the IP address of the targeted service. In the same way, it is easy to see how, by stringing together the database, authentication, transaction, mapping, and other services, they can be more easily modeled, deployed, scaled, monitored, and maintained than if they were all coupled to a centralized service manager.

Reducing memory usage

JavaScript was born and raised in the browser environment. For most of its history, this also implied that JavaScript programs were running on desktop systems with an enormous pool of available memory. For this reason, many JavaScript programmers have not traditionally thought much about managing memory in their applications.

In the world of Node, memory is not so cheap. According to Joyent (`https://github.com/joyent/node/wiki/FAQ#what-is-the-memory-limit-on-a-node-process`):

> *"Currently, by default, v8 has a memory limit of 512 MB on 32-bit systems and 1 GB on 64-bit systems. The limit can be raised by setting --max_old_space_size to a maximum of ~1024 (~1 GB) (32-bit) and ~1741 (~1.7 GiB) (64-bit), but it is recommended that you split your single process into several workers if you are hitting memory limits."*

Let's go over possible strategies to reduce the amount of memory your Node programs consume. We'll end with a discussion of how to make use of two memory-efficient data structures supported by Redis when developing your projects.

Use streams, not buffers

The design and implementation of Node.js native modules follow a simple directive: keep everything asynchronous. This design ethic, by convention, informs the design of modules contributed by the Node community.

When a process operates synchronously, it holds, or locks, the total amount of memory it needs to fully complete, at which point the memory it has held is flushed, usually returning this result to the calling method or process. For example, the following operation will load the entirety of a file into the memory prior to returning it:

```
var http = require('http')
var fs = require('fs')
http.createServer(function(req, res) {
  fs.readFile('./somefile.js', function(err, data) {
    res.writeHead(200);
    res.end(data)
  })
}).listen(8000)
```

When a request is made to `localhost:8000`, the `somefile.js` file is read off the filesystem *in its entirety* and returned to the client. That is the desired effect—but there is a slight problem. Because the entire file is being pushed into a buffer prior to being returned, an amount of memory equal to the byte size of the file must be allocated on each request. While the operation is itself asynchronous (allowing other operations to proceed), just a few requests for a very large file (of several MB, for example) can overflow the memory and take down the Node process.

Node excels at creating scalable web services. One of the reasons for this is the focus on providing robust `Stream` interfaces.

A better strategy is to stream the file directly to the HTTP response object (which is a writable stream):

```
http.createServer(function(req, res) {
  fs.createReadStream('./static_buffered.js').pipe(res);
}).listen(8000)
```

In addition to requiring less code, data is sent (piped) directly to the out stream, using very little memory.

On the other hand, we can use Stream to enable a very nice and composable pipeline of transformations. There are several ways to achieve this goal (such as with `Transform Stream`), but we'll just create our own transformer.

This script will take an input from `process.stdin` and convert what is received to uppercase, piping the result back to `process.stdout`:

```
var Stream = require('stream')
var through = new Stream;
through.readable = true;
through.writable = true;
through.write = function(buf) {
  through.emit('data', buf.toString().toUpperCase())
}
through.end = function(buf) {
  arguments.length && through.write(buf)
  through.emit('end')
}
process.stdin.pipe(through).pipe(process.stdout);
```

As much as possible, convert your program logic into discrete stream transformations, and compose useful pipelines that do good things with data without touching the memory.

Understanding prototypes

JavaScript is an **Object-oriented** (OO) prototype-based language. It is important for you to understand what this means and how this sort of design is more memory efficient than many traditional OO language designs when used correctly. Because the storage of state data within Node processes is a common practice (such as connection data lookup tables within a socket server), we should leverage the prototypal nature of the language to minimize memory usage. What follows is a brief but pointed comparison of the classical inheritance-based object model and the object system that JavaScript provides in terms of memory usage and efficiency.

In class-based systems, a **class** contains instructions on how to create instances of itself. In other words, a class describes a set containing objects built according to a class specification, which includes things such as default values for attributes of constructed objects. To create an instance of a class, there must be a class definition that describes how to build that instance. Classes can also inherit properties from each other, creating new instance blueprints that share characteristics with other blueprints—an inheritance model describing the provenance of objects.

The primary purpose of any OO system is to facilitate the sharing of common knowledge between related objects. For example, this is how you would create two Point instances using an inheritance model:

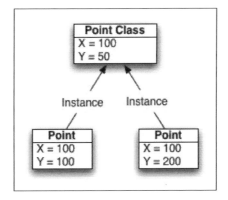

Note that both instances now maintain an identical attribute structure. Additionally, the property x of both point instances has been copied from the base point class. Importantly, notice that the value of x has been copied to each instance even though this attribute value is identical in both instances.

Objects in a prototypal language do not require a class to define their composition. For example, an object in JavaScript can be created literally:

```
var myPoint = {
    x : 100,
    y : 50
}
```

Not requiring the storage of a class definition prior to creating an object instance is already more memory efficient. Now, consider this use of prototypes to replicate the inheritance-based example discussed previously. In the following code, we see how a single object, myPoint, is passed as the first object to Object.create, which returns a new object with myPoint as its prototype:

```
var myPoint = {
  x: 100,
  y: 50
}
var pointA = Object.create(myPoint, {
  y: 100
})
var pointA = Object.create(myPoint, {
  y: 200
})
```

`Object.create` is the preferred method in modern JavaScript (ES5+) to create objects. Older browsers will not support this syntax. For more information on compatibility, visit `http://kangax.github.io/compat-table/es5/#Object.create`.

This creates the following object construct:

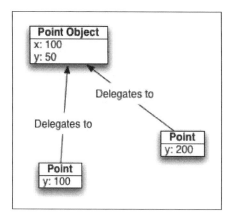

Note that each point instance *does not store copies* of attributes, the value of which is not explicitly declared. Prototypal systems employ message delegation, not inheritance. When a point instance receives the message *give me x*, and it cannot satisfy that request, it delegates the responsibility for satisfying that message to its prototype (which, in this case, does have a value for x). It should be obvious that, in real-world scenarios with large and complex objects, the ability to share default values across many instances without redundantly copying identical bytes will lead to a smaller memory footprint. Additionally, these instances can themselves function as prototypes for other objects, continuing a delegation chain indefinitely and enabling elegant object graphs using only as much memory as necessary to distinguish unique object properties.

Memory efficiency also speeds up instantiation. As should be clear from the preceding code, delegating responsibility for messages to a prototype implies that your extended receiver requires a smaller instance footprint—fewer slots need to be allocated per object. The following are two construction function definitions:

```
var rec1 = function() {}
rec1.prototype.message = function() { ... }
var rec2 = function() {
  this.message = function() { ... }
}
```

Even with these simple definitions, many instances built from the first constructor will consume much less memory than an equal number of instances constructed from the second—new Rec1() will complete well before new Rec2() due to the redundant copying seen in the second prototype-less constructor.

> You can see a performance comparison of the two instantiation methods at http://jsperf.com/prototype-speeds.

Use prototypes intelligently to reduce memory usage in your objects and to lower instantiation times. Determine the static or infrequently changed attributes and methods of your objects and put those into prototypes. This will allow you to create thousands of objects quickly, while reducing redundancy.

Memory-efficient data structures with Redis

While you should use the memory allotted to you in each Node process, more memory will likely be needed. In this section, we will look at Redis, an in-memory, high-speed database, and how it can be used to efficiently extend the amount of memory available to your programs.

At its most basic, Redis is a fast key-value store. We'll see later how it can be used as a cache for commonly used pieces of data. However, it also provides powerful data structures and an API allowing complex operations on those structures, thus helping with the modeling of sets of data and the relationships between sets of data. Here, we will discuss how to use Redis support for **Bit Operations (bitops)** and **HyperLogLog**—two space-efficient and, importantly, space-predictable memory structures to store and analyze the activity of data.

Using bitwise operations to analyze user actions over time

One of the more interesting features Redis provides is the ability to store binary numbers as values for keys. Multiple keys containing binary values can be compared by using the **bitwise operators** AND, OR, and XOR. By applying bitmasks mapping a range of bits to other binary values, you can make very rapid and memory-efficient analytical comparisons. In this section, we will learn some typical examples of how to use this technique.

Any key in a Redis database can store (2^32 - 1) bits or just under 512 MiB. This means that there are approximately 4.29 billion columns, or offsets, that can be set per key. This is a large number of data points referenced by a single key. We can set bits along these ranges to describe the characteristics of an item we would like to track, such as the number of users who have viewed a given article. Furthermore, we can use bit operations to gather other dimensions of information, such as what percentage of viewers of an article are female. Let's look at a few examples.

Setting, getting, and counting bits

Let's assume that we are serving many different articles and each article is assigned a unique identifier. Also assume that we have 100,000 active members on our website, and that each user also has a unique identifier—a number between 1 and 100,000. Using bit operations, we can easily track article view activity on a given day by creating a key in Redis, which can be done by combining the article's unique key and a date string and setting bits at that key corresponding to the user ID associated with an article view. For example:

```
article:324:01-03-2014 : 00010100111010001001111...
```

This key represents article 324 on a specific date, efficiently storing the unique user IDs of viewers on that day by *flipping a bit* at an offset corresponding to the user's assigned ID. Whenever a user views an article, fetch that user's ID, use that number as an offset value, and use the `setbit` command to set a bit at that offset:

```
redis.setbit('article:324:01-03-2014', userId, 1)
```

In what follows, we're going to demonstrate how to use Redis bitops to efficiently store and analyze data. First, let's create data for three articles:

```
var redis = require('redis');
var client = redis.createClient();
var multi = client.multi();
// Create three articles with randomized hits representing user views
var id = 100000;
while(id--) {
  multi.setbit('article1:today', id, Math.round(Math.random(1)));
  multi.setbit('article2:today', id, Math.round(Math.random(1)));
  multi.setbit('article3:today', id, Math.round(Math.random(1)));
}
multi.exec(function(err) {
  // done
})
```

Here, we simply created three Redis keys, `'article (1-3):today'`, and randomly set 100,000 bits on each key—either 0 or 1. Using the technique of storing user activity based on user ID offsets, we now have sample data for a hypothetical day of traffic against three articles.

 We're using Matt Ranney's `node_redis` module (`https://github.com/mranney`), which supports the Redis **multi** construct, allowing the execution of several instructions in one pipeline rather than suffering the cost of calling each individually. Always use `multi` when performing several operations in order to speed up your operations. Note also how the ordering guarantees provided by Redis ensure ordered execution and how its atomicity guarantees that either all or none of the instructions in a transaction will succeed. See `http://redis.io/topics/transactions`.

To count the number of users who have viewed an article, we can use `bitcount`:

```
client.bitcount('article1:today', function(err, count) {
  console.log(count)
})
```

This is straightforward: the number of users who saw the article equals the number of bits set on the key. Now, let's count the total number of article views:

```
client.multi([
  ["bitcount", "article1:today"],
  ["bitcount", "article2:today"],
  ["bitcount", "article3:today"]
]).exec(function(err, totals) {
  var total = totals.reduce(function(prev, cur) {
    return prev + cur;
  }, 0);
  console.log("Total views: ", total);
})
```

Once `multi` returns an array of results corresponding to the results returned by Redis for each operation (a count of bits), we `reduce` the count to a sum representing the total number of views of all our articles.

If we are interested, instead, in how many articles user 123 has viewed today, we can use `getbit`, which simply returns the value (either 0 or 1) at a given offset. The result will be in the range 0–3:

```
client.multi([
  ["getbit", "article1:today", 123],
  ["getbit", "article2:today", 123],
```

```
    ["getbit", "article3:today", 123]
]).exec(function(err, hits) {
  var total = hits.reduce(function(prev, cur) {
    return prev + cur;
  }, 0);
  console.log(total); // 0, 1, 2 or 3
})
```

These are very useful and direct ways to glean information from bit representations. Let's go a little further and learn about filtering bits using bitmasks and the AND, OR, and XOR operators.

Bitmasks and filtering results

Previously, we learned how to count the number of articles user 123 has seen. What if we want to check whether user 123 has read both articles? Using the bitop AND, this is easy to accomplish:

```
client.multi([
  ['setbit', 'user123', 123, 1],
  ['bitop', 'AND','123:sawboth','user123','article1:today',
    'article3:today'],
  ['getbit', '123:sawboth', 123]
]).exec(function(err, result) {
  var sawboth = result[2];
  console.log('123 saw both articles: ', !!sawboth);
});
```

First, we create a mask that isolates a specific user stored at the key `'user123'`, containing a single positive bit at offset 123 (again, representing the user's ID). The results of an AND operation on two or more bit representations is not returned as a value by Redis but rather written to a specified key, which is given in the preceding example as `'123:sawboth'`. This key contains the bit representation that answers the question whether *both* the article keys contain bit representations that also have a positive bit at the same offset as the 'user123' key.

What if we wanted to find the total number of users who have seen at least one article? The bitop OR works well in this case:

```
client.multi([
  ['bitop', 'OR','atleastonearticle','article1:today',
    'article2:today','article3:today'],
  ['bitcount', 'atleastonearticle']
]).exec(function(err, results) {
  console.log("At least one: ", results[1]);
});
```

Here, the `'atleastonearticle'` key flags bits at all offsets that were set in any one of the three articles.

We can use these techniques to create a simple recommendation engine. For example, if we are able to determine via other means that two articles are similar (based on tags, keywords, and so on), we can find all users that have read one and recommended the other. To do this, we will use XOR in order to find all users that have read the first article or the second article, but not both. We then break that set into two lists: those who have read the first article and those who have read the second article. We can then use these lists to offer recommendations:

```
client.multi([
  ['bitop','XOR','recommendother','article1:today',
    'article2:today'],
  ['bitop','AND','recommend:article1','recommendother',
    'article2:today'],
  ['bitop','AND','recommend:article2','recommendother',
    'article1:today'],
  ['bitcount', 'recommendother'],
  ['bitcount', 'recommend:article1'],
  ['bitcount', 'recommend:article2'],
  ['del', 'recommendother', 'recommend:article1',
    'recommend:article2']
]).exec(function(err, results) {
  //  Note result offset due to first 3 setup ops
  console.log("Didn't see both articles: ", results[3]);
  console.log("Saw article2; recommend article1: ", results[4]);
  console.log("Saw article1; recommend article2: ", results[5]);
})
```

While it is not necessary, we also fetch a count of each list and delete the result keys when we are done.

The total number of bytes occupied by a binary value in Redis is calculated by dividing the largest offset by 8. This means that storing access data for even 1,000,000 users on one article requires 125 KB—not a lot. If you have 1,000 articles in your database, you can store full-access data for 1,000,000 users in 125 MB—again, not a very large amount of memory or storage to spend in return for such a rich set of analytics data. Also, the amount of storage needed can be precisely calculated ahead of time.

View the code bundle for an example of building a *like this page* service, where we use a bookmarklet to trigger *likes* on any URL using bit operations to store the time at which each *like* occurs (offsetting by the current second on a given day).

Other useful ways to deploy bitwise ideas are easy to find. Consider that if we allocate 86,400 bits to a key (the number of seconds in a day) and set a bit corresponding to the current second in the day, whenever a particular action is performed (such as a login), we have spent *86400 / 8 / 1000 = 10.8 KB* to store login data that can easily be filtered using bitmasks to deliver analytics data.

As an exercise, use bitmasks to demonstrate gender breakdown in article readership. Assume that we have stored two keys in Redis, one reflecting the user IDs identified as female and the other as male:

```
users:female  : 00100001011000000011110010101...
users:male    : 11011110100111111100001101010...
```

Using bit operations, we filter articles by gender.

Using HyperLogLog to count unique anonymous visitors

One of the most common things done with databases is storing and counting unique things. How many events of a certain type have occurred? How many tags have been created?

Consider the nearly ubiquitous task of every marketer: counting the number of unique visitors to a web page. Traditionally, counting is done in databases by writing a row of data or in logs by writing a line of text whenever a visitor lands on a page. Each unique visit increments the set length by one. These are simple and straightforward techniques.

However, there is a problem: what if the same person arrives at the same page more than once? Whenever the user *John* lands on a page, some work must be done to determine whether this is a first-time occurrence (record it), or a repeat occurrence (don't record it). And there is another problem: the entire sequence of bytes representing a unique identifier — typically a very long hash — must be stored. Each unique item adds to the total memory expended in keeping track of item counts of the cardinality of a set. As we can't know in advance how many unique hits will occur, we cannot know how much memory will be needed to store this potential activity; we are, therefore, exposed to the risk of our system being overwhelmed when one page or another becomes very popular, goes viral, and so on, overnight.

HyperLogLog is a probabilistic data structure that allows a nearly infinite number of unique items to be counted within a fixed memory allocation. As Salvatore Sanfilippo puts it at `http://antirez.com/news/75`:

> *"HyperLogLog is remarkable as it provides a very good approximation of the cardinality of a set even using a very small amount of memory. In the Redis implementation it only uses 12kbytes per key to count with a standard error of 0.81%, and there is no limit to the number of items you can count, unless you approach 2^64 items (which seems quite unlikely)."*

In your code bundle, you will find the `/hyperloglog` folder containing a simple counting application. Start this application by running `server.js`, and then, in your browser, visit `localhost:8080`. When you get there, click on the **Send a specific value** button. You should see the following output:

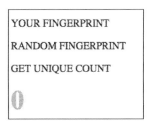

You have inserted the value `123` into a HyperLogLog key, and the number returned (1) is the cardinality of that key's set. Click on the same button a few times— given that this structure maintains a count of unique values, the number should not change. Now, try adding random values. You will see the numbers returned go up. Regardless of how many entries you make in the log key, the same amount of memory will be used. This sort of predictability is great when scaling out your application.

You can find the `index.html` page describing this client interface in the code bundle. All that the client needs to do is send an XHR request to `localhost:8080/log/<some value>`. Feel free to browse the code. More to the point, let's look at how the relevant route handler is defined on the server to insert values into HyperLogLog and retrieve log cardinality:

```
var http   = require('http');
var redis  = require('redis');
var client = redis.createClient();
var hyperLLKey = 'hyper:uniques';

...

http.createServer(function(request, response) {

  var route  = request.url;
```

```
      var val     = route.match(/^\/log\/(.*)/);

...

   if(val) {
      val = val[1];
      return client.pfadd(hyperLLKey, val, function() {
        client.pfcount(hyperLLKey, function(err, card) {
          respond(response, 200, JSON.stringify({
            count: err ? 0 : card
          }))
        })
      });
   }
}).listen(8080)
```

After validating that we have received a new value on the /log route, we add that value to hyperLLKey using the PFADD command (in Redis, if a key does not exist when performing an insert operation, it is automatically created). Once inserted successfully, the key is queried for its PFCOUNT, and the updated set's cardinality is returned to the client.

In addition, the PFMERGE command lets you merge (create the union of) several HyperLogLog sets and fetch the cardinality of the resulting set. The following code will result in a cardinality value of 10:

```
var redis  = require('redis');
var client= redis.createClient();
var multi  = client.multi();

client.multi([
   ['pfadd', 'merge1', 1, 2, 3, 4, 5, 6, 10],
   ['pfadd', 'merge2', 1, 2, 3, 4, 5, 6, 7, 8, 9],
   ['pfmerge', 'merged', 'merge1', 'merge2'],
   ['pfcount', 'merged'],
   ['del', 'merge1', 'merge2', 'merged']
]).exec(function(err, result) {
   console.log('Union set cardinality', result[3]);
});
```

The ability to approximate the cardinality of merged sets brings to mind the sort of efficient analytics possibilities we saw when exploring bitwise operations. Consider HyperLogLog when counts of many unique values are useful analytically and an imprecise but very closely approximated count is sufficient (such as tracking the number of users who logged in today, the total number of pages viewed, and so on).

Taming V8 and optimizing performance

V8 manages Node's main process thread. When executing JavaScript, V8 does so in its own process, and its internal behavior is *not* controlled by Node. However, we can write JavaScript in a way that helps V8 achieve optimal compilation results. In this section, we'll focus on how to write efficient JavaScript and take a look at special configuration flags we can pass to V8 that help with keeping our Node process fast and light.

 The version of V8 used by your Node installation can be viewed by typing the following:

```
node -e "console.log(process.versions.v8)"
```

Optimizing JavaScript

The convenience of a dynamic language is in avoiding the strictness that compiled languages impose. For example, you need not explicitly define object property types and can actually change those property types at will. This dynamism makes traditional compilation impossible but opens up interesting new opportunities for exploratory languages, such as JavaScript. Nevertheless, dynamism introduces a significant penalty in terms of execution speeds when compared to statically compiled languages. The limited speed of JavaScript has regularly been identified as one of its major weaknesses.

V8 attempts to achieve the sorts of speeds with JavaScript that one observes for compiled languages. V8 attempts to compile JavaScript into native machine code rather than interpreting bytecode or using other just-in-time techniques. Because the precise runtime topology of a JavaScript program cannot be known ahead of time (the language is dynamic), compilation consists of a two-stage, speculative approach:

1. Initially, a first-pass compiler converts your code into a runnable state as quickly as possible. During this step, type analysis and other detailed analysis of the code is deferred, achieving fast compilation—your JavaScript can begin executing as close to instantly as possible. Further optimizations are accomplished during the second step.

2. Once the program is up and running, an optimizing compiler then begins its job of watching how your program runs and attempting to determine its current and future runtime characteristics, optimizing and re-optimizing as necessary. For example, if a certain function is called many thousands of times with similar arguments of a consistent type, V8 recompiles that function with optimized code. While the first compile step was conservative with an as-yet unknown and untyped functional signature, this *hot* function's predictable texture impels V8 to assume a certain optimal profile and recompile based on that assumption.

Assumptions help us make decisions more quickly but can lead to mistakes. What if the hot function that V8's compiler just optimized against a certain type signature is now called with arguments violating that optimized profile? V8 has no choice in that case: it must de-optimize the function—V8 must admit its mistake and roll back the work it has done. It will re-optimize in the future if a new pattern is seen. However, if V8 must again de-optimize at a later time and if this binary switching of optimizing/de-optimizing continues, V8 simply *gives up* and leaves your code in a de-optimized state.

Two areas of focus for the V8 team are achieving fast property access and dynamically creating efficient machine code. Let's look at ways to approach the design and declaration of arrays, objects, and functions so that you are helping, rather than hindering, the compiler.

Numbers and tracing optimization/de-optimization

The ECMA-262 specification defines the Number value as a *primitive value corresponding to a double-precision, 64-bit binary format IEEE 754 value*. The point is that there is no integer type in JavaScript; there is a Number type defined as a double-precision floating-point number.

V8 uses 32-bit numbers for *all* values internally for performance reasons that are too technical to discuss here. It can be said that, should greater width be needed, one bit is used to point to another 32-bit number. Regardless, it is clear that there are two types of values tagged as numbers by V8 and switching between these types will cost you something. Try to restrict your needs to 31-bit signed integers where possible.

Because of the type ambiguity of JavaScript, switching the types of numbers assigned to a slot is allowed. The following code does not throw an error:

```
var a = 7;
a = 7.77;
```

However, a speculative compiler such as V8 will be unable to optimize this variable assignment given that its *guess* that a will always be an integer turned out to be wrong, forcing de-optimization.

We can demonstrate this using powerful V8 options available to you when executing code: executing V8 native commands in your Node program and tracing how V8 optimizes/de-optimizes your code.

Consider the following Node program:

```
var someFunc = function foo(){}
console.log(%FunctionGetName(someFunc));
```

If you try to run this normally, you receive an Unexpected Token error—the modulo (%) symbol cannot be used within an identifier name in JavaScript. What is this strange method with a % prefix? It is a V8 native command, and we can turn to the execution of these types of functions using the --allow-natives-syntax flag as follows:

```
node --allow-natives-syntax program.js

// foo
```

> You can learn about the available native functions by browsing the V8 source at https://code.google.com/p/v8/source/browse/trunk/src/runtime.cc?r=22500, and searching for **runtime_function**.

Now, consider the following code, which uses native functions to assert information about the optimization status of the square function using the %OptimizeFunctionOnNextCall native method:

```
var operand = 3;
function square() {
   return operand * operand;
}
//  Make first pass to gather type information
square();
//  Ask that the next call of #square trigger an optimization attempt;
//  Call
%OptimizeFunctionOnNextCall(square);
square();
```

Create a file using the preceding code and execute it using the following command:

```
node --allow-natives-syntax --trace_opt --trace_deopt myfile.js
```

You will see something like the following output returned:

```
[deoptimize context: c39daf14679]
[optimizing: square / c39dafca921 - took 1.900, 0.851, 0.000 ms]
```

We can see that V8 has no problem optimizing the `square` function as the operand is declared once and never changed. Now, append the following lines to your file and run it again:

```
%OptimizeFunctionOnNextCall(square);
operand = 3.01;
square();
```

On this execution, following the optimization report given earlier, you should now receive something like the following output:

```
**** DEOPT: square at bailout #2, address 0x0, frame size 8
[deoptimizing: begin 0x2493d0fca8d9 square @2]
...
[deoptimizing: end 0x2493d0fca8d9 square => node=3, pc=0x29edb8164b46,
state=NO_REGISTERS, alignment=no padding, took 0.033 ms]
[removing optimized code for: square]
```

This very expressive optimization report tells the story very clearly — the once-optimized `square` function was de-optimized following the change we made in one number's type. You are encouraged to spend time writing code and to test it using these methods now and as you move through this section.

Objects and arrays

As we learned when investigating numbers, V8 works best when your code is predictable. The same holds true with arrays and objects. Nearly all of the following *bad practices* are bad for the simple reason that they create unpredictability.

Remember that, in JavaScript, an object and an array are very similar *under the hood*. We won't be discussing those differences but only the important similarities, specifically in terms of how both these data constructs benefit from similar optimization techniques.

Avoid mixing types in arrays. It is always better to have a consistent data type, such as *all integers* or *all strings*. Also, avoid changing types in arrays or in property assignments after initialization, if possible. V8 creates *blueprints* of objects by creating hidden classes to track types, and, when those types change, the optimization blueprints will be destroyed and rebuilt—if you're lucky. See the following link for more information:

```
https://developers.google.com/v8/design
```

Don't create arrays with gaps, an example of which is shown as follows:

```
var a = [];
a[2] = 'foo';
a[23] = 'bar';
```

Sparse arrays are bad for this reason: V8 can either use a very efficient *linear storage* strategy to store (and access) your array data, or it can use a hash table (which is much slower). If your array is sparse, V8 must choose the less efficient of the two. For the same reason, always start your arrays at the zero index. Also, don't ever use `delete` to remove elements from an array. You are simply inserting an `undefined` value at that position, which is just another way of creating a sparse array. Similarly, be careful about populating an array with empty values—ensure that the external data you are pushing into an array is not incomplete.

Try not to pre-allocate large arrays—grow as you go. Similarly, do not pre-allocate an array and then exceed that size. You always want to avoid spooking V8 into turning your array into a hash table.

V8 creates a new hidden class whenever a new property is added to an object constructor. Try to avoid adding properties after an object is instantiated. Initialize all members in constructor functions in the same order. *Same properties + same order = same object.*

Remember that JavaScript is a dynamic language that allows object (and object prototype) modifications *after* instantiation. Since the shape and volume of an object can, therefore, be altered *after the fact*, how does V8 allocate memory for objects? It makes certain reasonable assumptions. After a set number of objects is instantiated from a given constructor (I believe 8 is the trigger number), the largest of these is assumed to be of the maximum size, and all further instances are allocated that amount of memory (and the initial objects are similarly resized). A total of 32 *fast property slots* is then allocated to each instance based on this assumed maximum size. Any *extra properties* are slotted into a (slower) overflow property array that can be resized to accommodate any further new properties.

With objects, just as with arrays, try as much as possible to define the shape of your data structures in a *futureproof* manner, with a set number of properties, types, and so on.

Functions

Functions are typically called often and should be one of your prime optimization focuses. Functions containing try-catch constructs are *not optimizable*, nor are functions containing other *unpredictable* constructs, such as `with` and `eval`. If, for some reason, your function is not optimizable, keep its use to a minimum.

A very common optimization error involves the use of polymorphic functions. Functions that accept variable function arguments will be de-optimized. Avoid polymorphic functions.

Caching strategies

Caching, generally, is the strategy of creating easily accessible intermediate versions of assets. When retrieving an asset is expensive—in terms of time, processor cycles, memory, and so on—you should consider caching that asset. For example, if a list of Canadian provinces must be fetched from your database each time a person from that country visits, it is a good idea to store that list in a static format, obviating the expensive operation of running a database query on each visit. A good caching strategy is essential to any web-based application that serves large numbers of rendered data views, be they HTML pages or JSON structures. Cached content can be served cheaply and quickly.

Whenever you deploy content that doesn't change often, you most likely want to cache your files. Two general types of *static* assets are commonly seen. Assets such as a company logo, existing as-is in a content folder, will change very rarely. Other assets do change more often but much less frequently than on every request of the asset. This second class encompasses such things as CSS style sheets, lists of user contacts, latest headlines, and so on. Creating a reliable and efficient caching system is a nontrivial problem:

> *"There are only two hard things in Computer Science: cache invalidation and naming things."*

> – *Phil Karlton*

In this section, we'll look at two strategies to cache your application content. First, we'll look at using Redis as an in-memory key-value cache for regularly used JSON data, learning about the Redis key expiry and key scanning. Finally, we'll investigate how to manage your content using the CloudFlare **content delivery network** (CDN), in the process learning something about using Node to watch for file changes and then invalidating a CDN cache when change events are detected.

Using Redis as a cache

In the example session-store implemented earlier, cookie values were stored in Redis and matched against incoming values to provide simple session management. This sort of regular checking of small, in-memory values is a common pattern in multiuser environments, for which technologies such as **memcached** were developed.

Redis is fully capable of functioning as a similar in-memory caching system. Let's implement a simple caching layer using Redis that intelligently manages key association and expiry.

Because many types of information will be cached, it is a good idea to namespace your cache keys. We'll structure our cache library such that individual namespace-aware cache APIs can be instantiated:

```
var redis   = require('redis');
var util    = require('util');
var Promise = require('bluebird');
var Cache = function(config) {
  config = config || {};
  this.prefix = config.prefix ? config.prefix + ':' : 'cache:';

  var port = config.port || 6379;
  var host = config.host || 'localhost';

  this.client = redis.createClient(port, host, config.options ||
    {});

  config.auth && this.client.auth(config.auth);
};
```

Typically, our caching layer will be decoupled from any given server, so here we design a constructor that expects Redis's connection and authentication information. Note the prefix argument. To instantiate a cache instance, use the following code:

```
var cache = new Cache({ prefix: 'articles:cache' });
```

Also note that we're going to implement the cache API using **Promises** via the bluebird library (https://github.com/petkaantonov/bluebird).

Getting a cached value is straightforward:

```
Cache.prototype.get = function(key) {
  key = this.prefix + key;
  var client = this.client;
  return new Promise(function(resolve, reject) {
    client.hgetall(key, function(err, result) {
      err ? reject() : resolve(result);
    });
  });
};
```

All cache keys will be implemented as Redis hashes, so a GET operation will involve calling hmget on a key. The Promises-powered API now enables the following easy-to-follow syntax:

```
cache.get('sandro').then(function(val) {
  console.log('cached: ' + val);
}).catch() {
  console.log('unable to fetch value from cache');
})
```

Setting a value is simply a matter of passing an object:

```
Cache.prototype.set = function(key, val, ttl) {
  var _this = this;
  var pkey = this.prefix + key;
  var client = this.client;
  var setArr = [];

  for(var k in val) {
    setArr[k] = val[k];
  }
  return new Promise(function(resolve, reject) {
    client.hmset(pkey, setArr, function(err) {
      err ? reject() : resolve();
      ttl && _this.expire(key, ttl);
    });
  });
};
```

When `val` is received, we reflect its key-value map in the Redis hash stored at `key`. The optional third argument, `ttl`, allows a flag to be set in Redis to expire this key after a number of seconds, flagging it for deletion. The key bit of code in `this.expire` is the following:

```
client.expire(key, ttl, function(err, ok) { // ...flagged for
  removal }
```

For more information on Redis `expire`, visit `http://redis.io/commands/expire`.

The `remove` method is simply a `del` operation on the Redis keyspace, so there is no need to explain it here. More interesting is the implementation of the `clear` method to remove all keys with a given prefix from Redis:

```
Cache.prototype.clear = function() {
 var prefixMatch = this.prefix + '*';
 var client    = this.client;
 return new Promise(function(resolve, reject) {
  var multi = client.multi();
  (function scanner(cursor) {
   client.scan([+cursor, 'match', prefixMatch], function(err, scn) {
    if(err) {
     return reject();
    }
    // Add new delete candidates
    multi.del(scn[1]);
    // More? Continue scan.
    if(+scn[0] !== 0) {
     return scanner(scn[0]);
    }
    // Delete candidates, then resolve.
    multi.exec(resolve);
   })
  })(0);
 });
};
```

Note the `scan` method we are using to target and delete keys matching our cache prefix. Redis is designed for efficiency, and, as much as possible, its designers aim to avoid adding slow features. Unlike other databases, Redis has no advanced *find* method of searching its keyspace, with developers limited to *keys* and basic glob pattern matching. Because it's common to have many millions of keys in a Redis keyspace, operations using *keys*, unavoidably or through sloppiness, can end up being punitively expensive because a long operation blocks other operations — transactions are atomic, and Redis is single-threaded.

The `scan` method allows you to fetch limited ranges of the keyspace in an iterative manner, enabling (nonblocking) asynchronous keyspace scanning. The scan object itself is stateless, passing only a cursor indicating whether there are further records to be fetched. Using this technique, we are able to clean out all keys prefixed with our target cache key (pattern: `this.prefix + '*'`). On each scan iteration, we queue up any returned keys for deletion using the `multi.del` function, continuing until the scanner returns a zero value (indicating that all sought keys have been returned), at which point we delete all those keys in one command.

Tie these methods together:

```
cache.set('deploying', { foo: 'bar' })
.then(function() {
 return cache.get('deploying');
})
.then(function(val) {
 console.log(val); // foo:bar
 return cache.clear();
})
.then(cache.close.bind(cache));
```

This is a simple caching strategy to get you started. While managing key expiration yourself is a perfectly valid technique, as you move into larger production implementations, consider configuring Redis's eviction policies directly. For example, you will want to set the `maxmemory` value in `redis.conf` to some maximum upper bound for the cache memory and configure Redis to use one of the six documented eviction policies when memory limits are reached, such as **Least Recently Used (LRU)**. For more information, visit: `http://redis.io/topics/lru-cache`.

Deploying CloudFlare as a CDN

A CDN is typically a globe-spanning network of servers leased out to companies unable to fund and build their own network. A CDN is set up to ensure that your application or other content remains available to anyone who wishes to access it, wherever they choose to access it in the world, and that your content is delivered quickly. Akamai is perhaps the most famous CDN, and CloudFlare is a recent arrival with a particular focus on security and "attack proofing" networks.

Usefully for our purposes, CloudFlare provides a free tier of service that satisfies the needs of most deployed applications. In the example that follows, you'll learn how to enable caching with CloudFlare. We'll then use the `cloudflare` module to purge your domain files when they change, in the process learning how to use Node's `fs.watch` method to watch for file changes.

CloudFlare has also embarked on an ambitious effort to host *all the JS* on its CDN at `https://cdnjs.com/`. Unlike other popular hosting services that only host the most popular JavaScript libraries, CloudFlare hosts all projects represented in the open GitHub project at `https://github.com/cdnjs/cdnjs`. Consider deploying your JavaScript files via this service.

To start, visit `https://www.cloudflare.com/sign-up` and set up a free account. You will need a domain to host files on—follow the instructions to configure your name servers and other DNS information. Once signed up, you will receive an authentication token and will use this to add CDN support to your application. CloudFlare does not cache HTML files by default. To enable HTML caching, visit your dashboard, locate your domain, open the options menu, and select **Page rules**. If your domain is `foo.com`, the following page rule will enable full caching: `*foo.com/*`. Finally, locate the **Custom Caching** dropdown on the page rules admin page and select **Cache everything**.

Now, let's establish a connection with CloudFlare:

```
var http = require('http');
var fs = require('fs');
var cloudflare = require('cloudflare');
var config = {
  "token": "your token",
  "email": "your account email",
  "domain": "yourdomain.com",
  "subdomain": "www",
  "protocol": "http"
};
var cloudflareClient = cloudflare.createClient({
  email: config.email,
  token: config.token
});
```

In our example, we will serve (and modify) a single `index.html` file. For this example, we will create a simple server:

```
var indexFile = './index.html';
http.createServer(function(request, response) {
  var route = request.url;
  if(route === "/index.html") {
    response.writeHead(200, {
      "content-type": "text/html",
      "cache-control": "max-age=31536000"
```

```
    });
      return fs.createReadStream(indexFile).pipe(response);
    }
}).listen(8080);
```

Note how `max-age` is set on the `cache-control` header. This will indicate to CloudFlare that we want this file cached.

With the server set up, we will now add the following `purge` method:

```
function purge(filePath, cb) {
  var head = config.protocol + '://';
  var tail = config.domain + '/' + filePath;
  //  foo.com && www.foo.com each get a purge call
  var purgeFiles = [
    head + tail,
    head + config.subdomain + '.' + tail
  ];
  var purgeTrack = 2;
  purgeFiles.forEach(function(pf) {
    cloudflareClient.zoneFilePurge(config.domain, pf,
      function(err) {
      (--purgeTrack === 0) && cb();
    });
  });
};
```

When this method is passed a file path, it asks CloudFlare to purge its cache of this file. Note how we must use two purge actions to accommodate subdomains.

With purging set up, all that is left to do is watch the filesystem for changes. This can be accomplished via the `fs.watch` command:

```
fs.watch('./index.html', function(event, filename) {
  if(event === "change") {
    purge(filename, function(err) {
      console.log("file purged");
    });
  }
});
```

Now, whenever the `index.html` file is changed, our CDN will flush its cached version. Create that file, start up the server, and point your browser to `localhost:8080`, bringing up your index file. In your browser's developer console, inspect the response headers—you should see a `CF-Cache-Status: MISS` record. This means that **CloudFlare (CF)** has fetched and served the original file from your server—on the first call, there is no cached version yet, so the cache was *missed*. Reload the page. The same response header should now read `CF-Cache-Status: HIT`. Your file is cached!

Go ahead and change the index file in some way. When you reload your browser, the changed version will be displayed—its cached version has been purged, the file has been fetched once again from your server, and you will see the `MISS` header value again.

You will want to expand this functionality to include a larger group of files and folders. To learn more about `fs.watch`, go to `http://nodejs.org/api/fs.html#fs_fs_watch_filename_options_listener`.

Managing sessions

The HTTP protocol is stateless. Any given request has no information about previous requests. For a server, this means that determining whether two requests originated from the same browser is not possible without further work. That's fine for general information, but targeted interactions require a user to be verified via some sort of unique identifier. A uniquely identified client can then be served targeted content— from lists of friends to advertisements.

This semipermanent communication between a client (often a browser) and a server persists for a period of time—at least until the client disconnects. That period of time is understood as a *session*. An application that manages sessions must be able to create a unique user session identifier, track the activity of an identified user during that session, and disconnect that user when requested or for some other reason, such as on reaching a session limit.

In this section, we'll implement a **JSON Web Token (JWT)** system for session management. JWT's have an advantage over traditional cookie-based sessions in that they do not require the server to maintain a session store as JWTs are self-contained. This greatly helps with deployments and scaling. They are also mobile friendly and can be shared between clients. While a new standard, JWTs should be considered as a simple and scalable session storage solution for your applications.

JSON Web Token authentication and sessions

A basic authentication system might require a client to send a username and password on each request. To initiate a token-based authenticated session, a client sends credentials just once, receives a token in exchange, and then sends only that token on subsequent requests, gaining any access that token provides. Incessantly passing around sensitive credentials is no longer required, as the following diagram demonstrates:

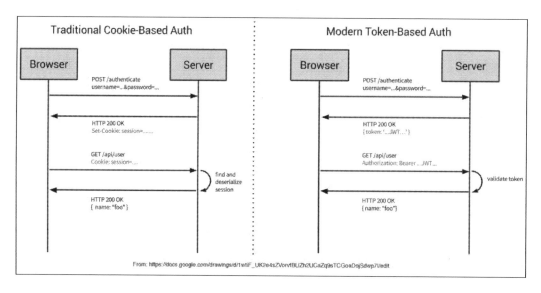

One particular advantage of JWTs is that servers are no longer responsible for maintaining access to a common database of credentials as only the *issuing authority* needs to validate an initial signin. There is no need to maintain a session store when you are using JWTs. The issued token (think of it as an access card) can, therefore, be used within any domain (or server) that recognizes and accepts it. In terms of performance, the cost of a request is now the cost of decrypting a hash versus the cost of making a database call to validate credentials. We also avoid the problems we can face using cookies on mobile devices, such as cross-domain issues (cookies are domain-bound), certain types of request forgery attacks, and so on.

Let's look at the structure of a JWT and build a simple example demonstrating how to issue, validate, and otherwise use JWTs to manage sessions.

A JWT token has the following format:

```
<base64-encoded header>.<base64-encoded claims>.<base64-encoded
   signature>
```

Each segment is described in the JSON format.

A **header** simply describes the token—its type and encryption algorithm. Take the following code as an example:

```
{
   "typ":"JWT",
   "alg":"HS256"
}
```

Here, we declare that this is a JWT token, which is encrypted using HMAC SHA-256.

> See http://nodejs.org/api/crypto.html for more information about encryption and how to perform encryption with Node. The JWT specification itself can be found at http://self-issued.info/docs/draft-ietf-oauth-json-web-token.html. Note that the JWT specification is in a draft state at the time of writing this, so changes may be made in the future.

The **claims** segment outlines security and other constraints that should be checked by any service receiving the JWT. Check the specification for a full accounting. Typically, a JWT claims manifest will want to indicate when the JWT was issued, who issued it, when it expires, who the subject of the JWT is, and who should accept the JWT:

```
{
   "iss" : "http://blogengine.com",
   "aud" : ["http://blogsearch.com", "http://blogstorage"],
   "sub" : "blogengine:uniqueuserid",
   "iat" : "1415918312",
   "exp" : "1416523112",
   "sessionData" : "<some data encrypted with secret>"
}
```

The iat (issued-at) and exp (expires) claims are both set to numeric values indicating the number of seconds since the Unix epoch. The iss (issuer) should be a URL describing the issuer of the JWT. Any service that receives a JWT must inspect the aud (audience), and that service must reject the JWT if it does not appear in the audience list. The sub (subject) of the JWT identifies the subject of the JWT, such as the user of an application—a unique value that is never reassigned, such as the name of the issuing service and a unique user ID.

Finally, useful data is attached using a key-value pairing of your choice. Here, let's call the token data sessionData. Note that we need to encrypt this data—the signature segment of a JWT prevents tampering with session data, but JWTs are not themselves encrypted (you can always encrypt the entire token itself though).

The last step is to create a signature, which, as mentioned, prevents tampering—a JWT validator specifically checks for mismatches between the signature and the packet received.

What follows is a scaffold server and client example demonstrating how to implement a JWT-driven authentication system. Rather than implementing the various signing and validation steps *by hand*, we'll use the jwt-simple package. Feel free to browse the /jwt folder in your code bundle, which contains the full code we'll be unpacking next.

To ask for a token, we will use the following client code:

```
var token;

function send(route, formData, cb) {
  if(!(formData instanceof FormData)) {
    cb = formData;
    formData = new FormData();
  }
  var caller = new XMLHttpRequest();
  caller.onload = function() {
    cb(JSON.parse(this.responseText));
  };
  caller.open("POST", route);
  token && caller.setRequestHeader('Authorization', 'Bearer ' +
    token);
  caller.send(formData);
}
// ...When we have received a username and password in some way
formData = new FormData();
formData.append("username", username);
formData.append("password", password);

send("/login", formData, function(response) {
  token = response.token;
  console.log('Set token: ' + token);
});
```

We'll implement the server code next. For now, note that we have a send method that expects, at some point, to have a global token set for it to pass along when making requests. The initial /login is where we ask for that token.

Using the Express web framework, we create the following server and /login route:

```
var express = require('express');
...
var jwt = require('jwt-simple');
var app = express();

app.set('jwtSecret', 'shhhhhhhhh');

app.post('/login', auth, function(req, res) {
  var nowSeconds    = Math.floor(Date.now()/1000);
  var plus7Days     = nowSeconds + (60 * 60 * 24 * 7);
  var token = jwt.encode({
    "iss" : "http://blogengine.com",
    "aud" : ["http://blogsearch.com", "http://blogstorage"],
    "sub" : "blogengine:uniqueuserid",
    "iat" : nowSeconds,
    "exp" : plus7Days
  }, app.get('jwtSecret'));

  res.send({
    token : token
  })
})
```

Note that we store jwtsecret on the app server. This is the key that is used when we are signing tokens. When a login attempt is made, the server will return the result of jwt.encode, which encodes the JWT claims discussed previously. That's it. From now on, *any* client that mentions this token to the correct audience will be allowed to interact with any services those audience members provide for a period expiring 7 days from the date of issue. These services will implement something like the following code:

```
app.post('/someservice', function(req, res) {
  var token = req.get('Authorization').replace('Bearer ', '');
  var decoded = jwt.decode(token, app.get('jwtSecret'));
  var now = Math.floor(Date.now()/1000);
  if(now > decoded.exp) {
    return res.end(JSON.stringify({
      error : "Token expired"
    }));
  }
  res.send(<some sort of result>);
})
```

Here, we are simply fetching the `Authorization` header (stripping out `Bearer`) and decoding via `jwt.decode`. A service must at least check for token expiry, which we do here by comparing the current number of seconds from the `epoch` to the token's **expiry** time.

Using this simple framework, you can create an easily scalable authentication/session system using a secure standard. No longer required to maintain a connection to a common credentials database, individual services (deployed perhaps as microservices) can use JWTs to validate requests, incurring little CPU latency or memory cost.

Summary

We covered a lot of ground in this chapter. Best practices for writing efficient JavaScript that the V8 interpreter can handle properly were outlined, including an exploration of garbage collection, the advantages of Node streams, and how JavaScript prototypes should be deployed in order to save memory. Continuing with the theme of reducing storage costs, we explored various ways in which Redis can help with storing large amounts of data in a space-efficient way.

Additionally, we looked at strategies to build composable, distributed systems. In the discussion on microservices, we touched on approaches to network many individual services and build the networks they can use to communicate with each other—from pub/sub to Seneca's pattern and action models. Joined with the examples of caching techniques, a reasonably complete picture of the issues you might want to consider when planning out resource management in your application was established.

After you build up a reasonably sophisticated architecture, it becomes more and more necessary to build probes and other monitoring tools to stay on top of what is going on. In the next chapter, we'll build tools to help you trace the changing topology of running applications.

5

Monitoring Applications

Distributed systems fail often. Worse, they often fail partially. When failures occur during operations responsible for altering a system's state (for instance, a write or delete operation), how can the correct state be recovered, especially when these operations are concurrent? To make matters even worse, some operations fail silently. Partial failures, then, can put applications in an indeterminate state. It is difficult to predict how an opaque system will behave.

Consider this quote from *The Datacenter as a Computer: An Introduction to the Design of Warehouse-Scale Machines*:

"Suppose a cluster has ultra-reliable server nodes with a stellar mean time between failures (MTBF) of 30 years (10,000 days) — well beyond what is typically possible to achieve at a realistic cost. Even with these ideally reliable servers, a cluster of 10,000 servers will see an average of one server failure per day. Thus, any application that needs the entire cluster to be up to work will see an MTBF of no better than 1 day."

Failure, especially on a large scale, is indifferent to the quality of your staff or your hardware. The point is that numerical ratios that seem large in common usage are less so in network environments where billions of transactions can happen in a matter of minutes or seconds and where hundreds or more separate systems are interacting. How failure evolves is often counterintuitive. It is a good idea, then, to prepare for failure, and, among other things, this means reducing the ability of any one failure to take down an entire system.

Typically, distributing the workload for a single user also requires distributing user data across many independent processes. Also, when a piece of the system fails, it must be restored in order to maintain two characteristics of the system — its capacity and any data or transactions that were in flight when the failure occurred.

In this chapter, I'll outline certain tools and tricks used to monitor what is going on across your application. We'll look at ways in which you can build your own monitoring and logging tools and discuss third-party tools. Along the way, you'll learn about the following:

- Remotely controlling Node processes
- Using New Relic to monitor servers
- Catching errors
- Other options for tracking and logging activity in your application

Dealing with failure

As we outlined in *Chapter 4, Managing Memory and Space*, isolating operations and intelligently monitoring an applications help to minimize the chances of one failed subsystem taking down the larger system. In this section, we'll look at how to catch errors and exceptions within a Node program and how to gracefully shut down and/or restart a process that has become unstable individually and within clusters.

 The following comprehensive article on handling errors with Node.js is recommended:

http://www.joyent.com/developers/node/design/errors

Peppering a codebase with try/catch blocks and trying to anticipate all errors can become unmanageable and unwieldy. Additionally, what if an exception you didn't anticipate occurs? How do you *pick up where you left off*?

Node does not yet have a good built-in way to handle uncaught critical exceptions. This is a weakness of the platform. An exception that is uncaught will continue to bubble up through the execution stack until it hits the event loop where, like a wrench in the gears of a machine, it will take down the entire process.

One option is to attach an uncaughtException handler to the process itself, as shown in the following code:

```
process.on('uncaughtException', function(err) {
  console.log('Caught exception: ' + err);
});
setTimeout(function() {
  console.log("The exception was caught and this can run.");
}, 1000);
throwAnUncaughtException();
```

The output of the preceding code will be as follows:

> `Caught exception: ReferenceError: throwAnUncaughtException is not defined`

> `The exception was caught and this can run.`

While nothing that follows our exception code will execute, the timeout will still fire as the process managed to catch the exception, thus saving itself. However, this is a very clumsy way of handling exceptions.

The `domain` module makes a good attempt at fixing this hole in Node's design. We will discuss the domain module next as a better tool to handle exceptions.

The 'domain' module

Error handling in asynchronous code is also difficult to trace:

```
function f() {
    throw new error("error somewhere!")
}
setTimeout(f, 1000*Math.random());
setTimeout(f, 1000*Math.random());
```

Which function caused the error? It is difficult to say. It is also difficult to intelligently insert exception management tools. It is difficult to know what to do next. Node's `domain` module attempts to help with this and other exception localization issues. In this way, code can be tested and errors can be handled with more precision.

At its simplest, a **domain** sets up a context within which a function or other "chunk" of code can be run such that any errors occurring within that implicit domain binding will be routed to a specific domain error handler. Take the following code as an example:

```
var domain = require('domain');
var dom = domain.create();
dom.on('error', function(err) {
    console.error('error', err.stack);
});

dom.run(function() {
    throw new Error("my domain error");
});
// error Error: my domain error
//   at /js/basicdomain.js:10:8
//   ...
```

Here, we establish a domain and execute code within that domain via the `run` command within the context of that domain. This enables us to intelligently catch those exceptions, implicitly binding all event emitters, timers, and other requests created within that context.

Sometimes, a method might be created elsewhere (not within the implicit context of a given `domain.run` function call) but is nevertheless best associated with an external domain. The `add` method exists for just such explicit binding, as shown in the following code:

```
var dom = domain.create();
dom.on("error", function(err) {
   console.log(err);
});

var somefunc = function() {
   throw new Error('Explicit bind error');
};
dom.add(somefunc);
dom.run(function() {
   somefunc();
});
// [Error: Explicit bind error]
```

Here, we see how a function that is not implicitly bound within the `run` context can still be added to that context explicitly. To remove an execution context from a domain, use `domain.remove`. An array of all timers, functions, and other emitters added explicitly or implicitly to a domain is accessible via `domain.members`.

In the same way that JavaScript's `bind` method binds a function to a context, the `domain.bind` method similarly allows an independent function to be bound to a domain. This is shown in the following code:

```
var domain = require('domain');
var fs = require('fs');
var dom = domain.create();
dom.on("error", ...);
fs.readFile('somefile', dom.bind(function(err, data) {
   if(err) { throw new Error('bad file call'); }
}));
// { [Error: bad call]
//   domain_thrown: true,
//   ...
```

Here, we see how any function can be wrapped by a particular error domain *inline*, a feature especially useful to manage exceptions in callbacks. Error objects emitted from a domain have the following special properties

- `error.domain`: This is the domain that handled the error.

- `error.domainEmitter`: If `EventEmitter` fires an `error` event within a domain, this will be flagged.

- `error.domainBound`: This is the callback that passed an error as its first argument.

- `error.domainThrown`: This is a Boolean indicating whether the error was thrown or not. For example, the following callback will pass an ENOENT error as its first argument, so `domainThrown` would be false:

```
fs.createReadStream('nofile', callback)
```

 Another method, `domain.intercept`, functions similarly to `domain.bind` but simplifies error handling in callbacks such that the developer will no longer need to repetitively check (or even set) the first argument of every callback, `cb(err, data)`, for errors. An example can be found in the `js/domainintercept.js` file in your code bundle.

You may also need to move between domains, entering and exiting them as needed. For this, we use the `domain.enter` and `domain.exit` methods. Assuming that we have set up two domains, `dom1` and `dom2`, the first emitting `domain 1 error` and the second `domain 2 error`, we can move between domain contexts, as shown here:

```
dom1.add(aFuncThatThrows);
dom1.run(function() {
  dom1.exit();
  dom2.enter();
  aFuncThatThrows();
});
// domain 2 error
```

Any number of `enter` and `exit` events can be used. Note that no changes are made to the domain objects themselves—`exit` does not close the domain or do any such thing. If a domain needs to be destroyed, you should use the `domain.dispose` method, which will also try to clean up any inflight domain I/O—aborting streams, clearing timers, ignoring callbacks, and so on.

Catching process errors

Process-oriented designs are common in Node.js applications, where independent processes communicate with each other through evented streams. Errors in these channels, and in the processes themselves, must be tracked. In this section, we'll look at how to track and how to properly throw errors related to process events.

We covered the `child_process` module in *Chapter 3, Scaling Node*. Here, we will go into a little more detail about how to handle errors in child processes and their parents.

To spawn a Node program, use the `fork` method of the `child_process` module. This creates a new child process under the calling parent. Also, an IPC channel is automatically set up between the two processes, where the child calls `process.send` to send messages to its parent, and the parent can listen to `child.on('message')`. Create two files, the first named `parent.js` and the other named `child.js`:

```
// parent.js
var fork = require('child_process').fork;
var proc = fork('./child.js');

proc.on('message', function(msg) {
  console.log("Child sent: " + msg);
});
// Keeps the parent running even if no children are alive.
process.stdin.resume();

// child.js
var cnt = 0;
setInterval(function() {
  process.send(++cnt);
}, 1000);
```

The child process upon which fork has been used by the parent will increment and emit a value at a 1-second interval, which the parent will listen for and echo to your console. How do we catch an error in the child process from the parent process?

Let's cause an error in our child process by making it `throw`. Add the following line to `child.js`:

```
...
process.send(++cnt);
throw new Error('boom!');
```

Running the parent process again will result in an error, and the message we set will be displayed. Typically, the parent will want to act when a child dies—such as using `fork` on a new child or logging the error, or both. To catch child errors in the parent, add the following line to `parent.js`:

```
proc.on('exit', function() {
    console.log("Child exited: ", arguments);
});
```

Running the parent script again will result in the following being displayed in addition to the original error:

```
Child exited:   { '0': 1, '1': null }
```

The first argument received is the exit code passed by the child process when it is terminated (if the parent had sent a kill signal, for example, `child.kill('SIGTERM')`, the second argument here would contain `'SIGTERM'`).

In addition to handling child errors from within a parent process, using the Domain module to catch and handle errors within the child process itself is recommended. In this way, you properly clean up after a child error and use `process.send()` to broadcast any additional error information to the parent.

> The exit codes that Node will return when a process exits abnormally can be found at `https://github.com/joyent/node/blob/master/doc/api/process.markdown#exit-codes`. (Note that this is for Node 0.11.x—earlier versions always return exit code 8.)

A child process can also be created via `spawn`, which differs from `fork` in that it is not Node-specific; any OS process can be started by using `spawn`. For example, this is a roundabout way of executing the `ls` command; you should receive a directory listing when this runs:

```
var spawn = require('child_process').spawn;
var proc = spawn('ls',['-l']);
proc.stdout.setEncoding('utf8');
proc.stdout.on('data', function(data) {
    console.log(data)
});
```

Note the differences from `fork`. The first argument is an OS command, and the second argument is an array of options passed to that command — the equivalent of `> ls -l`. Secondly, we do not have access to a custom IPC (as with `fork` — no `send` or `on('message')`), but we do have access to the standard process pipes: `stdin`, `stdout`, and `stderr`. Because pipes will default to speaking in buffers, we have set the desired encoding and simply display any data that the spawned process writes to `stdout`.

Another way to catch subprocess errors should be clear to you. Modify the preceding code with the following:

```
var spawn = require('child_process').spawn;
var proc = spawn('ls',['-l', '/nonexistent/directory']);
proc.stderr.setEncoding('utf8');
proc.stderr.on('data', function(err) {
  console.log("Error", err)
});
```

When this attempt to list the contents of a nonexistent directory is executed, you should see the following:

Error ls: /nonexistent/directory: `No such file or directory`

By listening on the `stderr` pipe, errors in child processes can be caught. We can also change the `stdio` settings such that errors are automatically logged to a file. Rather than catching the child output in the parent, we use `spawn` on the child using a customized `stdio` option, redirecting the child's `stdout` directly to a file:

```
var spawn = require('child_process').spawn;
// This will be the file we write to
var out = require('fs').openSync('./out.log', 'w+');
var proc = spawn('node', ['./spawn_child.js'], {
  // The options are: 0:stdin, 1:stdout, 2:stderr
  stdio : ['pipe', out, 'pipe']
});
```

Next, we'll go a little deeper into logging strategies.

Logging

Why log data? One answer might be that the amount of activity data a modern application produces exceeds the capacity of any one person's analytical abilities. We can't react to that much information usefully in real time. It is, therefore, necessary to store, or log, the mass of details and use smart tools to slice and sort that data into forms that we humans can comprehend. We can look for patterns in the logs and perhaps find bottlenecks or even bugs in our application, helping us improve the design of our system. We can garner business intelligence from logs, discovering usage patterns that help us understand customer preferences or ones that can help us design new features or enhance existing ones.

In what follows, I'll take you through some of the information available to all Node processes, how those might be logged using **UDP**, and how to use Morgan for simple request logging.

 A popular open source project from the Etsy team for logging and statistical reporting is **StatsD** (`https://github.com/etsy/statsd`), for which there is a good Node client at `https://github.com/sivy/node-statsd`.

Let's create a logging module that uses UDP. Detailed information on how UDP works was provided in *Chapter 3, Scaling Node*—go ahead and refresh your memory if necessary. The important concept to remember is that UDP achieves extremely high performance by making no guarantee that messages will arrive. Note that in 99 percent of cases, very few messages will drop, making UDP an excellent balance of speed and accuracy for applications that do not need perfect fidelity, such as logging applications.

Logging with UDP

The goal of our UDP logging module is to have a straightforward interface for any Node program to do logging. Also, we'll want to allow many independent processes to write to the same log file. The full code for this module can be found in the udp/logger folder of your code bundle.

Starting from the end, let's go over the client code first before diving into the logger itself. All clients will send (at least) a log file path, optional information about the port or host, a few handler functions if necessary, and the system will just work:

```
var dgram = require('dgram');
var Logger = require('./logger');

logger = new Logger({
  file : './out.log',
  port : 41234,
  host : 'localhost',
  encoding : 'utf8',
  onError : function(err) {
    console.log("ERROR: ", err);
  },
  onReady : function() {
...
  }
});
```

We can see that our module starts a server on the port provided and is configured to notify the client of any errors as well as its ready state. By fleshing out the remaining code for onReady, we can also see the ways that we expect clients to hit the UDP logger:

```
console.log("READY");
var client = dgram.createSocket("udp4");
var udpm;
//  Flood it a bit.
for(var x=0; x < 10000; x++) {
  udpm = new Buffer("UDP write #" + x);
  logger.log('Test write #' + x);
  client.send(udpm, 0, udpm.length, 41234, "localhost");
}
```

The client will be able to either call the module's log function or send a UDP message directly. Also, we expect that it is possible to receive many messages. Besides, we expect that any number of processes could be logging to *the same file*, so we must deal with managing a flood of messages.

The logging module is as follows:

```
var dgram = require('dgram');
var fs = require('fs');

module.exports = function(opts) {

  opts = opts || {};

  var file = opts.file;
  var host = opts.host || 'localhost';
  var port = opts.port || 41234;
  var encoding = opts.encoding || 'utf8';
  var onError = opts.onError || function() {};
  var onReady = opts.onReady || function() {};
  var socket = dgram.createSocket("udp4");
  var writeable = true;
  var _this = this;
  var stream;

  if(!file) {
    throw new Error("Must send a #file argument");
  }

  stream = fs.createWriteStream(file, {
    flags : 'a+'
  });
  stream.setMaxListeners(0);

  socket.bind(port, host);

  socket.on("listening", onReady);
  socket.on("error", onError);
  socket.on("message", function(msg) {
    this.log(msg.toString());
  });

  this.log = function(msg) {
    if(!stream) {
      throw new Error('No write stream available for logger.');
    }

    try {
```

```
        if(typeof msg !== 'string') {
           msg = JSON.stringify(msg);
        }
     } catch(e) {
        return onError("Illegal message type sent to #log. Must be a
           string, or JSON");
     };


     // You'll likely want to create retry limits here.
     //
     var writer = function() {
        if(!stream.write(msg + '\n', encoding)) {
           stream.once('drain', writer);
        }
     }
     writer();
   };
};
```

This is all the code necessary to manage the setting up of a UDP server and our client interface. Note how the `log` function will either be called directly by a client or will be called via the `on('message')` handler of our UDP binding. This allows clients the flexibility of calling our logging server from any environment—using this module, using another language, using another server, without using this module, and so on.

The last important bit is the management of backpressure in `log`. Because many independent sources may be hitting our log file, the write stream managing that resource could be at its high watermark (*full*) when we try to use `write`. When that happens, a call to `stream.write` will return `false`, which the caller should take as a signal to *stop sending data*. When that happens, we bind to the `drain` event (only once—see `http://nodejs.org/api/events.html#events_emitter_once_event_listener`), which is fired when the consumer (the write manager for our log file) is ready to accept more data.

Logging with Morgan

Morgan (`https://github.com/expressjs/morgan`) is an HTTP logger for the **Express** framework. If logging HTTP connection data for a server is all you need, it serves very well and is easy to use. We'll close out this section with a few short examples using Express.

The following is the most basic usage of Morgan:

```
var express = require('express')
var morgan = require('morgan')
var app = express()
app.use(morgan('combined'))
app.get('/', function (req, res) {
  res.send('hello, world!')
});
app.listen(8080);
```

This code will create a server listening on port 8080 and will dump a log entry in Apache **Combined Log Format** (httpd.apache.org/docs/1.3/logs.html#combined) to stdout:

```
127.0.0.1 - - [20/Nov/2014:23:02:58 +0000] "GET / HTTP/1.1" 200 13 "-"
"Mozilla/5.0 (Macintosh; Intel Mac OS X 10_10_1) AppleWebKit/537.36
(KHTML, like Gecko) Chrome/39.0.2171.99 Safari/537.36"
```

In addition to the format parameter, Morgan also accepts various options. For example, to stream log data to a file, use the stream option. For this example, replace the app.use declaration with the following:

```
app.use(morgan('combined', {
  stream : require('fs').createWriteStream('./out.log')
}));
```

Log entries will now be written to out.log.

The combined argument reflects one of the built-in Morgan log formatters. These formatters are composed of tokenized strings, with several tokens available by default. For example, the combined formatter interpolates the following string:

```
:remote-addr - :remote-user [:date[clf]] ":method :url HTTP/:http-
version" :status :res[content-length] ":referrer" ":user-agent"
```

It should be clear how the preceding fully qualified output is generated via the given formatter with tokens mapping to the standard properties of the ClientRequest and ClientResponse objects managed by Node's http module.

Morgan logs data reflecting the states of the `ClientRequest` and `ClientResponse` objects. The `skip` option allows you to filter logging based on the state of these objects. By default, Morgan logs every request. To only log errors, you would add the following to your middleware definition:

```
skip: function(req, res) {
  return res.statusCode < 400;
}
```

You can also add new tokens. Here, we create one named `'cache'`:

```
morgan.token('cache', function(req, res) {
  return req.headers['cache-control'];
});
```

This new token (and/or existing tokens) can be used in custom formatters:

```
app.use(morgan('cache-control is :cache'))
```

Morgan is now initialized with a custom formatter that will write something like `cache-control is max-age=0` to your log.

For more information on additional built-in formatters and other advanced options, visit the project page. Given its flexibility, Morgan can be customized to satisfy many logging needs.

Other popular options are available for consideration:

- **Bunyan** (`https://github.com/trentm/node-bunyan`): Bunyan is a simple but sufficiently powerful logging tool for most needs.

- **Winston** (`https://github.com/flatiron/winston`): The key selling point of Winston is the number of logging transport plugins it supports—you can configure it to log to Redis, a file, or a third-party service, such as `loggly.com`.

Modifying behavior in changing environments

Modifying application data in a running system has been compared to changing the engine of a jet while it is in flight. Luckily, we developers work in a virtual world where the *laws of physics* are more forgiving. In this section, we will learn how to create a *remote control* for your Node applications using examples demonstrating how to monitor processes remotely.

Node REPL

Node's **Read-Eval-Print-Loop** (**REPL**) represents the Node shell. To enter the shell prompt, enter Node via your terminal without passing a filename:

```
> node
```

You now have access to a running Node process and can pass JavaScript commands to this process. For example, after entering 2+2, the shell would send 4 to stdout. Node's REPL is an excellent place to try out, debug, test, or otherwise play with JavaScript code.

Because REPL is a native object, programs can also use instances as a context in which to run JavaScript interactively. For example, here, we create our own custom function sayHello, add it to the context of an REPL instance, and start REPL, emulating a Node shell prompt:

```
require('repl').start("> ").context.sayHello = function() {
    return "Hello"
};
```

Entering sayHello() at the prompt will result in Hello being sent to stdout.

What this also means is that your Node process can expose an REPL instance to the outside world that can access that process in some way, providing a *backdoor* through which you can connect to a process, modify its context, change its behavior, or even shut it down if it has gone bad in some way. Let's explore possible applications related to monitoring processes.

Create two files, repl_client.js and repl_server.js, using the following code, and run each in its own terminal window so that both terminal windows are visible to you:

```
/*  repl_client.js   */
var net = require('net');
var sock = net.connect(8080);
process.stdin.pipe(sock);
sock.pipe(process.stdout);
```

The repl_client file simply creates a new socket connection to port 8080 through net.connect and pipes any data coming from stdin (your terminal) through that socket. Similarly, any data arriving from the socket is piped to stdout (your terminal). It should be clear that we have created a way to take input and send it via a socket to port 8080, listening for any data that the socket may send back to us. The following code shows this:

```js
/*   repl_server.js   */
var repl = require('repl')
var net = require('net')
net.createServer(function(socket) {
  var inst = repl.start({
    prompt : 'repl_server> ',
    input      : socket,
    output   : socket,
    terminal   : true
  })

  inst.on('exit', function () {
    socket.end()
  })
}).listen(8080)
```

The repl_server file closes the loop. We will first create a new **Transmission Control Protocol (TCP)** server with net.createServer, binding to port 8080 via .listen. The callback passed to net.createServer will receive a reference to the bound socket. Within the enclosure of that callback, we instantiate a new REPL instance, giving it a nice prompt ('repl_server>' in this case, but it could be any string), indicating that it should both listen for input from, and broadcast output to, the passed socket reference, indicating that the socket data should be treated as terminal data (which has special encoding).

We can now type something, such as console.log("hello"), in the client terminal, and see hello displayed—the REPL server has executed the command we sent via our REPL client and sent back the evaluated response.

To confirm that the execution of our JavaScript commands is occurring in the repl_server process, type process.argv in the client terminal, and the server will display an object containing the current process path, which will be /.../repl_server.js.

Additionally, we can add custom methods to the REPL `context` that are then accessible through clients. For example, add the following line to `repl_server.js`:

```
inst.context.sayHello = function() {
    return "Hello";
}
```

Restart the server and the client, and enter `sayHello()` in the client terminal. You will see `Hello` displayed. It should be clear from this demonstration that we have created a way to remotely monitor Node processes.

Finally, REPL provides custom commands, in particular `.save` and `.load` (the dot (.) prefix is intentional). The .save command will save the current REPL session to a file—all the commands you have sent to REPL will be written to a specified file, meaning that they can be replayed. To see this in action, open an REPL session and run some commands, building up a session history. Then, enter the following two commands:

```
.save test.js
.load test.js
// Session saved to:test.js
// ... the output of the session commands, replayed
```

Now, let's create a demonstration module, which, when included in a process, opens it up to remote management via REPL.

Remotely monitoring and managing Node processes

In your code bundle, you will find the `repl-monitor` package. This module will expose a server on a given port, which will provide the current process memory usage, allowing a remote process to read this information and send instructions to the monitored process. For this example, we'll be able to tell the process to stop storing things in memory when the process heap exceeds a limit and to start storing things again when it is back below the given threshold.

We'll also demonstrate the usefulness of `.load` to create highly dynamic monitoring solutions that can be adjusted without restarting targeted processes.

Note that creating this sort of access point in the internals of your application should be done with caution. While these techniques are very useful, you must take care to secure access to the various ports, and so on, primarily by limiting access to those within a properly secured private network.

The monitor code is as follows:

```
var repl = require('repl');
var net = require('net');
var events = require('events');
var Emitter = new events.EventEmitter();

module.exports = function(port) {
  net.createServer(function(socket) {
    var inst = repl.start({
      prompt : '',
      input      : socket,
      output   : socket,
      terminal   : false
    })

    inst.on('exit', function () {
      socket.end();
    })

    inst.context.heapUsed = function() {
      return process.memoryUsage().heapUsed;
    }

    inst.context.send = function(msgType, msg) {
      Emitter.emit(msgType, msg);
    }

  }).listen(port);

  return Emitter;
};
```

This module creates REPL on a specified port and exposes two custom methods via the REPL context that clients can use. The `heapUsed` method returns a specific memory reading, and `send` is used by connecting clients to broadcast messages to monitored processes via the returned `EventEmitter` instance. It is important to note that the `output` pipe for this REPL is the connecting socket (identical to the `input` pipe). As we discussed earlier, this means that the calling process will receive the results of executing the JavaScript code it sends. We will provide more information on this later.

Next, we will create a process to be monitored, which will require the monitoring module:

```
var listener = require('./monitor')(8080);

store = true;
var arr = [];

listener.on('stop', function() {
  console.log('stopped');
  store = false;
})

listener.on('start', function() {
  store = true;
})

var runner = function() {
  if(store === true) {
    arr.push(Math.random()*1e6);
    process.stdout.write('.');
  }
  setTimeout(runner, 100);
};

runner();
```

Here, we have a process that keeps adding to an array. Via the monitor module, a client can connect to this process, check memory usage, and broadcast either a start or a stop message, which this process will listen for and act upon.

The last step is to create a client that does remote process management. The control client is straightforward. We connect to REPL via a TCP (net) connection and periodically poll the memory state of the targeted process:

```
var net = require('net');
var sock = net.connect(8080);

var threshold = 0;
var stopped = false;
sock.on('end', function() {
  clearInterval(writer);
  console.log('**** Process ended ****');
});
// Keep checking for memory usage, stringifying the returned
  object
var writer = setInterval(function() {
  sock.write('heapUsed()\n');
}, 1000);
```

Recalling how we added the heapUsed method to the monitor's REPL context, we should expect some value back when we write to the REPL input socket. This means that we must add a data listener to sock:

```
sock.setEncoding('ascii');
sock.on('data', function(heapUsed) {

  // Convert to number
  heapUsed = +heapUsed;

  // Responses from commands will not be numbers
  if(isNaN(heapUsed)) {
    return;
  }

  if(!threshold) {
    threshold = heapUsed;
    console.log("New threshold: " + threshold)
  }

  console.log(heapUsed);

  // If heap use grows past threshold, tell process to stop
  if((heapUsed - threshold) > 1e6) {
    !stopped && sock.write('.load stop_script.js\n');
    stopped = true;
```

```
    } else {
      stopped && sock.write('.load start_script.js\n');
      stopped = false;
    }
});
```

When we receive a memory probe reading, it is converted to an integer and checked against the threshold value (based on whatever the first reading was). If the reading exceeds a predetermined limit, we tell the process to stop allocating memory; when the memory frees up, the process is told to resume.

Importantly, the particular opportunity afforded by REPL is the ability to *run a script* in the context of a remote process. Note the commands sent to `socket.write`, each of which loads an external file containing JavaScript:

```
// Stop script
send("stop")
// Start script
send("start")
```

While these *one-liners* simply exercise the messaging interface we discussed earlier, there is nothing that stops your implementation from using a much longer list of commands in the service of more realistic deployment needs. Crucially, this decoupling of process control facilitates dynamic process management as the script that you use `.load` on today can be changed in the future without requiring any alteration of the target process.

Now, let's take a look at more comprehensive techniques for deep analysis of application performance.

Profiling processes

When tracing memory leaks and other hard-to-find bugs, it is useful to have profiling tools at the ready. What we will look at in this section is how to take snapshots of running processes and how to draw useful information out of them.

Node already provides some process information natively. Basic tracking of how much memory your Node process is using is easy to fetch with `process.memoryUsage()`:

```
{ rss: 12361728, heapTotal: 7195904, heapUsed: 2801472 }
```

There are also modules available to track a little more information on processes. For example, the usage module (github.com/arunoda/node-usage) delivers straightforward memory and CPU usage information. To probe the current process, use the following code:

```
var usage = require('usage');
usage.lookup(process.pid, function(err, result) {
  console.log(result);
});
```

This delivers the following result:

```
{ memory: 15093760,
  memoryInfo: { rss: 15093760, vsize: 3109531648 },
  cpu: 3.8 }
```

Here, we see the total process memory usage in bytes and the CPU usage percentage.

 A good resource to learn about JavaScript memory profiling can be found at https://developer.chrome.com/devtools/docs/javascript-memory-profiling.

It is more interesting to be able to get a look into what V8 sees when it is running your process. Any node process can have v8.log generated simply by passing the --prof (for profile) flag. Let's create a log reader and check its performance using the tick module (https://github.com/sidorares/node-tick), which will read v8 logs and generate a breakdown of the execution profile.

To begin with, install the package globally:

```
npm install -g tick.
```

In your code bundle, under the /profiling directory for this chapter, there will be a file called logreader.js. This simply reads the dummy.log file (also in that folder) and dumps its contents to the console. It's a good example of how to use a Transform stream to process log files:

```
var fs = require('fs');
var stream = require('stream');
var lineReader = new stream.Transform({
  objectMode: true
});
lineReader._transform = function $transform(chunk, encoding, done)
  {
  var data = chunk.toString()
  if(this._lastLine) {
```

```
      data = this._lastLine + data;
    }
    var lines = data.split('\n');
    this._lastLine = lines.pop();
    lines.forEach(this.push.bind(this));
    done();
  }

  lineReader._flush = function $flush(done) {
    if(this._lastLine) {
      this.push(this._lastLine);
    }
    this._lastLine = null;
    done();
  }
  lineReader.on('readable', function $reader() {
    var line;
    while(line = lineReader.read()) {
      console.log(line);
    }
  });
  fs.createReadStream('./dummy.log').pipe(lineReader);
```

The important thing to note is that the main functions have been named and prefixed with $. This is good practice generally—you should always name your functions. The reason is specifically relevant to debugging. We want those names to show up in the reports we're about to generate.

To generate a v8 log, run this script using the --prof (profile) argument and --nologfile-per-isolate to suppress default log file generation:

node --prof logreader --nologfile-per-isolate > v8.log

You should now see a log file in the current working directory with the name v8.log. Go ahead and take a look at it—the log is somewhat intimidating. This is where the tick module comes into play:

node-tick-processor > profile

This command will generate a more readable profile and dump that to the `profile` file. Open that file and take a look. There is a lot of information and doing a deep dive into what it all means is well beyond the scope of this chapter. However, it is very clear how many ticks are being consumed by various functions in our script, such as `$transform`, and we can also see whether or not the functions are optimized. For example:

```
16    21.6%      0    0.0%    LazyCompile: ~$transform /Users/sandro/
profiling/logreader.js:8
```

Here, we see that `$transform` occupied 16 ticks and was lazily compiled, and the tilde (~) indicates that the function is not optimized—if it was optimized, you would see an asterisk (*) prefix.

As an experiment, create a script with the following code and run it with the `--prof` flag:

```
while((function $badidea() {
   return 1;
})());
```

Let this endless loop run for a while and then terminate the process by using *Ctrl* + *C*. Create a profile file, as we did previously, and view it. It should be clear how easy it would be to catch an expensive function using these profiling tools.

An extremely useful visualization tool available to those running the latest Node.js build (0.11.x or higher and io.js) is accessible simply by running the following in a version of the Chrome browser—`chrome://tracing/`:

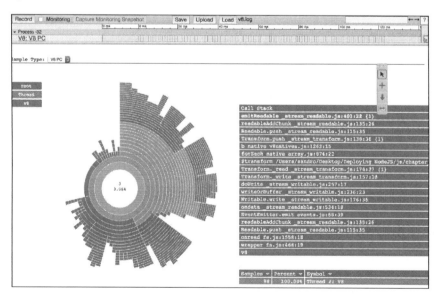

Once you have this ready in your browser, click on the **Load** button and upload your `v8.log` file. The execution timeline is laid out across the top, and, by clicking on the link (V8: V8 PC) on the left, you can access the starburst navigation tool. Starbursts radiate call stacks, nicely visualizing where the work in our application is being done. Note how our `$transform` function is listed to the right—name your functions!

These are a few helpful links if you'd like to learn more about profiling v8:

- `https://developers.google.com/v8/profiler_example`
- `https://groups.google.com/forum/#!msg/nodejs/oRbX5eZvOPg/`
  `jM6TINytVhoJ`

Using third-party monitoring tools

Node is a new technology for which there are few mature application monitoring tools. Some independent developers, along with established companies in the application monitoring space, have jumped in to fill this gap. In this section, we'll look at PM2 as a process manager and monitor and also have a look at Nodetime.

PM2

PM2 is designed to be an enterprise-level process manager. As discussed elsewhere, Node runs within a Unix process, and its `child_process` and `cluster` modules are used to spawn further processes, typically when scaling an application across multiple cores. PM2 can be used to implement the deployment and monitoring of your Node processes both via the command line and programmatically. Here, I will focus on programmatically using PM2 for process management and show you how to use it to monitor and display process activity.

Install PM2 globally:

```
npm install pm2 -g
```

The most straightforward way to use PM2 is as a simple process runner. The following program will increment and log a value every second:

```
// script.js
var count = 1;
function loop() {
  console.log(count++);
  setTimeout(loop, 1000);
};
loop();
```

Here, we use `fork` on a new process from `script.js`, running it in the background *forever*, until we stop it. This is a great way to run a daemonized process:

```
pm2 start script.js
// [PM2] Process script.js launched
```

Once the script launches, you should see something like this in your terminal:

App name	id	mode	PID	status	restarted	uptime	memory	watching
script	0	**fork**	7255	online	0	0s	14.344 MB	disabled

The meaning of most of the values should be clear, such as the amount of memory your process is using, whether or not it is online, how long it has been up, and so on (the `mode` and `watching` fields will be explained shortly). The process will continue to run until it is stopped or deleted.

To set a custom name for your process when you start it, pass the `--name` argument to PM2 as follows: `pm2 start script.js --name 'myProcessName'`.

This overview of all running PM2 processes can be brought up at any time via the `pm2 list` command. PM2 offers other straightforward commands:

- `pm2 stop <app_name | id | all>`: This is used to stop a process by name or ID or stop all processes. A stopped process remains in the process list and can be restarted later.

- `pm2 restart <app_name | id | all>`: This is used to restart a process. The number of process restarts is displayed under `restarted` in all process lists. To automatically restart a process when it reaches a maximum memory limit (say, 15 M), use the `pm2 start script.js --max-memory-restart 15M` command.

- `pm2 delete <app_name | id | all>`: This deletes a process. This process cannot be restarted.

- `pm2 info <app_name | id >`: This provides detailed information on a process, as shown here:

```
status              online
name                script
id                  1
path                /Users/sandro/Desktop/chapter_five/pm2/script.js
args
exec cwd            /Users/sandro/Desktop/chapter_five/pm2/script.js
error log path      /Users/sandro/.pm2/logs/script-error-1.log
out log path        /Users/sandro/.pm2/logs/script-out-1.log
pid path            /Users/sandro/.pm2/pids/script-1.pid
mode                fork_mode
node v8 arguments
watch & reload      ✗
interpreter         node
restarts            0
unstable restarts   0
uptime              2m
created at          2014-07-20T04:16:52.297Z
```

Note the paths given for error and other logs. Remember that our script increments an integer by one every second and logs that count. If you use `cat /path/to/ script/ out/log`, your terminal will show what has been written to the out log, which should be a list of incrementing numbers. Errors are similarly written to a log. Furthermore, you can stream the output logs in real time with `pm2 logs`. For example, our `script.js` process is still pumping out incremented values:

```
PM2: 2014-07-19 23:20:51: Starting execution sequence in -fork mode- for
app name:script id:1
PM2: 2014-07-19 23:20:51: App name:script id:1 online
script-1 (out): 2642
script-1 (out): 2643
script-1 (out): 2644
...
```

To clear all logs, use `pm2 flush`.

You can also use PM2 programmatically. First, you will need to install PM2 locally in your application's `package.json` file with the standard `npm install pm2` command. To replicate the steps we took to run `scripts.js` with PM2, first create the `programmatic.js` script as follows:

```
// programmatic.js
var pm2 = require('pm2');
pm2.connect(function(err) {
  pm2.start('script.js', {
    name: 'programmed script runner',
    scriptArgs: [
      'first',
```

```
        'second',
        'third'
    ],
    execMode : 'fork_mode'
}, function(err, proc) {
    if(err) {
        throw new Error(err);
    }
  });
});
```

This script will use the pm2 module to run script.js as a process. Go ahead and run it with node programmatic.js. Executing a PM2 list should show that programmed script runner is alive. To make sure this is so, try pm2 logs—you should see numbers being incremented, just as before.

Monitoring

PM2 makes process monitoring easy. To view real-time statistics on the CPU and memory usage for your processes, simply enter the command pm2 monit:

```
○ PM2 monitoring :

● script                            [                    ] 0 %
[1] [fork_mode]                     [██████████████      ] 17.684 MB
```

Here, we see a constantly updated graph of the CPU and memory usage for our process. What could be easier?

PM2 also makes it easy to create web-based monitoring interfaces—it's as simple as running pm2 web. This command will start a monitored process listening on port 9615—running pm2 list will now list a process named pm2-http-interface. Run the web command and then navigate to localhost:9615 in your browser. You will see a detailed snapshot of your processes, OS, and so on, as a JSON object:

```
...
  "monit": {
    "loadavg": [
       1.89892578125,
       1.91162109375,
       1.896484375
    ],
    "total_mem": 17179869184,
    "free_mem": 8377733120,
...
```

```
  "pm_id": 1, // our script.js process
    "monit": {
      "memory": 19619840,
      "cpu": 0
    }
  ...
```

Creating a web-based UI that polls your server every few seconds, fetches process information, and then graphs it is made much simpler due to this built-in feature of PM2.

PM2 also has an option to set a watcher on all managed scripts so that any changes to the watched script will cause an automatic process restart. This is very useful when developing. As a demonstration, let's create a simple HTTP server and run it through PM2:

```
// server.js
var http = require('http');
http.createServer(function(req, resp) {
  if(req.url === "/") {
    resp.writeHead(200, {
      'content-type' : 'text/plain'
    });
    return resp.end("Hello World");
  }
  resp.end();
}).listen(8080);
```

This server will echo **"Hello World"** whenever `localhost:8080` is hit. Start it using `pm2 start server.js --watch --name 'watchedHTTPServer'`. Note that if you now list the running processes, our named process will show `enabled` in the `watching` column. Bring up this server in your browser. You should see **"Hello World"**. Now, navigate to the `server.js` script and change `"Hello World"` to `"Hello World, I've changed!"`. Reload your browser. Note the change. Run a process list, and you'll see that this server process indicates a restart. Do it a few more times. Live development of your server applications just got easier thanks to PM2.

 A process management tool with features similar to those of PM2 that is more focused on delivering a full-featured web UI out of the box is **Guvnor**: `https://github.com/tableflip/guvnor`. Other popular process monitors can be found at `https://github.com/remy/nodemon` and `https://github.com/foreverjs/forever`.

We will talk about application deployment strategies using PM2 in *Chapter 7, Deploying and Maintaining*, including using PM2's `cluster` mode.

Nodetime

Nodetime is an easy-to-use Node-monitoring tool. Visit www.nodetime.com and sign up. Once you do so, you will be presented with a page containing code to include in your application. Keep this page open as it will update when we start our application.

To begin with, we'll create a simple HTTP server application that returns `"Hello World"` for every request:

```
"use strict";
require('nodetime').profile({
  accountKey: 'your_account_key',
  appName: 'monitoring'
});

var http    = require('http');

http.createServer(function(request, response) {

  response.writeHead(200, {
    "content-type" : "text/html"
  });
  response.end('Hello World');

}).listen(8080)
```

Save this as server.js. Execute it:

node server.js

Note how, on the Nodetime page in your browser, you will see **monitoring** show up under the **Applications** section. Click on that link—you will now see Nodetime's monitoring interface:

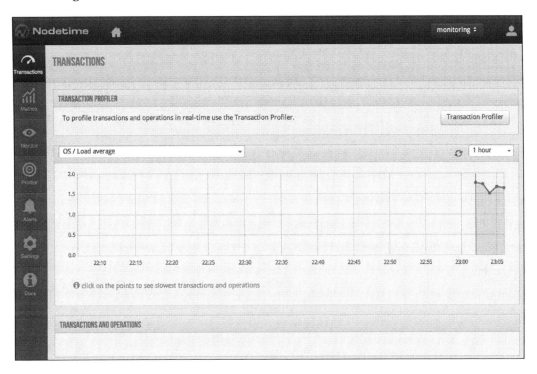

Go ahead and hit the server by visiting `localhost:8080` in your browser. After doing that a number of times, go back to your Nodetime interface and use the dropdown listing **OS / Load average**, selecting other useful metrics. Try `Process/V8 heap total (MB)` to see how V8 is allocating memory. Other metrics allow you to check the profile of the machine executing this server process, and so on.

Using New Relic for monitoring

New Relic is a well-known tool to monitor servers and applications that has been upgraded to support Node. It is intended to be used by those looking to monitor the memory and CPU usage as well as things such as network activity and the health of your Node processes. In this section, we'll look into how to install it on your server and provide examples of its use.

Installation involves applying for a license key from the New Relic website at `newrelic.com`. Setting up your account is straightforward. After signing up, you'll be presented with a list of monitoring tools that New Relic provides—you'll want to select New Relic Servers. In the next steps, you'll select Node.js as your development environment and the OS you'll be working within. I'll use CentOS. After selecting your OS, you should see the installation instructions generated for you, with your license key included—just cut and paste.

You are installing and starting a server that will probe system processes and report results to New Relic. This server must authenticate with New Relic by using your license key, and that means you must store that key in an accessible location. For this reason, a configuration file will be stored on your system. For most Unix installs, this file will be stored in `/etc/newrelic/nrsysmond.cfg`. Read through the configuration options described in that file, such as the location of log files.

Many third-party deployment environments/hosts often provide easy integration with New Relic, such as Heroku (`https://devcenter.heroku.com/articles/newrelic`).

Once New Relic is running, a log file will be created, and if all goes well, that file should contain a line similar to the following, indicating that New Relic is now tracking:

```
{
  "v": 0,
  "level": 30,
  "name": "newrelic",
  "hostname": "your.server.net",
  "pid": 32214,
  "time": "2015-02-16T19:52:20.295Z",
  "msg": "Connected to collector-114.newrelic.com:443 with agent
    run ID 39366519380378313.",
  "component": "collector_api"
}
```

We'll connect to this server via the `newrelic` package. Once that package is installed into your application directory, you will need to configure it. Somewhat awkwardly, this means copying the `newrelic.js` file from `node_modules/newrelic` into your application's root folder, modifying its contents, and adding your license key and a name for your application. The log level field corresponds to the log levels used by Bunyan, so you may want to visit the project page for more information: `https://github.com/trentm/node-bunyan`.

You'll want to avoid storing your license key in the `newrelic.js` file when you go into production. You can pass configuration parameters to New Relic via environment variables rather than hardcoding them via environment variables. For example, you can pass your license key via the `NEW_RELIC_LICENSE_KEY` environment variable.

The `newrelic` package repository can be found at `https://github.com/newrelic/node-newrelic`. This project page contains extensive information on New Relic's usage and configuration, environment variables, and so on. Also, there are examples for setting up client-side monitoring.

Let's add New Relic monitoring to an example application. Create the following Express server:

```
var newrelic = require('newrelic');
var express = require('express');

var app = express();

app.get('/', function(req, res) {
  res.send('Hello World');
});

app.get('/goodbye', function(req, res) {
  res.send('Goodbye World');
});
app.listen(3000);
console.log('Server started on port 3000');
```

You can add additional routes or change the route names if you'd like. What we're going to do is run this server, hit it a few times, and then check with New Relic to see what it has picked up. Start the server and make some requests.

Once you've exercised the server a bit, head over to newrelic.com and log in. Across the top of the page, you will see a navigation menu, and you'll be in the **APM** section. Here is where you can access various monitoring tools for you applications. You should see a list including the application name you set earlier. Click on that name, and you'll be brought to a dashboard overview (there won't be much information yet). You should, however, see some information about the server route activity:

Transactions	App server time
get /	8.35 ms
Transaction traces: n/a	
get /goodbye	1.75 ms
Transaction traces: n/a	

Along the left-hand side, there will be a more detailed navigation pane. Go to **Reports | Web transactions**, and you'll see more detailed information on the routes you've set up. If you navigate to the **SERVERS** section, you'll see a dashboard for your host containing detailed system information.

Now, let's create server load and see how New Relic does with monitoring. If you have a favorite load stress tool, go ahead and send some traffic to your application. If you'd like to learn a simple and common stress-testing tool, learn and use the Apache Bench tool (http://httpd.apache.org/docs/2.2/programs/ab.html). There are also free online stress-testing services, such as http://loader.io and https://loadimpact.com.

Once you've started the stress test, return to the New Relic dashboard for your application and host server. You'll see regularly updated statistics as the New Relic monitor reports the effect of requests on the memory, CPU load, and other key metrics.

Summary

In this chapter, we engaged with one of the most important aspects of deployment—monitoring running processes. Starting at the most basic and necessary level—catching errors—you learned how to trap errors at the individual process level and across processes. After discussing techniques to log errors with both UDP and third-party tools, we looked at how to build remote process monitors using Node's REPL, leading to a deeper discussion on how to do extensive application profiling and memory analysis. Finally, we looked at how to deploy the PM2 process runner in an effort to manage processes and visualize their activity. We also looked at how to use the cloud-based Nodetime and New Relic services to monitor your applications.

Direct monitoring provides crucial real-time insights into any potential threats, but we must also try to limit the possibility of future errors by writing resilient code that we can be confident of. In the next chapter, we will look at how to build and test our applications such that they inspire confidence. Advice on how best to build and organize your applications so that their design is clear will be presented. This way, applying the remaining chapter content on testing strategies to your application can flow naturally with your ongoing development.

6

Building and Testing

Perfect code is a unicorn; what good developers do is introduce the smallest amount of bad code. Any code is, therefore, somewhat flawed, so errors and inefficiency are an inescapable pathology in software development. Accordingly, **technical debt** naturally compounds as more code is written. Some of the more expensive technical realities of modern application development are listed here:

- There are rigidly coupled components that do not easily allow change at either the technical level or the business level. Allowing such unprincipled interpenetration leads to complex capillary networks growing throughout the body of your code. The edges of these networks are nearly impossible to trace, concretizing entanglements that obscure how a change in one function might affect other functions.

- Poor gatekeeping allows untested code to enter production, often leading to quick fixes, which, in turn, can lead to intractable patches and bridge code as well as relentless bugs that regularly resurface.

- There are code units built in isolation in parallel without objective *big picture* guidelines that are merged into a single codebase sloppily and joined together by undocumented, ad hoc bindings.

- The need for refactoring reaches a critical point, and further development, in any sense, becomes nearly impossible. Scaling ceilings typify this situation, and wholesale rewrites are inevitable and nearly always doomed.

Debt accumulates interest. Software, like many long-term pursuits, requires constant debt management. It is in your interest to reduce debt. In the previous chapter, we learned how to profile *deployed* applications at a level of detail sufficient to expose errors, weaknesses, and other unwanted characteristics. In this chapter, we will explore strategies that help software developers and teams catch errors before the membranes of their applications are breached. We will also explore workflows to manage the integration of independently written programs.

Building with Gulp, Browserify, and Handlebars

The JavaScript you are working on will likely be transformed and augmented before it makes it to production. At the very least, it will be checked for errors, minified, packaged, and so on. It will be deployed only after that. Deployment, therefore, follows a build step and how each step in the build is instrumented must be clearly defined.

Over time, certain patterns of development have emerged within the Node community. Many of these patterns map to other environments, while others are unique to the *full-stack JavaScript* Node.js world. The ability to run identical code on the client and server is perhaps the most prominent example. Because deployed codebases often contain the end result of transpilation (for example, CoffeeScript, and SASS), deployment workflows are assembled to run preprocessors, concatenate files, create source maps, compress images, and so on.

In this section, we will look at three technologies that are regularly seen in the Node build/deploy process. We'll use **Gulp** to create a build system, using **Browserify** to bundle application code and **Handlebars** as a templating language for compiling static pages. Finally, we'll look at how to improve our development experience by using **BrowserSync**

Using Gulp

Create a new folder and initialize a `package.json` file in that folder with `npm init`. When this is done, you'll end up with a `package.json` file that looks somewhat like the following:

```
{
  "name": "building",
  "version": "1.0.0",
  "description": "",
  "main": "index.js",
  "scripts": {
    "test": "echo \"Error: no test specified\" && exit 1"
  },
  "author": "",
  "license": "ISC"
}
```

This basic scaffold will be fleshed out and explained as we proceed. The point is simply that you will now hang the modules and other dependencies of your application on this scaffold, using npm, neatly describing dependencies, test harnesses, and more. Since we'll use the Gulp build system, it is reasonable to install the Gulp module first and to assert that it is a dependency of this package. Run these two commands:

```
npm install gulp --global
npm install gulp --save-dev
```

The first command installs Gulp globally, meaning that you can now use the gulp command directly from the command line (you can also abbreviate --global with -g). The next command installs Gulp locally, adding the following new property to the package.json file:

```
"devDependencies": {
    "gulp": "^3.8.10"
}
```

Gulp has been installed and saved as a dependency. We are prepared to construct a build system.

One goal of a build system is the instrumentation of your development environment such that you can work naturally with uncompressed, unminified code while developing and, later, issue commands to convert your *raw* code and assets into an optimized state suitable for staging environments, production environments, and so on. Providing developers with an expressive and simple syntax for describing how to convert source code into deployable code is what Gulp aims to provide.

Create two new folders in your working directory: a /source folder and a /build folder. We're going to create a set of instructions for transforming the files in source/ into files in /build. This set of instructions is stored in a file that is specifically called gulpfile.js. Create that file and insert the following code:

```
"use strict";
var fs = require('fs');
var gulp = require('gulp');
var buildDirectory = './build';
gulp.task('default', function(cb) {
  fs.exists(buildDirectory, function(yes) {
```

```
        if(yes) {
          return cb();
        }
        fs.mkdirSync(buildDirectory);
        cb();
      });
    });
```

Gulp works on the idea of running a number of tasks in a certain order. The general format is `gulp.task(<task name>, <task runner>)`. A Gulpfile is typically extended with several such task definitions. As we'll see, tasks can be named anything you'd like, but there must always be a default task named *default*, and the preceding code establishes such a task to do one simple thing: ensure that a `/build` folder exists, and, if not, to create one.

One thing to notice is the first argument a task runner function receives: a callback function, here named `cb`. Because Node programs customarily run asynchronous code, it is important to have a mechanism to *tell* `gulp` that a task is finished. We're running asynchronous code to check for the existence of a folder, so we use this callback system, but note that, if your code either runs synchronously or if the moment of task completion is irrelevant to subsequent tasks, you can skip running a callback, and Gulp will simply continue with the next task as soon as the task runner exits.

Go ahead and run the `gulp` command in the folder containing your Gulpfile. You should see something like the following:

```
Using gulpfile ~/building/gulpfile.js
Starting 'default'...
Finished 'default' after 720 µs
```

To check that the task is doing its job correctly, delete the `/build` folder and run `gulp` again. You'll see that the folder is recreated.

 Given that Gulp expects its Gulpfile to contain a *default* task, the `gulp` command is simply a shortcut for `gulp default`. You can execute a specific task by running `gulp <taskname>`.

In a typical build, many tasks will be run. Each task should be as simple and specific as possible, and the Gulpfile should neatly organize them so that they execute in a certain order. For this reason, the default task, typically, doesn't do much on its own but is used as a way to hint at the list of tasks that will be run. Let's rewrite the preceding code in a more directed way:

```
gulp.task('initialize',function(cb) {
    fs.exists(buildDirectory, function(yes) {
```

```
   . . .
   cb();
 });
});
```

```
gulp.task('default', ['initialize'], function() {
  console.log('Build is complete');
});
```

Here, we see more clearly how `gulp` works. A second array argument is passed to the `gulp` task's definition, listing other tasks on which the current task depends—a task will not run until all of its dependencies have completed. Let's add another task to this execution chain that copies files in the `/source` folder to the `/build` folder. Add the following to your Gulpfile:

```
gulp.task('move', function() {
  gulp
  .src('./source/**')
  .pipe(gulp.dest('./build'))
});
```

Now, tell `gulp` about this new task:

```
gulp.task('default', ['initialize', 'move'], function() ...)
```

In addition to `task`, you will use the `src`, `pipe`, and `dest` Gulp commands frequently. Gulp is a *streaming* build system—within a task, you will normally identify a collection of files, run a chain of transformations against them, and put the transformed files somewhere useful, typically the folder containing a deployable application. The `src` command is used to identify this collection and convert the contained files into streamable objects such that `pipe` can be used on them to gulp plugins. We will provide more information on this later.

> Arguments to Gulp's `src` command often contain *globs* (for example, `/source/**`), flavors of pattern matching that are useful when we target files within folders. More on how they work can be found at `https://github.com/isaacs/node-glob#glob-primer`.

The preceding code creates a collection of files in the /source directory and pipes them to the (built-in) dest gulp plugin, which writes them to /build. Run gulp again. You will see something like the following:

```
Starting 'initialize'...
Starting 'move'...
Finished 'move' after 3.66 ms
Finished 'initialize' after 4.64 ms
Starting 'default'...
Build is complete
Finished 'default' after 19 µs
```

Did you see anything problematic? The move task ran prior to the completion of initialize, which creates a race condition—will the /build directory be created before move tries to add files to it? A build should be as fast as possible, and, to that end, Gulp aims for maximum concurrency—unless you specify otherwise, Gulp will run all of its tasks concurrently. As illustrated in the preceding code, initialize and move start simultaneously. How can a specific ordering be enforced?

The ordering of the dependency list passed to default does *not* reflect their execution order. However, it does represent a list of tasks that must complete prior to the execution of default. To ensure that move follows initialize, simply make initialize a dependency of move:

```
gulp.task('move', ['initialize'], function() {
    ...
});
```

Erecting a build scaffold

Now that you have an idea of how Gulp works, let's build a representative build process. We'll develop a Gulpfile step by step. To start with, use the following code:

```
"use strict";

// npm install coffee-script -> this is used for test task
require('coffee-script/register');

var path = require('path');
var mkdirp = require('mkdirp');
var del = require('del');
var source = require('vinyl-source-stream');
var buffer = require('vinyl-buffer');
```

```javascript
var browserSync = require('browser-sync');
var gulp = require('gulp');
var coffee = require('gulp-coffee');
var coffeelint = require('gulp-coffeelint');
var sourcemaps = require('gulp-sourcemaps');
var changed = require('gulp-changed');
var concat = require('gulp-concat');
var handlebars = require('gulp-handlebars');
var browserify = require('browserify');
var sass = require('gulp-sass');
var wrap = require('gulp-wrap');
var mocha = require('gulp-mocha');
var uglify = require('gulp-uglify');
var minifyHTML = require('gulp-minify-html');

// A map of relevant source/build folders
var buildDir       = './build';
var sourceDir      = './source';
var s_scriptsDir   = './source/scripts';
var b_scriptsDir   = './build/js';
var s_stylesDir    = './source/styles';
var b_stylesDir    = './build/css';
var s_templatesDir = './source/templates';
var b_templatesDir = './build/templates';
var s_testsDir     = './source/tests';

// Clean out build directories before each build
gulp.task('clean', function(cb) {
  del([
    path.join(b_scriptsDir, '**/*.js'),
    path.join(b_stylesDir, '**/*.css'),
    path.join(b_templatesDir, '*.js'),
    path.join(buildDir, '*.html')
  ], cb);
});
gulp.task('scaffold', ['clean'], function() {
  mkdirp.sync(s_scriptsDir);
  mkdirp.sync(b_scriptsDir);
  mkdirp.sync(s_stylesDir);
  mkdirp.sync(b_stylesDir);
  mkdirp.sync(s_templatesDir);
```

```
      mkdirp.sync(b_templatesDir);
      mkdirp.sync(s_testsDir);
    });


    ...


    gulp.task('default', [
      'clean',
      'scaffold',
      'lint',
      'scripts',
      'styles',
      'templates',
      'browserify',
      'views',
      'test',
      'watch',
      'server'
    ]);
```

At the head of this file, you'll see a lot of require statements. Excepting `path`, they will all be used as either Gulp plugins or helpers. You can just copy the `package.json` file found in the `/building` folder of you code bundle for this chapter, or go ahead and install them using the `--save-dev` directive: `npm install --save-dev gulp-coffee gulp-changed [...]`.

Also, install the `jquery` and `handlebars` npm modules as dependencies using `npm install --save jquery handlebars`. We will provide more information on why we do this when we discuss Browserify.

The `clean` and `scaffold` tasks exist to build a folder structure for your app and to clean the relevant build directories whenever a new build happens (making room for newly built files without leaving the residue of old ones). Take a look at those tasks; they ultimately ensure the following folder structure:

```
build
  css
  js
  templates
source
  scripts
  styles
  templates
tests
```

In the following demonstration, we'll write our JavaScript in **CoffeeScript**, storing `.coffee` files in the `source/scripts` directory, which will be compiled and moved to the `build/js` directory. The `build/css` directory will receive transformed `.scss` files contained in `source/styles`. Handlebars templates will be precompiled and moved from `source/templates` to `build/templates`. Finally, the `.html` files forming the main "pages" of our application will be located in `/source` and moved to the root `/build` folder. Later on, we will add tasks to expose these HTML views via a web server.

At the bottom of the snippet, you will see the list of tasks that we'll define bound as dependencies of the default Gulp task. Let's go over those one by one.

Linting files involves running a syntax checker on your scripts, enforcing various rules, such as indentation, whether or not certain constructs are allowed, whether to force the use of the semicolon, and so on. We'll use CoffeeScript exclusively, so we implement a lint task using the `gulp-coffeelint` plugin:

```
gulp.task('lint', ['scaffold'], function() {
    return gulp.src(path.join(s_scriptsDir, '**/*.coffee'))
    .pipe(coffeelint('./coffeelint.json'))
    .pipe(coffeelint.reporter('default'))
});
```

We're simply checking the syntax of the CoffeeScript files that will be transpiled into JavaScript files residing in the `/js` build folder. Any discrepancies will be reported to `stdout` but will not stop the build. A `coffeelint.json` file containing syntax rules is applied. You should investigate this file and modify it to fit your needs—more information can be found at `http://www.coffeelint.org`.

The next step is to build these newly linted scripts:

```
gulp.task('scripts', ['lint'], function() {
    return gulp.src(path.join(s_scriptsDir, '**/*.coffee'))
    .pipe(changed(b_scriptsDir, {extension: '.js'}))
    .pipe(sourcemaps.init())
    .pipe(coffee({bare: true}))
    .pipe(sourcemaps.write())
    .pipe(gulp.dest(b_scriptsDir))
});
```

There are several build steps happening here. We could simply transform CoffeeScript files to JavaScript files and copy them to the `build/scripts` folder. However, as the transpiled JavaScript file is not the original source file, we need to create a **sourcemap** — an essential tool that will map errors in JavaScript to *the original CoffeeScript source* that generated the said JavaScript. This is invaluable when we are debugging in a browser. As you saw in the code, we simply use the `gulp-sourcemaps` plugin to track the compilation step, and it automatically appends a sourcemap to the generated JavaScript file, which looks somewhat like the following:

```
//# sourceMappingURL=data:application/json;base64,
    eyJ2ZXJzaW9uIjozLCJzb3VyY2VzIjpbInNhbXBsZS5jb2ZmZWUiXS
    wibmFtZXMiOltdLCJtYXBwaW5ncyI6IkFBQUEsSUFBQSxJQUFBBOztBQUFBL
    ElBQUEsR0FFTTTyxxQkFFUUCxDQUFBBIiwiZmlsZSI6InNhbXBsZS5qcyIsInNvdX
    JjZVJvb3QiOiIvvc291cmNlLyIsInNvdXJjZXNDb250ZW50IjpbImRheHggPSB
    bMS4uNjldcbiJdfQ==
```

The `gulp-changed` plugin intelligently tracks whether any targeted files have changed, and, if they have not, the plugin removes them from processing. This plugin can drastically reduce the execution time of any task processing a large numbers of files. Note that we set the extension argument to `.js` as an option as the original file extension (`.coffeescript`) will be changed and the plugin must be told about this naming change.

We will create styles in our system using the **Sass** CSS preprocessor (`http://sass-lang.com/`) denoted by their `.scss` extension. In the following task definition, they are converted to standard CSS. In addition, they are bundled up into a single output file (`app.css`) using the `gulp-concat` plugin:

```
gulp.task('styles', function() {
  return gulp.src(path.join(s_stylesDir, '**/*.scss'))
  .pipe(sass())
  .pipe(concat('app.css'))
  .pipe(gulp.dest(b_stylesDir));
});
```

Bundled into a single file at the build step, global styles can be added to any view with a single `<link>` tag, while maintaining the necessary separation of style documents during development.

The next step is slightly more complicated. We are going to use Handlebars templates, which (might) look like this:

```
<ul>
  {{#each days}}
    <li>{{this}}</li>
  {{/each}}
</ul>
```

For Handlebars to feed the preceding iterator some JSON to process, the template must be compiled into a JavaScript function via the `Handlebars.template` method. While this could be done on the client side, it is much more efficient to simply precompile our templates at the build step. So, what we're going to do is export each template as an individual Node module such that they can be used as one normally uses modules. To accomplish this, we'll use the `gulp-wrap` plugin:

```
gulp.task('templates', function () {
  return gulp.src(path.join(s_templatesDir, '/**/*.hbs'))
  .pipe(handlebars())
  .pipe(wrap('var Handlebars = require
    ("handlebars/runtime")["default"];module.exports =
    Handlebars.template(<%= contents %>);'))
  .pipe(gulp.dest(b_templatesDir));
});
```

This task wraps each source file in code that will use the Handlebars runtime to compile the source code into an exportable JavaScript function. Now, the template can be used in your client code without the overhead of loading Handlebars at runtime or using it for compilation. For example, use the following code:

```
var myTemplate = require("build/templates/myTemplate.js");
$(document.body).append(myTemplate({days:
  ['mon','tue','wed'...]}));
```

You might be saying to yourself, "But wait...client-side JavaScript doesn't have a `require` statement!"...and you'd be right! Enter the power of Browserify:

```
gulp.task('browserify', ['scripts', 'templates', 'views'],
  function() {
  return browserify(b_scriptsDir + '/app.js')
  .bundle()
  // Converts browserify out to streaming vinyl file object
  .pipe(source('app.js'))
  // uglify needs conversion from streaming to buffered vinyl file
    object
  .pipe(buffer())
  .pipe(uglify())
  .pipe(gulp.dest(b_scriptsDir));
});
```

As mentioned at `http://browserify.org/`:

> *"With Browserify, you can write code that uses require in the same way that you would use it in Node."*

This allows us to write our client application code as if it was running within Node, with a DOM document thrown in. In the preceding task, Browserify automatically fetches all app.js dependencies (instances of require), bundles them up into a file that will run on the client, runs the gulp-uglify plugin to minify the resulting JavaScript, and replaces the old file with the Browserified bundle. The app.js file can contain all of the code we need, in one file, thus simplifying and standardizing client integration.

Browserify isn't just about concatenation, however. The point is that, with Browserify, we can use npm modules on both the client and the server, *normalizing* our process, and, therefore, leveraging intelligent package management for client-side JavaScript. This is new and important: we have gained the power of package management and its standardized loading system on the client side. While some client frameworks provide something resembling module management systems, none of these *hacks* can replace the solid npm system. Consider this example source/scripts/app.coffee file:

```
$ = require("jquery")
days = require("../../build/js/sample.js")
complimentTemplate = require("../../build/templates/compliment.js")
helloTemplate = require("../../build/templates/hello.js")
daysTemplate = require("../../build/templates/days.js")
$ ->
  $("#hello").html helloTemplate(name: "Dave")
  $("#compliment").html complimentTemplate(compliment: "You're
great!")
  $("#days").html daysTemplate(days: days)
```

If you check your code bundle, you will find this file. Notice how we require the npm module version of jQuery, as well as the precompiled templates we created previously from Handlebars templates. Yet, we are running in the client, so we can use jQuery operations to add HTML to the DOM—the best of both worlds.

The task for views is very simple:

```
gulp.task('views', ['scaffold'], function() {
  return gulp.src(path.join(sourceDir, '*.html'))
  .pipe(minifyHTML({
    empty: true
  }))
  .pipe(gulp.dest(buildDir))
});
```

We're just compressing HTML and moving the file, with no further changes, to the build directory.

Running and testing your build

At this point, we have all the tasks set up to manage the key files for our repository. Let's use `browser-sync` to automatically spawn a server and a browser window that will load the `index.html` file from our build directory:

```
gulp.task('server', ['test','watch'], function() {
  browserSync({
    notify: false,
    port: 8080,
    server: {
      baseDir: buildDir
    }
  });
});
```

The `test` and `watch` tasks will be explained next. For now, notice how easy it is to add a server to your build process. This task starts a server on the provided port and automatically loads `index.html` found in `baseDir` onto an automatically spawned browser window. The `notify` option tell BrowserSync not to display debugging notifications in connected browsers. Now, every time we run Gulp, our app will load up in a browser. Your terminal should display information similar to the following:

```
[BS] Access URLs:
    ----------------------------------------------------------
         Local: http://localhost:8080
      External: http://192.168.2.23:8080
    ----------------------------------------------------------
            UI: http://localhost:3001
   UI External: http://192.168.2.23:3001
    ----------------------------------------------------------
[BS] Serving files from: ./build
```

BrowserSync allows multiple clients to view your build, so an external access URL is provided. Additionally, they will see your interactions. For example, if you scroll the page, the pages of connected clients will also scroll. Additionally, the UI URL will expose a sort of dashboard for your build, allowing you to control connected clients, reload their views, and so on. This is a great tool when you are doing demonstrations for your team or for a client. To learn more about BrowserSync and its configuration, visit `http://www.browsersync.io/`.

A good build system should provide a testing harness as the final arbiter of whether the build should be certified. We'll do a deep dive into testing with **Mocha**, **Chai**, and **Sinon** later in this chapter, so here we'll just demonstrate a very simple testing stub that you can build on when designing your Gulp workflow:

```
gulp.task('test', ['browserify'], function() {
  return gulp.src(path.join(s_testsDir, '**/*.coffee'), {
    read: false
  })
  .pipe(coffee({bare: true}))
  .pipe(mocha({
  reporter: 'spec'
  }));
});
```

There is a test file written in CoffeeScript within the tests directory:

```
days = require('../../build/js/sample.js')
assert = require("assert")
describe "days() data", ->
  it "should have a length of 7", ->
    assert.equal days().length, 7
```

This test will load one of our template modules, which exports an array with seven members—the days of the week. The test uses Node's core `assert` library (discussed in detail later in this chapter) to test whether this array has the correct length of seven characters. Mocha provides the testing harness, via `describe` and `it`, allowing you to design tests that read like a natural language. When you run through Gulp, you should see something like this (if everything goes right):

```
[17:27:40] Starting 'test'...
  days array
    ✓ should have a length of 7
  1 passing (2ms)
```

The final task is provided by another native Gulp method: `watch`. The purpose of `watch` is to bind file watchers to certain directories such that any file change will automatically trigger a rerun of the relevant build tasks. For example, you might want to run the `scripts` task again if any file in `source/scripts` changes. The following code demonstrates how (changes in) certain folders automatically trigger a number of build tasks:

```
gulp.task('watch', ['scaffold'], function() {
  gulp.watch(path.join(s_scriptsDir, '**/*'), [
    'browserify', browserSync.reload
```

```
  ]);
  gulp.watch(path.join(s_templatesDir, '**/*'), [
    'browserify', browserSync.reload
  ]);
  gulp.watch(path.join(s_stylesDir, '**/*'), [
    'styles', browserSync.reload
  ]);
  gulp.watch(path.join(sourceDir, '*.html'), [
    'views', browserSync.reload
  ]);
});
```

You will notice that BrowserSync is bound to changes as well, thus creating a very natural development process. Once you have a running build displayed in a browser, any change you make to, for example, `index.html`, will be *automatically* reflected in that view. As you change the CSS, you will see the change immediately, and so on. There will be no more constant reloading when you are developing; BrowserSync pushes changes for you.

There are many other things you might need to do. For example, you might want to compress images before pushing them to production. As a practice, create the relevant image folders in your source and build directory and implement an `images` task using `gulp-imagemin` (`https://github.com/sindresorhus/gulp-imagemin`).

 The people behind Gulp provide a good collection of suggested patterns to implement common build tasks at `https://github.com/gulpjs/gulp/tree/master/docs/recipes`.

Here's a final note: you will regularly *hand-code* these sorts of build systems, typically reusing the same patterns. For this reason, certain automated tools have been created that can often reduce the creation of boilerplate build code to a few commands. A popular one is **Yeoman** (`http://yeoman.io/`), which makes it easy to construct common "stacks" of build steps, databases, servers, and frameworks. Other notable solutions are **Brunch** (`http://brunch.io/`) and **Mimosa** (`http://mimosa.io/`).

Using Node's native testing tools

Testing is simply the act of checking whether your assumptions about the state of something are false. In this way, testing software follows the scientific method in that you will express a theory, make a prediction, and run an experiment to see whether the data matches your prediction.

Unlike scientists, software developers can change reality—Einstein's joke about changing the facts if they don't fit the theory actually applies, without irony, to the testing process. In fact, it is required! When your tests (theories) fail, you must change "the world" until the tests do not fail.

In this section, you will learn how to use Node's native debugger for *live* code testing and how to use the `assert` module to make predictions, run experiments, and test results.

The Node debugger

Most developers have used an IDE for development. A key feature of all good development environments is access to a debugger, which allows breakpoints to be set in a program in places where the state or other aspects of the runtime need to be checked.

V8 is distributed with a powerful debugger (commonly seen powering the Google Chrome browser's developer tools panel), and this is accessible to Node. It is invoked using the `debug` directive, as shown here:

```
> node debug somescript.js
```

Simple stepthrough and inspection debugging can now be achieved within a Node program. Consider the following program:

```
myVar = 123;
setTimeout(function () {
  debugger;
  console.log("world");
}, 1000);
console.log("hello");
```

Note the `debugger` directive. Executing this program *without* using the `debug` directive will result in `"hello"` being displayed, followed by `"world"` one second later. When using the directive, you will see this:

```
> node debug somescript.js
< debugger listening on port 5858
connecting... ok
break in debug-sample.js:1
  1 myVar = 123;
  2 setTimeout(function () {
  3   debugger;
debug>
```

Once a breakpoint is hit, we are presented with a CLI to the debugger itself, from within which we can execute standard debugging and other commands:

- `cont`, `c`: This continues execution from the last breakpoint until the next breakpoint

- `step`, `s`: Step in — this keeps running until a new source line (or breakpoint) is hit; after that, return control to the debugger

- `next`, `n`: This is like the preceding command, but function calls made on the new source line are executed without stopping

- `out`, `o`: Step out — this executes the remainder of the current function and back out to the parent function

- `backtrace`, `bt`: This traces the steps to the current execution frame in a manner similar to the following:

  ```
  ...
  #3 Module._compile module.js:456:26
  #4 Module._extensions..js module.js:474:10
  #5 Module.load module.js:356:32
  ... etc.
  ```

- `setBreakpoint()`, `sb()`: This sets a breakpoint on the current line

- `setBreakpoint(Integer)`, `sb(Integer)`: This sets a breakpoint on the specified line

- `clearBreakpoint()`, `cb()`: This clears a breakpoint on the current line

- `clearBreakpoint(Integer)`, `cb(Integer)`: This clears a breakpoint on the specified line

- `run`: If the debugger's script has terminated, this will start it again

- `restart`: This terminates and restarts the script

- `pause`, `p`: This pauses the running code

- `kill`: This kills the running script

- `quit`: This exits the debugger

- `version`: This displays the V8 version

- `scripts`: This lists all loaded scripts

> To repeat the last debugger command, simply hit *Enter* on your keyboard.

Returning to the script we are debugging, entering `cont` in the debugger results in the following output:

```
debug> cont
< hello // ... a pause of 1000 ms will now occur, then...
break in debug-sample.js:3
  1 myVar = 123;
  2 setTimeout(function () {
  3   debugger;
  4   console.log("world");
  5 }, 1000);
debug>
```

Notice how "`hello`" was not printed when we started the debugger even though you would expect the `console.log('hello')` command to execute prior to the breakpoint being reached in the `setTimeout` callback. The debugger does not execute at runtime; it is evaluating at compile time *as well as at run time*, giving you deep visibility into how the bytecode for your program is being assembled and, eventually, will be executed, not simply a postcompilation printout, which `console.log` gives.

It is normally useful at a breakpoint to do some inspection, such as of the value of variables. There is an additional command available to the debugger, `repl`, which enables this. Currently, our debugger has stopped after having successfully parsed the script and executed `console.log('hello')`, the first function pushed into the event loop. What if we wanted to check the value of `myVar`? Use `repl`:

```
debug> repl
Press Ctrl + C to leave debug repl
> myVar
123
```

Play around with REPL here, experimenting with how it might be used.

At this point, our program has a single remaining instruction to execute—printing "`world`". An immediate `cont` command will execute this last command, the event loop will have nothing further to do, and our script will terminate:

```
debug> cont
< world
program terminated
debug>
```

As an experiment, run the script again, using next instead of cont just before the execution of this final context. Keep hitting *Enter* and try to follow the code that is being executed. You will see that, after "world" is printed, the timers.js script will be introduced into this execution context as Node cleans up after firing a timeout. Run the scripts command in the debugger at this point. You will see something like this:

```
debug> next
break in timers.js:125
 123
 124    debug(msecs + ' list empty');
 125    assert(L.isEmpty(list));
 126    list.close();
 127    delete lists[msecs];
debug> scripts
* 37: timers.js
  46: debug-sample.js
debug>
```

It will be useful to experiment with various methods, learning about what happens when Node executes scripts at a deep level as well as about Node helping with your debugging needs.

It can be useful to read the following document, describing how the Google Chrome debugger interface is used: https://developers.google.com/chrome-developer-tools/docs/javascript-debugging#breakpoints.

Miroslav Bajtos's **node-inspector** module is strongly recommended for debugging, allowing a developer to remotely debug a Node application from the Chrome browser. You can find more information on this at https://github.com/node-inspector/node-inspector.

The 'assert' module

Node's assert module is used for simple unit testing. In many cases, it suffices as a basic scaffolding for tests or is used as the assertion library for testing frameworks (such as Mocha, as we'll see later). Its usage is straightforward; we want to assert the truth of something and throw an error if our assertion is not true. For example, use the following commands:

```
> require('assert').equal(1,2,"Not equal!")
AssertionError: Not equal!
    at repl:1:20
  ...
```

If the assertion was `true` (both values are equal), nothing would be returned:

```
> require('assert').equal(1,1,"Not equal!")
undefined
```

Following the UNIX Rule of Silence, *when a program has nothing surprising, interesting, or useful to say, it should say nothing*, assertions only return a value when the assertion fails. The value returned can be customized by using an optional message argument, as seen in the preceding code.

The `assert` module API is composed of a set of comparison operations with identical call signatures—the actual value, the expected value, and an optional message to display when comparison fails. Alternate methods functioning as shortcuts or handlers for special cases are also provided.

A distinction must be made between **identity comparison (===)** and **equality comparison (==)**; the former is often referred to as *strict equality comparison* (as is the case of the `assert` API). Because JavaScript employs dynamic typing, when two values of different types are compared using the equality operator ==, an attempt is made to coerce (or cast) one value into the other—a sort of *common denominator* operation. For example, use the following code:

```
1 == "1" // true
false == "0" // true
false == null // false
```

As you might expect, these sorts of comparisons can lead to surprising results. Notice the more predictable results when identity comparison is used:

```
1 === "1" // false
false === "0" // false
false === null // false
```

The thing to remember is that the === operator *does not perform type coercion* prior to the comparison, while the equality operator compares *after type coercion*. Additionally, because objects in JavaScript are passed by reference, the identity of two objects with the same values is distinct—for objects, identity requires that both operands *refer to the same object*:

```
var a = function(){};
var b = new a;
var c = new a;
var d = b;
console.log(a == function(){}) // false
console.log(b == c) // false
console.log(b == d) // true
console.log(b.constructor === c.constructor); // true
```

Finally, the concept of *deep equality* is used for object comparisons where identity need not be exact. Two objects are deeply equal if they both posses the same number of owned properties, the same prototype, the same set of keys (though not necessarily in the same order), and equivalent (not identical) values for each of their properties:

```
var a = [1,2,3];
var b = [1,2,3];
assert.deepEqual(a, b);   // passes
assert.strictEqual(a, b);  // throws AssertionError: [1,2,3] ===
  [1,2,3]
```

It is useful to test your assumptions about how values are understood in comparison to each other by designing assertion tests. The results may surprise you.

The following rounds out the assertions you can make using this module:

- `assert.equal(actual, expected, [message])`: This is used to test coerced equality with ==.

- `assert.notEqual(actual, expected, [message])`: This is used to test coerced equality with !=.

- `assert.deepEqual(actual, expected, [message])`: This is used to test for deep equality.

- `assert.notDeepEqual(actual, expected, [message])`: This is used to test for deep inequality.

- `assert.strictEqual(actual, expected, [message])`: This is used to test identity equivalence ===.

- `assert.notStrictEqual(actual, expected, [message])`: This is used to test for identity mismatch !==.

- `assert(value, [message])`: This throws an error if the sent value is not truthy.

- `assert.ok(value, [message])`: This is identical to `assert(value)`.

- `assert.ifError(value)`: This throws an error if the value is truthy.

- `assert.throws(block, [error], [message])`: This is used to test whether or not the supplied code block throws. The optional error value can be an error constructor, regular expression, or a validation function returning a Boolean value.

- `assert.doesNotThrow(block, [error], [message])`: This is used to test whether the supplied code block does not throw an error.

- `assert.fail(actual, expected, message, operator)`: This throws an exception. This is most useful when the exception is trapped by a try/catch block.

A shortcut method to log assertion results is available in the `console` API:

```
> console.assert(1 == 2, "Nope!")
AssertionError: Nope!
```

 For a more detailed explanation of how comparison is done in JavaScript, consult `https://developer.mozilla.org/en-US/docs/Web/JavaScript/Reference/Operators/Comparison_Operators`.

Now, let's look at testing with more advanced testing frameworks and tools.

Testing with Mocha, Chai, Sinon, and npm

One of the great benefits of writing tests for your code is that you will be forced to think through how what you've written works. A test that is difficult to write might indicate code that is difficult to understand. On the other hand, comprehensive coverage with good tests helps others (and you) understand how an application works.

There are at least three notions to consider when setting up your test environment.

The purpose of testing is to make comparisons between the value of what is received and what is expected by your application code. As we saw earlier, Node's `assert` module is designed for this purpose, but its functionality is limited to individual, isolated assertions. We'll use the Chai library (`http://chaijs.com`), which provides you with a richer choice of languages and idioms to make assertions with.

It is not unusual for an application to be covered by several hundred tests. When assertions are grouped, say by feature or business unit, these groups can provide a clearer picture of your application's state. Designing and instrumenting tools to do this grouping, especially with asynchronous code, is difficult. Thankfully, several well-known, well-designed test runners exist for you to use. We'll use Mocha (`http://mochajs.org`), which makes it easier to organize, control, and display the results of your tests.

Testing is normally done on development boxes and not in live production environments. How can you write tests for code that does not run in a real environment? For example, how do I test my code's ability to handle responses from a network endpoint that I cannot connect to locally? How do I check the arguments a function is being sent without rewriting the function? We'll use Sinon (`http://sinonjs.org/`), which lets you create synthetic methods and other simulations.

 Other popular test runners are Jasmine (`https://github.com/jasmine/jasmine`) and Vows (`https://github.com/vowsjs/vows`). Should (`https://github.com/shouldjs/should.js`) is a popular assertion library.

To start with, set up a folder containing the following structure:

```
scripts
spec
  helpers
```

The `/scripts` folder contains the JavaScript we'll test. The `/spec` folder contains configuration and test files.

Now, initialize a `package.json` file with `npm init`. You can just hit *Enter* at the prompts, but when you are asked for a test command, enter the following:

```
mocha ./spec --require ./spec/helpers/chai.js --reporter spec
```

This will make more sense as we move forward. For now, recognize that this assignation to npm's `test` attribute asserts that we will use Mocha for testing. Mocha's test report will be of the `spec` type and that test will exist in the `/spec` directory. We will also require a configuration file for Chai, which will be explained in one of the following sections. Importantly, this has now created a script declaration in npm that will allow you to run your test suite with the `npm test` command. Use that command whenever you need to run the Mocha tests we'll be developing in the following section.

If you haven't already, install Mocha globally with `npm install mocha -g`. Also, install the local modules that we'll need for testing using the `npm install mocha chai sinon redis --save-dev` command.

Mocha

Mocha is a test runner that does not concern itself with test assertions themselves. Mocha is used to organize and run your tests, primarily through the use of the `describe` and `it`. operators. The following code shows this:

```
describe("Test of Utility Class", function() {
  it("Running #date should return a date", function(){
    // Test date function
  });
  it("Running #parse should return JSON", function() {
    // Run some string through #parse
  });
});
```

As illustrated, the Mocha harness leaves open how the tests are described and organized and makes no assumptions about how test assertions are designed.

You can set up tests that run synchronously, as described in the preceding code, or asynchronously, using the completion handler passed to all `it` callbacks:

```
describe("An asynchronous test", function() {
  it("Runs an async function", function(done) {
    // Run async test, and when finished call...
    done();
  });
});
```

Blocks can also be nested:

```
describe("Main block", function() {
  describe("Sub block", function() {
    it("Runs an async function", function() {
      // A test running in sub block
    });
  });
  it("Runs an async function", function() {
    // A test running in main block
  });
});
```

Finally, Mocha offers *hooks* that enable you to run code before and/or after tests:

- `beforeEach()` runs before each test in a `describe` block
- `afterEach()` runs after each test in a `describe` block
- `before()` runs code once prior to any test—prior to any run of `beforeEach`
- `after()` runs code once after all tests have run—after any run of `afterEach`

Usually, these are used to set up test contexts, such as creating variables before certain tests and cleaning those up prior to certain other tests.

This simple collection of tools is expressive enough to handle most testing needs. Additionally, Mocha provides various test reporters that offer differently formatted results. We'll see those in action later as we build realistic test scenarios.

Chai

As we saw earlier with Node's native `assert` module, at its base, testing involves asserting what we expect a chunk of code to do, executing that code, and checking whether our expectations were met. Chai is an assertion library with a more expressive syntax, offering three assertion styles: **expect**, **should**, and **assert**. We will use Chai to provide the assertions (tests) to be wrapped within Mocha `it` statements, favoring the *expect* style of assertion.

 Note that while `Chai.assert` is modeled after the core Node `assert` syntax, Chai augments the object with additional methods.

To begin with, we are going to create a configuration file called `chai.js`:

```
var chai = require('chai');
chai.config.includeStack = true;
global.sinon = require('sinon');
global.expect = chai.expect;
global.AssertionError = chai.AssertionError;
global.Assertion = chai.Assertion;
```

Place this file in the `/spec/helpers` folder. This will tell Chai to display the full-stack trace of any errors and to expose the `expect` assertion style as a `global` variable. Similarly, Sinon is also exposed as a `global` variable. This file will augment the Mocha test run context such that we can use these tools without having to redeclare them in each test file.

The `expect` style of assertion reads like a sentence, with *sentences* composed from words like *to*, *be*, *is*, and more. Take the following code as an example:

```
expect('hello').to.be.a('string')
expect({ foo: 'bar' }).to.have.property('foo')
expect({ foo: 'bar' }).to.deep.equal({ foo: 'bar' });
expect(true).to.not.be.false
expect(1).to.not.be.true
expect(5).to.be.at.least(10) // fails
```

To explore the extensive list of *words* available when you are creating `expect` test chains, consult the full documentation at `http://chaijs.com/api/bdd/`.

As stated earlier, Mocha does not have an opinion on how you create assertions. We will use `expect` to create assertions in the tests that follow.

Consider testing the `capitalize` function in the following object:

```
var Utils = function() {
  this.capitalize = function(str) {
    return str.split('').map(function(char) {
      return char.toUpperCase();
    }).join('');
  };
};
```

We might do something like this:

```
describe('Testing Utils', function() {
  var utils = new Utils();
  it('capitalizes a string', function() {
    var result = utils.capitalize('foobar');
    expect(result).to.be.a('string').and.equal('FOOBAR');
  });
});
```

This Chai assertion will be `true` and Mocha will report the same results. This is shown in the following screenshot:

```
Running tests
  Testing Utils
    ✓ capitalizes a string
```

Next, we'll look at how to add Sinon to our test process.

Sinon

Within a testing environment, you typically emulate the realities of a production environment as access to real users, data, or other live systems is unsafe or otherwise undesirable. Being able to simulate environments is, therefore, an important part of testing. Also, you will often want to inspect more than just call results—you might want to test whether a given function is being called in the right context or with the right examples. Sinon is a tool that helps you to simulate external services, emulate functions, track function calls, and so on.

 The `sinon-chai` module extends Chai with Sinon assertions. For more information on `sinon-chai`, visit `https://github.com/domenic/sinon-chai`.

The key Sinon technologies are **spies**, **stubs**, and **mocks**. Additionally, you can set fake timers, create fake servers, and more (see `http://sinonjs.org/`). This section focuses on the first three. Let's go over examples of each.

Spies

Take a look at this text from the Sinon documentation that defines a test spy:

"A test spy is a function that records arguments, return value, the value of this and exception thrown (if any) for all its calls. A test spy can be an anonymous function or it can wrap an existing function."

A spy gathers information on the function it is tracking. For example:

```
var sinon = require('sinon');
var argA = "foo";
var argB = "bar";
var callback = sinon.spy();

callback(argA);
callback(argB);

console.log(
  callback.called,
  callback.callCount,
  callback.calledWith(argA),
  callback.calledWith(argB),
  callback.calledWith('baz')
);
```

This will log the following:

```
true 2 true true false
```

The spy was called twice, once with `foo`, once with `bar`, and never with `baz`.

Let's suppose we wanted to test whether our code properly connects to the pub/sub functionality of Redis:

```
var redis = require("redis");
var client1 = redis.createClient();
var client2 = redis.createClient();

//  Testing this
function nowPublish(channel, msg) {
  client2.publish(channel, msg);
};
describe('Testing pub/sub', function() {
  before(function() {
    sinon.spy(client1, "subscribe");
  });
  after(function() {
    client1.subscribe.restore();
  });
  it('tests that #subscribe works', function() {
    client1.subscribe("channel");
    expect(client1.subscribe.calledOnce);
  });
  it('tests that #nowPublish works', function(done) {
    var callback = sinon.spy();
    client1.subscribe('channel', callback);
    client1.on('subscribe', function() {
      nowPublish('channel', 'message');
      expect(callback.calledWith('message'));
      expect(client1.subscribe.calledTwice);
      done();
    });
  });
});
```

In this example, we do more with spy and with Mocha. We deploy spy to proxy the native `subscribe` method of `client1`, importantly setting up and tearing down the spy proxy (restoring original functionality) within Mocha's `before` and `after` methods. The Chai assertions prove that both `subscribe` and `nowPublish` are functioning correctly and receiving the right arguments.

More information on spies can be found at `http://sinonjs.org/docs/#spies`.

Stubs

A stub, when used as a spy, can be wrapped around an existing function such that it can fake the behavior of that function (rather than simply recording function execution as we saw earlier). Take a look at this definition of test stubs taken from the Sinon documentation:

> "*Test stubs are functions (spies) with pre-programmed behavior. They support the full test spy API in addition to methods which can be used to alter the stub's behavior.*"

Let's assume that you have a functionality in your application that makes calls to an HTTP endpoint. The code may be something like the following:

```
http.get("http://www.example.org", function(res) {
  console.log("Got status: " + res.statusCode);
}).on('error', function(e) {
  console.log("Got error: " + e.message);
});
```

When it's successful, the call will log Got status: 200. Should the endpoint be unavailable, you'll see something like Got error: getaddrinfo ENOTFOUND.

It is likely that you will need to test the ability of your application to handle alternate status codes, and, of course, explicit errors. It may not be in your power to force endpoints to emit these, yet you must prepare for them should they occur. Stubs are useful here to create synthetic responses such that your response handlers can be comprehensively tested.

We can use stubs to emulate a response without actually calling the `http.get` method:

```
var http = require('http');
var sinon = require('sinon');
sinon.stub(http, 'get').yields({
  statusCode: 404
});
// This URL is never actually called
http.get("http://www.example.org", function(res) {
  console.log("Got response: " + res.statusCode);
  http.get.restore();
});
```

This stub yields a simulated response by wrapping the original method, which is never called, resulting in a 404 error being returned from a call that would normally return a status code of 200. Importantly, note how we restore the stubbed method to its original state when we are done with it.

For example, the following *pseudo* code describes a module that makes HTTP calls, parses the response, and responds with 'handled' if everything went OK and 'not handled' if the HTTP response was unexpected:

```javascript
var http = require('http');
module.exports = function() {
  this.makeCall = function(url, cb) {
    http.get(url, function(res) {
      cb(this.parseResponse(res));
    }.bind(this))
  }
  this.parseResponse = function(res) {
    if(!res.statusCode) {
      throw new Error('No status code present');
    }
    switch(res.statusCode) {
      case 200:
      return 'handled';
      break;
      case 404:
      return 'handled';
      break;
      default:
      return 'not handled';
      break;
    }
  }
}
```

The following Mocha test ensures that the Caller.parseReponse method can handle all response codes we need handled using stubs to simulate the entire expected response range:

```javascript
var Caller = require('../scripts/Caller.js');

describe('Testing endpoint responses', function() {
  var caller = new Caller();
  function setTestForCode(code) {
    return function(done) {
      sinon.stub(caller, 'makeCall').yields(caller.parseResponse({
```

```
            statusCode: code
        }));
        caller.makeCall('anyURLWillDo', function(h) {
            expect(h).to.be.a('string').and.equal('handled');
            done();
        });
    }
}
afterEach(function() {
    caller.makeCall.restore();
});
it('Tests 200 handling', setTestForCode(200));
it('Tests 404 handling', setTestForCode(404));
it('Tests 403 handling', setTestForCode(403));
});
```

By proxying the original `makeCall` method, we can test `parseResponse` against a range of status codes without the difficulty of forcing remote network behavior. Noting that the preceding test should fail (there is no handler for 403 codes), the output of this test should look something like the following:

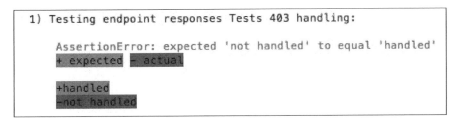

The full API for stubs can be seen at `http://sinonjs.org/docs/#stubs`.

Mocks

Rather than checking expectations *after the fact*, mocks can be used to check whether the unit under test is being used correctly—they enforce implementation details. Take a look at this definition of mocks taken from the Sinon documentation:

> "*Mocks (and mock expectations) are fake methods (like spies) with pre-programmed behavior (like stubs) as well as pre-programmed expectations. A mock will fail your test if it is not used as expected.*"

In the following example, we check not only the number of times a specific function is called (easy with spies) but also whether it is called with specific, expected arguments. Specifically, we again test the `capitalize` method of `Utils`, this time using mocks:

```
var sinon = require('sinon');
var Utils = require('./Utils.js');
var utils = new Utils();
var arr = ['a','b','c','d','e'];
var mock = sinon.mock(utils);

// Expectations
mock.expects("capitalize").exactly(5).withArgs.apply(sinon,arr);

arr.map(utils.capitalize);
console.log(mock.verify());
```

After setting up a mock on `utils`, we map a five-element array to `capitalize`, expecting `capitalize` to be called exactly five times, with the array's elements as arguments (using `apply` to spread the array into individual arguments). The well-named `mock.verify` function is then checked to see whether our expectations were satisfied. As usual, when we are done with it, we unwrap the `utils` object with `mock.restore`. You should see `true` logged to your terminal.

Now, remove one element from the tested array, frustrating expectations. When you run the test again, you should see the following near the top of the output:

ExpectationError: Expected capitalize([...]) 5 times (called 4 times)

This should clarify the type of test results that mocks are designed to produce.

> Note that mocked functions do not execute — mock overrides its target. In the preceding example, no array members are ever run through `capitalize`.

Let's revisit our earlier example, this time testing Redis pub/sub using mocks:

```
var redis = require("redis");
var client = redis.createClient();

describe('Mocking pub/sub', function() {
  var mock = sinon.mock(client);
  mock.expects('subscribe').withExactArgs('channel').once();
  it('tests that #subscribe is being called correctly', function()
    {
```

```
      client.subscribe('channel');
      expect(mock.verify()).to.be.true;
    });
  });
```

Rather than checking for conclusions, here we assert our expectation that the mocked `subscribe` method will receive the exact argument `channel` only `once`. Mocha expects `mock.verify` to return `true`. To make this test fail, add one more `client.subscribe('channel')` line, producing something like the following:

ExpectationError: Unexpected call: subscribe(channel)

 More information on how to use mocks can be found at `http://sinonjs.org/docs/#mocks`.

Automated browser testing with PhantomJS and CasperJS

One way to test whether a UI is working is to pay several people to interact with a website via a browser and report any errors they find. This can become a very expensive and ultimately unreliable process. Also, it requires putting potentially failing code into production in order to test it. It is better to test whether application views are rendering correctly from within the build process itself prior to releasing any views "into the wild". PhantomJS was created to address this need, among others.

A browser, stripped of its buttons and other controls, is, at its heart, a program that validates and runs JavaScript, HTML, and CSS. That the validated HTML is rendered visually on your screen is simply a consequence of humans being able to see only with their eyes. A server can interpret the logic of compiled code and see the results of interactions with that code without a visual component. Perhaps because eyes are usually found in one's head, a browser running on a server is typically referred to as a headless browser. PhantomJS provides a headless version of the WebKit engine that is scriptable via a JavaScript API.

Headless testing with PhantomJS

PhantomJS (`http://phantomjs.org/build.html`) allows you to create scripts that can be executed in a headless browser context. It allows you to capture a browser context within a scriptable environment, enabling various operations, such as loading an HTML page into that context. This allows you to perform operations on that browser context, such as manipulating the DOM of a loaded page.

For example, fetching a Twitter user's recent tweets can be accomplished by hitting the following endpoint in your browser: `http://mobile.twitter.com/<twitter user>`. We can also use PhantomJS to do the same thing within a headless, scriptable environment and then write code to fetch those tweets. Create a `phantom-twitter.js` file containing the following code:

```
var page = require('webpage').create();
var system = require('system');
var fs = require('fs');
var twitterId = system.args[1];

page.open(encodeURI("http://mobile.twitter.com/" + twitterId),
function(status) {
  if(!status) {
    throw new Error("Can't connect to Twitter!");
  }
  var tweets = page.evaluate(function() {
    var _tweets = [];
    var coll = Array.prototype.slice.call(document.query
      SelectorAll('div.tweet-text'))
    coll.forEach(function(tweet) {
      _tweets.push(tweet.innerText);
    });
    return _tweets
  });
  fs.write(twitterId + '.json', JSON.stringify(tweets));
  phantom.exit();
});
```

Now, use the CLI to pass that script to PhantomJS, sending the Twitter handle of the person you'd like to read as an argument:

```
phantomjs phantom-twitter.js kanyewest
```

A new file called `kanyewest.json` will be created, containing recent tweets in the JSON format. Let's examine the code.

We first require some of PhantomJS's core modules, importantly the `page` library that allows us to load pages, and the `system` and `fs` modules (which resemble Node's `process` and `fs` modules, respectively). We'll use `system` to fetch command-line arguments and `fs` to write fetched tweets to the filesystem.

The `page.open` command does what you would expect—loading a web page into the PhantomJS context. We can now perform operations on the rendered DOM. In this case, we are going to use `evaluate` on JavaScript within the context of that page, fetching the elements containing tweets identified by the `div.tweet-text` CSS selector and stripping out `innerText`. Because `evaluate` is running in the context of a headless WebKit, there is no way for us to access the outer PhantomJS scope, so we simply return what we find within the evaluation scope to the outer scope, where a file can be generated using `fs`.

PhantomJS offers an extensive API to interact with WebKit (`http://phantomjs. org/api/`), allowing script injection, creating screen captures, navigating rendered pages, and so on. A whole range of client tests can be created using these tools.

When writing server tests, you will probably not want to use PhantomJS from the CLI. For this reason, various Node-PhantomJS bridges have been written that let you interact with PhantomJS via a Node module. A good one is `phantomjs` (`https:// github.com/sgentle/phantomjs-node`). For example, the following will load a page, as shown earlier, and execute JavaScript to fetch the page's title attribute:

```
var phantom = require('phantom');
phantom.create(function(ph) {
  ph.createPage(function(page) {
    page.open("http://www.example.org", function(status) {
      page.evaluate(function() {
        return document.title;
      }, function(title) {
        console.log('Page title: ' + title);
        ph.exit();
      });
    });
  });
});
```

Running the preceding code should result in something like the following being logged:

```
Page title: Example Domain
```

Navigation scenarios with CasperJS

Because PhantomJS is not specifically designed to be a test runner, others have created tools to simplify testing with PhantomJS. **CasperJS** (http://casperjs. org/) is a navigation and testing utility for PhantomJS and **SlimerJS** (which uses the Gecko engine that powers Firefox).

CasperJS offers an extensive toolkit to create complex chains of interactions using an expressive Promises-like interface. Describing page interaction tests with CasperJS requires much less code and is clearer. For example, the earlier phantom example demonstrating how to fetch a page title can be simplified:

```
casper.start('http://example.org/', function() {
  this.echo('Page title: ' + this.getTitle());
});
casper.run();
```

If the preceding code were saved as a file called pagetitle.js and run with the casperjs test pagefile.js command, you would see the following logged:

Page title: Example Domain

A much terser syntax produces identical results. Let's look at another example that demonstrates how to fetch one page, click on a link on that page, and read some information from the resulting page:

```
casper.start('http://google.com/', function() {
  this
  .thenEvaluate(function(term) {
    document.querySelector('input[name="q"]').setAttribute
      ('value', term);
    document.querySelector('form[name="f"]').submit();
  }, 'node.js')
  .then(function() {
    this.click('h3.r a');
  })
  .then(function() {
    this.echo('New location: ' + this.getCurrentUrl());
  });
});
casper.run();
```

Here, we can see how a Promise-like chaining of interactions results in clear and expressive code. After fetching Google's search page, we will evaluate a piece of JavaScript that inserts the `node.js` string into its famous search box and submit the search form. Then, CasperJS is asked to click on the first result link (`h3.r a`) and to finally display the current URL:

```
New location: http://nodejs.org/
```

This demonstrates that a full-page navigation has occurred, at which point we can chain even more interaction steps.

Finally, let's use some of the CasperJS test assertions and demonstrate how to take snapshots of web pages while testing Google's translation service:

```
casper.start('http://translate.google.com/', function() {
  this
  .sendKeys('#source', 'Ciao')
  .waitForText('Hello')
  .then(function() {
    this.test.assertSelectorHasText('#result_box', 'Hello');
  })
  .then(function() {
    this.capture('snapshot.png');
  });
});
casper.run();
```

Google's translation page is dynamic. As you type into the translation box, the service detects keyboard events, attempts to infer the language you are using based on any available text, and, in "real time", provides a translation, all without refreshing the page. In other words, we are not submitting a form and waiting for the resulting page.

Therefore, once we have the page loaded, we send keystrokes (`sendKeys`) into the `#source` input box with the Italian word `"Ciao"`. Testing that this results in the correct translation, we wait for `"Hello"` to arrive—`waitForText` fires when the text passed appears on a page. To ensure that the text has arrived in the right place, we assert that the element with the `#result_box` selector contains `"Hello"`. If all is well, you will see the following logged:

```
PASS Find "Hello" within the selector "#result_box"
```

Additionally, within the same folder, you will find the `snapshot.png` image visualizing the DOM-based interactions just executed:

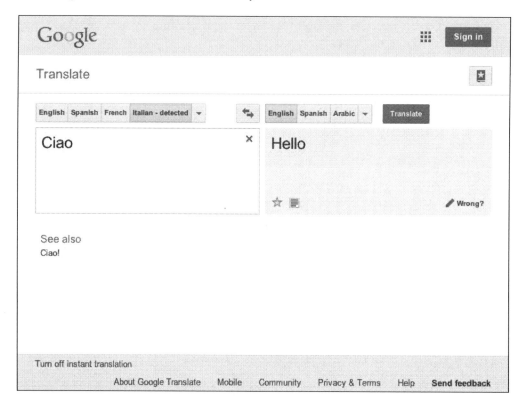

Hopefully, this demonstrates how CasperJS can be used to harness the power of PhantomJS when you're writing client tests. If you'd like to use CasperJS as a Node module, give SpookyJS (`https://github.com/SpookyJS/SpookyJS`) a try.

Summary

In this chapter, we took a look at testing and building your application such that you can get a good sense of its ability to *stand up* in production. We worked through a representative build system that used Gulp and Browserify, along with some other tools, to show how a codebase can be optimized and packaged for deployment. Also, you learned about Node's native debugging tools and assertion library.

The Node community has embraced testing from the beginning, and many testing frameworks and native tools are made available to developers. You learned how to set up a proper test system using Gulp, Mocha, Chai, and Sinon, in the process experimenting with headless browser testing.

The next chapter will be focused on taking the builds you have tested and deploying them to production servers. You'll learn about setting up local development environments on virtual machines, provisioning remote servers, setting up continuous integration with webhooks and Jenkins, maintaining your application dependencies and, generally, keeping your applications running smoothly as changes are made.

7
Deploying and Maintaining

In this book, we have seen the advantages of composing applications out of well defined components. This assembly process involves the installation of many support systems, from the operating system your application will run on, to the version of Node you will support, to the various npm modules, testing frameworks, profiling tools, and other subsystems that power an application. It is likely that you have been doing all this on a single machine—manually starting and stopping servers, updating configurations, and altering application code. Are you adding a new module? Stop the server, add the module, and restart the server.

In a production environment, this sort of ad hoc development is almost impossible, and it remains tedious regardless. How can this process be automated and streamlined so that altering the number of servers being balanced or incrementally pushing out new deployments can be done with minimum work, thus making life simpler for the folks responsible for operations?

In this chapter, we will learn about the following:

- Automating the deployment of applications, including a look at the differences between continuous integration, delivery, and deployment

- Using Git to track local changes and triggering deployment actions via webhooks when appropriate

- Using Vagrant to synchronize your local development environment with a deployed production server

- Provisioning a server with Ansible

- Implementing continuous integration and deployment using Jenkins and working through a complete example of how to automate builds and deploys when the source code changes

- Maintaining npm packages and dependency trees, outlining how to track version changes, and keeping your deployed applications up to date

Note that application deployment is a complex topic with many dimensions that are often considered within unique sets of needs. This chapter is intended as an introduction to some of the technologies and themes you will encounter. Also, note that the scaling issues discussed in *Chapter 3, Scaling Node*, are part and parcel of deployment. Also, our discussion in *Chapter 2, Installing and Virtualizing Node Servers*, is relevant here. You may want to revisit those topics while working through the following deployment scenarios.

Using GitHub webhooks

At the most basic level, deployment involves automatically validating, preparing, and releasing new code into production environments. One of the simplest ways to set up a deployment strategy is to trigger releases whenever changes are committed to a Git repository through the use of **webhooks**. Paraphrasing the GitHub documentation, webhooks *provide a way for notifications to be delivered to an external web server whenever certain actions occur on a repository.*

In *Chapter 2, Installing and Virtualizing Node Servers*, we saw a simplified example of this process, where pushing changes to a Heroku instance caused your production build to automatically update. One problem with this simple solution is that no validation was performed—if you pushed bad code, your production server would blindly run bad code. In this section, we'll use GitHub webhooks to create a simple continuous deployment workflow, adding more realistic checks and balances.

We'll build a local development environment that lets developers work with a clone of the production server code, make changes, and see the results of those changes immediately. As this local **development** build uses the same repository as the **production** build, the build process for a chosen environment is simple to configure, and multiple production and/or development *boxes* can be created with no special effort.

The first step is to create a GitHub (`www.github.com`) account if you don't already have one. Basic accounts are free and easy to set up.

Now, let's look at how GitHub webhooks work.

Enabling webhooks

Create a new folder and insert the following `package.json` file:

```
{
    "name": "express-webhook",
    "main": "server.js",
    "dependencies": {
```

```
    "express": "~4.0.0",
    "body-parser": "^1.12.3"
  }
}
```

This ensures that Express 4.x is installed and includes the `body-parser` package, which is used to handle POST data. Next, create a basic server called `server.js`:

```
var express     = require('express');
var app         = express();
var bodyParser  = require('body-parser');
var port        = process.env.PORT || 8082;

app.use(bodyParser.json());
app.get('/', function(req, res) {
  res.send('Hello World!');
});
app.post('/webhook', function(req, res) {
  // We'll add this next
});
app.listen(port);
console.log('Express server listening on port ' + port);
```

Enter the folder you've created, and build and run the server with `npm install`; `npm start`. Visit `localhost:8082/` and you should see **"Hello World!"** in your browser.

Whenever any file changes in a given repository, we want GitHub to push information about the change to /webhook. So, the first step is to create a GitHub repository for the Express server mentioned in the code. Go to your GitHub account and create a new repository with the name `'express-webhook'`. The following screenshot shows this:

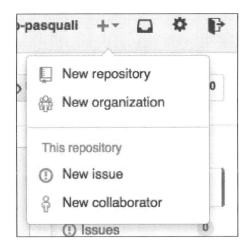

Once the repository is created, enter your local repository folder and run the following commands:

```
git init
git add .
git commit -m "first commit"
git remote add origin git@github.com:<your username>/express-webhook
```

You should now have a new GitHub repository and a local linked version. The next step is to configure this repository to broadcast the push event on the repository. Navigate to the following URL:

```
https://github.com/<your_username>/express-webhook/settings
```

From here, navigate to **Webhooks & Services | Add webhook** (you may need to enter your password again). You should now see the following screen:

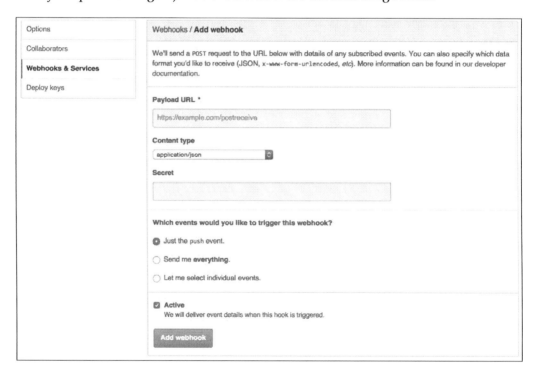

This is where you set up webhooks. Note that the push event is already set as default, and, if asked, you'll want to disable SSL verification for now. GitHub needs a target URL to use POST on change events. If you have your local repository in a location that is already web accessible, enter that now, remembering to append the /webhook route, as in `http://www.example.com/webhook`.

If you are building on a local machine or on another limited network, you'll need to create a secure tunnel that GitHub can use. A free service to do this can be found at `http://localtunnel.me/`. Follow the instructions on that page, and use the custom URL provided to configure your webhook.

Other good forwarding services can be found at `https://forwardhq.com/` and `https://meetfinch.com/`.

Now that webhooks are enabled, the next step is to test the system by triggering a push event. Create a new file called `readme.md` (add whatever you'd like to it), save it, and then run the following commands:

```
git add readme.md

git commit -m "testing webhooks"

git push origin master
```

This will push changes to your GitHub repository. Return to the **Webhooks & Services** section for the `express-webhook` repository on GitHub. You should see something like this:

This is a good thing! GitHub noticed your push and attempted to deliver information about the changes to the webhook endpoint you set, but the delivery failed as we haven't configured the `/webhook` route yet—that's to be expected. Inspect the failed delivery payload by clicking on the last attempt—you should see a large JSON file. In that payload, you'll find something like this:

```
"committer": {
  "name": "Sandro Pasquali",
  "email": "spasquali@gmail.com",
  "username": "sandro-pasquali"
},
"added": [
  "readme.md"
],
"removed": [],
"modified": []
```

It should now be clear what sort of information GitHub will pass along whenever a push event happens. You can now configure the /webhook route in the demonstration Express server to parse this data and do something with that information, such as sending an e-mail to an administrator. For example, use the following code:

```
app.post('/webhook', function(req, res) {
  console.log(req.body);
});
```

The next time your webhook fires, the entire JSON payload will be displayed.

Let's take this to another level, breaking down the autopilot application to see how webhooks can be used to create a build/deploy system.

Implementing a build/deploy system using webhooks

To demonstrate how to build a webhook-powered deployment system, we're going to use a starter kit for application development. Go ahead and use fork on the repository at https://github.com/sandro-pasquali/autopilot.git. You now have a copy of the **autopilot** repository, which includes scaffolding for common Gulp tasks, tests, an Express server, and a deploy system that we're now going to explore.

The autopilot application implements special features depending on whether you are running it in production or in development. While autopilot is a little too large and complex to fully document here, we're going to take a look at how major components of the system are designed and implemented so that you can build your own or augment existing systems. Here's what we will examine:

- How to create webhooks on GitHub programmatically
- How to catch and read webhook payloads
- How to use payload data to clone, test, and integrate changes
- How to use PM2 to safely manage and restart servers when code changes

If you haven't already used fork on the autopilot repository, do that now. Clone the autopilot repository onto a server or someplace else where it is web-accessible. Follow the instructions on how to connect and push to the fork you've created on GitHub, and get familiar with how to pull and push changes, commit changes, and so on.

 PM2 delivers a basic deploy system that you might consider for your project (https://github.com/Unitech/PM2/blob/master/ADVANCED_README.md#deployment).

Install the cloned autopilot repository with `npm install; npm start`. Once npm has installed dependencies, an interactive CLI application will lead you through the configuration process. Just hit the *Enter* key for all the questions, which will set defaults for a local development build (we'll build in production later). Once the configuration is complete, a new development server process controlled by PM2 will have been spawned. You'll see it listed in the PM2 manifest under `autopilot-dev` in the following screenshot:

You will make changes in the `/source` directory of this development build. When you eventually have a production server in place, you will use `git push` on the local changes to push them to the autopilot repository on GitHub, triggering a webhook. GitHub will use `POST` on the information about the change to an Express route that we will define on our server, which will trigger the build process. The build runner will `pull` your changes from GitHub into a temporary directory, install, build, and test the changes, and if all is well, it will replace the relevant files in your deployed repository. At this point, PM2 will restart, and your changes will be immediately available.

Schematically, the flow looks like this:

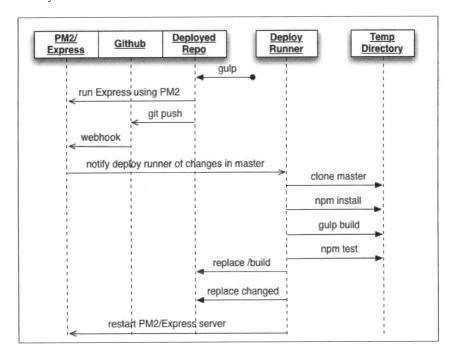

To create webhooks on GitHub programmatically, you will need to create an access token. The following diagram explains the steps from A to B to C:

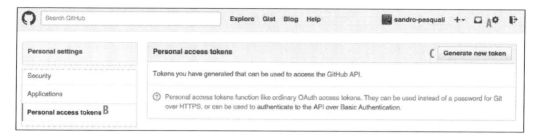

We're going to use the Node library at `https://github.com/mikedeboer/node-github` to access GitHub. We'll use this package to create hooks on GitHub using the access token you've just created.

Once you have an access token, creating a webhook is easy:

```
var GitHubApi = require("github");

github.authenticate({
  type: "oauth",
  token: <your token>
});
github.repos.createHook({
  "user": <your github username>,
  "repo": <github repo name>,
  "name": "web",
  "secret": <any secret string>,
  "active": true,
  "events": [
    "push"
  ],
  "config": {
    "url": "http://yourserver.com/git-webhook",
    "content_type": "json"
  }
}, function(err, resp) {
  ...
});
```

Autopilot performs this on startup, removing the need for you to manually create a hook.

Now, we are listening for changes. As we saw previously, GitHub will deliver a payload indicating what has been added, what has been deleted, and what has changed. The next step for the autopilot system is to integrate these changes.

It is important to remember that, when you use webhooks, you do not have control over how often GitHub will send changesets—if more than one person on your team can push, there is no predicting when those pushes will happen. The autopilot system uses Redis to manage a queue of requests, executing them in order. You will need to manage multiple changes in a way. For now, let's look at a straightforward way to build, test, and integrate changes.

In your code bundle, visit `autopilot/swanson/push.js`. This is a process runner on which fork has been used by `buildQueue.js` in that same folder. The following information is passed to it:

- The URL of the GitHub repository that we will clone
- The directory to clone that repository into
  (`<temp directory>/<commit hash>`)
- The changeset
- The location of the production repository that will be changed

Go ahead and read through the code. Using a few shell scripts, we will clone the changed repository and build it using the same commands you're used to— `npm install`, `npm test`, and so on. If the application builds without errors, we need only run through the changeset and replace the old files with the changed files.

The final step is to restart our production server so that the changes reach our users. Here is where the real power of PM2 comes into play.

When the autopilot system is run in production, PM2 creates a cluster of servers (similar to the Node `cluster` module). This is important as it allows us to restart the production server incrementally. As we restart one server node in the cluster with the newly pushed content, the other clusters continue to serve old content. This is essential to keeping a zero-downtime production running.

Hopefully, the autopilot implementation will give you a few ideas on how to improve this process and customize it to your own needs.

Synchronizing local and deployed builds

One of the most important (and often difficult) parts of the deployment process is ensuring that the environment an application is being developed, built, and tested within perfectly simulates the environment that application will be deployed into. In this section, you'll learn how to emulate, or virtualize, the environment your deployed application will run within using Vagrant. After demonstrating how this setup can simplify your *local* development process, we'll use Ansible to provision a remote instance on DigitalOcean.

Developing locally with Vagrant

For a long while, developers would work directly on running servers or cobble together their own version of the production environment locally, often writing ad hoc scripts and tools to smoothen their development process. This is no longer necessary in a world of virtual machines. In this section, we will learn how to use Vagrant to emulate a production environment within your development environment, advantageously giving you a realistic *box* to work on testing code for production and isolating your development process from your local machine processes.

By definition, Vagrant is used to create a virtual box emulating a production environment. So, we need to install Vagrant, a virtual machine, and a machine image. Finally, we'll need to write the configuration and provisioning scripts for our environment.

Go to `http://www.vagrantup.com/downloads` and install the right Vagrant version for your box. Do the same with VirtualBox here at `https://www.virtualbox.org/wiki/Downloads`.

You now need to add a box to run. For this example, we're going to use Centos 7.0, but you can choose whichever you'd prefer. Create a new folder for this project, enter it, and run the following command:

```
vagrant box add chef/centos-7.0
```

> Usefully, the creators of Vagrant, HashiCorp, provide a search service for Vagrant boxes at `https://atlas.hashicorp.com/boxes/search`.

You will be prompted to choose your virtual environment provider—select `virtualbox`. All relevant files and machines will now be downloaded. Note that these boxes are very large and may take time to download.

You'll now create a configuration file for Vagrant called `Vagrantfile`. As with npm, the `init` command quickly sets up a base file. Additionally, we'll need to inform Vagrant of the box we'll be using:

```
vagrant init chef/centos-7.0
```

Vagrantfile is written in Ruby and defines the Vagrant environment. Open it up now and scan it. There is a lot of commentary, and it makes a useful read. Note the `config.vm.box = "chef/centos-7.0"` line, which was inserted during the initialization process.

Now you can start Vagrant:

```
vagrant up
```

If everything went as expected, your box has been booted within Virtualbox. To confirm that your box is running, use the following code:

```
vagrant ssh
```

If you see a prompt, you've just set up a virtual machine. You'll see that you are in the typical home directory of a CentOS environment.

To destroy your box, run `vagrant destroy`. This deletes the virtual machine by cleaning up captured resources. However, the next `vagrant up` command will need to do a lot of work to rebuild. If you simply want to shut down your machine, use `vagrant halt`.

Vagrant is useful as a virtualized, production-like environment for developers to work within. To that end, it must be configured to emulate a production environment. In other words, your box must be provisioned by telling Vagrant how it should be configured and what software should be installed whenever `vagrant up` is run.

One strategy for provisioning is to create a shell script that configures our server directly and point the Vagrant provisioning process to that script. Add the following line to Vagrantfile:

```
config.vm.provision "shell", path: "provision.sh"
```

Now, create that file with the following contents in the folder hosting Vagrantfile:

```
# install nvm
curl https://raw.githubusercontent.com/creationix/nvm/v0.24.1/install.
sh | bash
# restart your shell with nvm enabled
source ~/.bashrc
```

```
# install the latest Node.js
nvm install 0.12
# ensure server default version
nvm alias default 0.12
```

Destroy any running Vagrant boxes. Run Vagrant again, and you will notice in the output the execution of the commands in our provisioning shell script.

When this has been completed, enter your Vagrant box as the root (Vagrant boxes are automatically assigned the root password "vagrant"):

vagrant ssh

su

You will see that Node v0.12.x is installed:

node -v

 It's standard to allow password-less sudo for the *Vagrant* user. Run visudo and add the following line to the sudoers configuration file:
vagrant ALL=(ALL) NOPASSWD: ALL

Typically, when you are developing applications, you'll be modifying files in a project directory. You might bind a directory in your Vagrant box to a local code editor and develop in that way. Vagrant offers a simpler solution. Within your VM, there is a /vagrant folder that maps to the folder that Vagrantfile exists within, and these two folders are automatically synced. So, if you add the server.js file to the right folder on your local machine, that file will also show up in your VM's /vagrant folder.

Go ahead and create a new test file either in your local folder or in your VM's /vagrant folder. You'll see that file synchronized to both locations regardless of where it was originally created.

Let's clone our express-webhook repository from earlier in this chapter into our Vagrant box. Add the following lines to provision.sh:

```
# install various packages, particularly for git
```

```
yum groupinstall "Development Tools" -y
```

```
yum install gettext-devel openssl-devel perl-CPAN perl-devel zlib-devel
-y
```

```
yum install git -y
```

```
# Move to shared folder, clone and start server
```

```
cd /vagrant
git clone https://github.com/sandro-pasquali/express-webhook
cd express-webhook
npm i; npm start
```

Add the following to Vagrantfile, which will map port 8082 on the Vagrant box (a guest port representing the port our hosted application listens on) to port 8000 on our host machine:

```
config.vm.network "forwarded_port", guest: 8082, host: 8000
```

Now, we need to restart the Vagrant box (loading this new configuration) and re-provision it:

```
vagrant reload
vagrant provision
```

This will take a while as yum installs various dependencies. When provisioning is complete, you should see this as the last line:

```
==> default: Express server listening on port 8082
```

Remembering that we bound the guest port 8082 to the host port 8000, go to your browser and navigate to localhost:8000. You should see **"Hello World!"** displayed.

Also note that in our provisioning script, we cloned to the (shared) /vagrant folder. This means the clone of express-webhook should be visible in the current folder, which will allow you to work on the more easily accessible codebase, knowing it will be automatically synchronized with the version on your Vagrant box.

Provisioning with Ansible

Configuring your machines *by hand*, as we've done previously, doesn't scale well. For one, it can be overly difficult to set and manage environment variables. Also, writing your own provisioning scripts is error-prone and no longer necessary given the existence of provisioning tools, such as Ansible.

With Ansible, we can define server environments using an organized syntax rather than ad hoc scripts, making it easier to distribute and modify configurations. Let's recreate the provision.sh script developed earlier using Ansible **playbooks**:

> *Playbooks are Ansible's configuration, deployment, and orchestration language. They can describe a policy you want your remote systems to enforce or a set of steps in a general IT process.*

Playbooks are expressed in the **YAML** format (a human-readable data serialization language). To start with, we're going to change Vagrantfile's provisioner to Ansible. First, create the following subdirectories in your Vagrant folder:

```
provisioning
   common
      tasks
```

These will be explained as we proceed through the Ansible setup.

Next, create the following configuration file and name it `ansible.cfg`:

```
[defaults]
roles_path = provisioning
log_path = ./ansible.log
```

This indicates that Ansible **roles** can be found in the `/provisioning` folder, and that we want to keep a provisioning log in `ansible.log`. Roles are used to organize tasks and other functions into reusable files. These will be explained shortly.

Modify the `config.vm.provision` definition to the following:

```
config.vm.provision "ansible" do |ansible|
ansible.playbook = "provisioning/server.yml"
ansible.verbose = "vvvv"
end
```

This tells Vagrant to defer to Ansible for provisioning instructions, and that we want the provisioning process to be verbose — we want to get feedback when the provisioning step is running. Also, we can see that the playbook definition, `provisioning/server.yml`, is expected to exist. Create that file now:

```
---
- hosts: all
  sudo: yes
  roles:
    - common
  vars:
    env:
      user: 'vagrant'
    nvm:
      version: '0.24.1'
      node_version: '0.12'
    build:
      repo_path: 'https://github.com/sandro-pasquali'
      repo_name: 'express-webhook'
```

Playbooks can contain very complex rules. This simple file indicates that we are going to provision all available hosts using a single role called common. In more complex deployments, an inventory of IP addresses could be set under hosts, but, here, we just want to use a general setting for our one server. Additionally, the provisioning step will be provided with certain environment variables following the forms env.user, nvm.node_version, and so on. These variables will come into play when we define the common role, which will be to provision our Vagrant server with the programs necessary to build, clone, and deploy express-webhook. Finally, we assert that Ansible should run as an administrator (sudo) by default—this is necessary for the yum package manager on CentOS.

We're now ready to define the common role. With Ansible, folder structures are important and are implied by the playbook. In our case, Ansible expects the role location (./provisioning, as defined in ansible.cfg) to contain the common folder (reflecting the common role given in the playbook), which itself must contain a tasks folder containing a main.yml file. These last two naming conventions are specific and required.

The final step is creating the main.yml file in provisioning/common/tasks. First, we replicate the yum package loaders (see the file in your code bundle for the full list):

```
---

- name: Install necessary OS programs
  yum: name={{ item }} state=installed
  with_items:
    - autoconf
    - automake
    ...
    - git
```

Here, we see a few benefits of Ansible. A human-readable description of yum tasks is provided to a looping structure that will install every item in the list. Next, we run the nvm installer, which simply executes the auto-installer for nvm:

```
- name: Install nvm
  sudo: no
  shell: "curl https://raw.githubusercontent.com/creationix/nvm/v{{ nvm.
version }}/install.sh | bash"
```

Note that, here, we're overriding the playbook's `sudo` setting. This can be done on a per-task basis, which gives us the freedom to move between different permission levels while provisioning. We are also able to execute shell commands while at the same time interpolating variables:

```
- name: Update .bashrc
  sudo: no
  lineinfile: >
    dest="/home/{{ env.user }}/.bashrc"
    line="source /home/{{ env.user }}/.nvm/nvm.sh"
```

Ansible provides extremely useful tools for file manipulation, and we will see here a very common one—updating the `.bashrc` file for a user. The `lineinfile` directive makes the addition of aliases, among other things, straightforward.

The remainder of the commands follow a similar pattern to implement, in a structured way, the provisioning directives we need for our server. All the files you will need are in your code bundle in the `vagrant/with_ansible` folder. Once you have them installed, run `vagrant up` to see Ansible in action.

One of the strengths of Ansible is the way it handles contexts. When you start your Vagrant build, you will notice that Ansible gathers facts, as shown in the following screenshot:

```
PLAY [all] ****************************************************************

GATHERING FACTS **********************************************************
ok: [default]

TASK: [common | Install necessary OS programs] ***************************
ok: [default] => (item=autoconf,automake,binutils,bison,flex,gcc,gcc-c++,gettext,
libtool,make,patch,pkgconfig,redhat-rpm-config,rpm-build,rpm-sign,gettext-devel,o
penssl-devel,perl-CPAN,perl-devel,zlib-devel,git)
```

Simply put, Ansible analyzes the context it is working in and only executes what is necessary to execute. If one of your tasks has already been run, the next time you try `vagrant provision`, that task will not run again. This is *not* true for shell scripts! In this way, editing playbooks and reprovisioning does not consume time redundantly changing what has already been changed.

Ansible is a powerful tool that can be used for provisioning and much more complex deployment tasks. One of its great strengths is that it can run remotely—unlike most other tools, Ansible uses SSH to connect to remote servers and run operations. There is no need to install it on your production boxes. You are encouraged to browse the Ansible documentation at `http://docs.ansible.com/index.html` to learn more.

Integrating, delivering, and deploying

In this chapter, we've been looking at using deployment systems that encourage agile development, generally facilitating safe delivery into production environments of code updates in near real time. Variations in how deployments can be structured and/or understood, which usually depend on factors such as team size and management structure, are common. A brief summary of each of the three typical categories, **continuous integration**, **continuous delivery**, and **continuous deployment**, will be provided in the following sections. Finally, we'll set up a build/deploy system for a Node application using Jenkins, a CI server, configured to automatically deploy changes to a Heroku server.

Continuous integration

Continuous integration is the process of merging changes into a master branch continuously (typically, several times a day). The goal of CI is to make errors impatient and noisy, arriving early and failing loudly, rather than emerging later from much larger and more complex **bulk** merges comprising several days or weeks of work. Unit tests are typically run here. Note that an updated integration branch is not necessarily continuously deployed, though it may be. The goal is to keep a master branch fresh, current, and ready to be deployed when necessary.

Continuous delivery

"Delivery" is the key word here. In environments where all changes must be tested/vetted by a quality assurance team or some other group of stakeholders prior to being released, changes are delivered and reviewed as they are proposed. While continuous delivery does not preclude delivery into production, the general goal is to deliver new code where it can be subjected to further functional tests, tests of business logic, and so on, prior to it reaching real customers.

This test environment should be equivalent to the production environment and, when tests pass, there should be confidence that the changes will also be deployable to production. Because this stage is typically understood as preceding deployment, it is often described as the *staging environment*.

Staged changes are normally deployable in one step, a single system command, or the click of a button in a GUI.

Continuous deployment

Continuous deployment is the aggressive, optimistic strategy of building your application in a way such that it can be released into production at any time, typically as soon as it passes certain automated tests. This strategy generally leads to many releases per day and requires that the validation pipeline, which changes move through, is as close to production-like as possible.

Because there is limited (or nonexistent) oversight of the code being released, continuous post-release inspection of application performance is normal. That is, trust but verify: push changes into production after automated testing, but regularly check whether your visitor counts are dropping, response times are rising, or other metrics are behaving abnormally.

While similar to continuous delivery, the two should not be confused.

Building and deploying with Jenkins

You've learned how to use GitHub webhooks to trigger a build process whenever new code is pushed to a repository. From pulling and testing a changed repository to notifying a chat server that a new build has occurred, Jenkins helps you to trigger deployment workflows. As your deployment needs become more complex than simply testing a single branch, the benefits of a more powerful CI tool become apparent. Jenkins provides tools to manage build permissions, task scheduling, triggering deploys, displaying build logs, and more. Let's deploy an application using Jenkins.

To install Jenkins, run the installer for your environment that can be found at `http://jenkins-ci.org/`. There are also services that allow you to install Jenkins in the "cloud", but we're going to build a local service. Upon successful installation, a browser will open up with the Jenkins "home page" UI, as shown here:

You will use this Jenkins **dashboard** often as you manage builds.

Note that Jenkins will, by default, run on port `8080`. You will, as with webhooks, need to map this location to a web-accessible URL directly, via proxy, via forwarding, or in some other way. Move to **Manage Jenkins | Configure System** and find the **Jenkins Location** section. Add the Jenkins URL, as shown in the following screenshot:

If you are running Jenkins on `localhost`, jump back to earlier in this chapter when we discussed using forwarding services, such as `http://localtunnel.me/`.

> You may be warned about an unsecured Jenkins instance. This is a valid complaint! While we will not set up authentication, you should do so in any real production environment. It isn't hard. Visit **Manage Jenkins | Configure Global Security** to do so and/or visit `https://wiki.jenkins-ci.org/display/JENKINS/Securing+Jenkins`.

The next thing to do is configure Jenkins to work with Node.js and GitHub. From the dashboard, navigate to **Manage Jenkins | Manage Plugins | Available**. You should see a list of available plugins, from which you will search for and install *NodeJS Plugin* and *GitHub Plugin*. This may take a while as these plugins, and their dependencies, are installed. If any of the installs prompt you to restart Jenkins, you will find instructions on how to do that in the installs list provided further on in this section.

The key integration that we'll have to do is with GitHub. In a new browser window, visit your GitHub account and generate a new access token.

Copy the generated key. You will now give Jenkins this access token so that it can perform operations on GitHub on your behalf, in particular around webhooks. Return to **Manage Jenkins | Configure**, and add this OAuth token and your user information to the **GitHub Web Hook** section, as shown here:

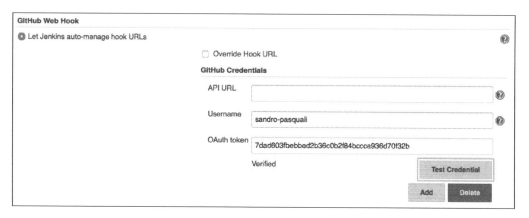

Run **Test Credential** to ensure that Jenkins can connect to GitHub using the token you've provided.

Finally, we need to provide our GitHub credentials to Jenkins so that it can pull our repository when changes happen. Navigate to **Credentials** and click on **Global credentials**. Select **Username with Password** and add your credentials, which will ensure that you give these credentials a useful name (you'll need to refer to these credentials later).

Because you have already built your own webhook-powered CI system, it may already be apparent to you why Jenkins is being configured in this way. In the end, we are configuring Jenkins to respond to push events on a GitHub repository, pull the changed repository, and automatically build it. To that end, we will need to provision Jenkins so that it is configured with Node and can, therefore, build Node repositories.

Navigate to **Configure System** and add a NodeJS installation, as shown here:

You will now configure the Node environment that Jenkins will use. You should match that environment with the environment your production servers will run in. Click on **Add NodeJS** and follow the instructions. You can select **Install automatically** and, when presented with installer options, select **Install from nodejs. org**. Make sure that you add any global npm packages you need—tools such as gulp, pm2, mocha, and others that are necessary to your build environment.

If you would rather manage the install yourself, just use the "Run Shell command" option and something like the following command, adding any global installs you'd like:

```
curl https://raw.githubusercontent.com/creationix/nvm/v0.24.1/install.sh
| bash; nvm install 0.12; nvm alias default 0.12; npm install gulp -g
```

Remember to save your changes!

We're almost done configuring Jenkins for CI. The last step is to create a build project. Navigate to **New Item**, add a useful item name in the **Item name** field, select **Freestyle project**, and click on **OK**. Now, navigate to **Source Code Management**, select **Git**, add a GitHub repository name, select the credentials to access that repository, click on **Save**, and you'll be ready to build, as shown in the following screenshot:

Return to the Jenkins dashboard, and you'll see your build project listed. Click on the name, and select **Build Now** from the menu on the left-hand side. If all goes well, you'll see a build history table quickly populate, as shown here:

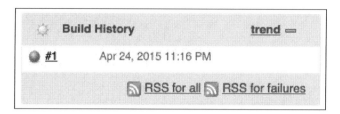

Click on the number and, if all is well, you'll see information on your build, indicating *no changes* (you have just pulled off a masterstroke), some information about the Git revision number, and so on. Now, the real test—make a change to your GitHub repository, either by pushing a change or simply editing a file using GitHub's editing tools. If you return to the dashboard, you will see that Jenkins has added a new build to **Build Queue**; shortly the build will complete, and you'll see the changes you've just made listed in your project's build history. You've just created a CI environment for your project!

Now, we need to deploy. We'll use Heroku to deploy, but feel free to try your provider of choice—as long as it *speaks* Git, Jenkins will be able to push your repository.

Deploying to Heroku

It might be useful to return to *Chapter 2, Installing and Virtualizing Node Servers,* and refresh your memory about how to build on Heroku. At the very least, you will need to install Heroku Toolbelt and authenticate. Once you are connected to Heroku via the toolbelt, clone the `express-webhook` repository we created earlier and enter that folder. Now, run `heroku create` to build a machine on Heroku. You should receive both a URL and a Git endpoint resembling the following:

```
https://floating-shelf-4947.herokuapp.com/ | https://git.heroku.com/
floating-shelf-4947.git

Git remote heroku added
```

Now, it is time to push something for that server to run. Execute the following command to push the `express-webhook` application to Heroku:

```
git push heroku master
```

The express-webhook application is now deployed to Heroku. Heroku will have automatically built and started the application. Go ahead and visit the URL we received before in a browser. The next step is to use Jenkins to automatically deploy to Heroku whenever you make changes to the application repository.

You are now connected to two Git repositories, which you can see by running `git remote -v`:

```
heroku   https://git.heroku.com/floating-shelf-4947.git (fetch)
heroku   https://git.heroku.com/floating-shelf-4947.git (push)
origin   https://github.com/sandro-pasquali/express-webhook (fetch)
origin   https://github.com/sandro-pasquali/express-webhook (push)
```

The `origin` URL is our GitHub repository, and `heroku` represents the Git repository maintained by Heroku. We'll synchronize these two via Jenkins.

As Jenkins will eventually be doing the pushing for us, we need to give it permission to access your Heroku box. What we're going to do is generate a key pair for the `jenkins` user and associate these local SSH keys with Heroku, allowing Jenkins to perform pushes and so on. Log in as the `jenkins` user, and run the following two commands:

```
ssh-keygen -t rsa
heroku keys:add ~/.ssh/id_rsa.pub
```

Jenkins can now authenticate with Heroku. All that is left to do is inform Jenkins about the Heroku repository and to instruct Jenkins to deploy to Heroku whenever it is informed, via the webhook we configured earlier, that changes have been made.

Return to your Jenkins project, click on **Configure**, and add the Heroku Git endpoint as another repository to the **Source Code Management** section by clicking on **Add Repository**. Fill in the **Repository URL** field to match the one you received earlier:

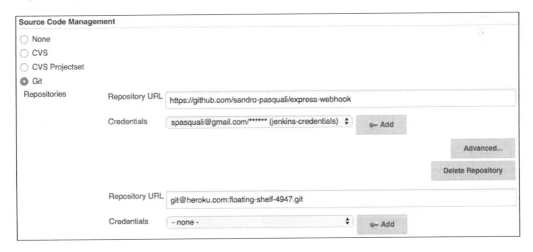

Note that you will *not* fill in **Credentials** as we've earlier linked Jenkins to Heroku using SSH keys.

Now, click on the "Advanced" button underneath the new repository, and give it a name—you'll need this for the next step. Here we use **heroku**, but it can be anything:

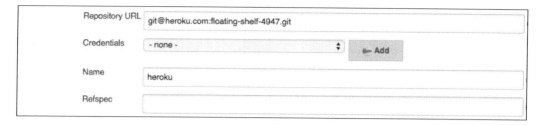

Now, Jenkins has been made aware of our GitHub repo and our Heroku repo. The final step is to configure Jenkins to push GitHub changes to Heroku.

Scroll down to **Post-build Actions** in your Jenkins project. Click on **Add post-build action** and select **Git publisher**. Fill out the form provided exactly as shown here:

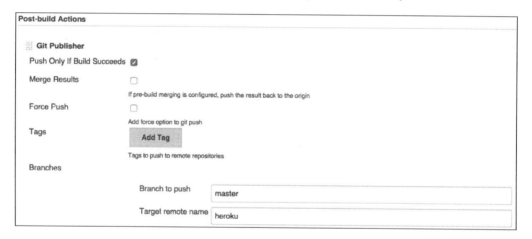

We are telling Jenkins to push to the `master` branch of the `express-webhook` GitHub repository to `heroku` after each successful build. This is the deploy step. Save your changes—you're done!

To test that everything is working, modify the default route of `server.js` in your local clone of `express-webhook` such that it produces a different message, and push that change to GitHub. If you return to the Jenkins dashboard, you will soon see something like the following progress indicator on the build status of your project:

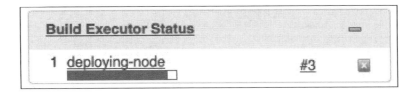

If all goes well, your project will be listed on the dashboard as having been successfully built. If you refresh your Heroku URL, you will also see the changes you've made. Congratulations on successfully setting up continuous deployment for your project!

Now that you have the structure set up for CI and deployment, start adding tests and other build steps and run them either in your Node environment or using the many Jenkins tools available to you. Happy building!

Package maintenance

JavaScript itself does not provide a native package management system; npm does this job for Node applications. A good package management strategy is, therefore, a key part of a good deployment strategy.

Packages offer the benefit of encapsulation. Running packages are accessible only through the API they've exported. This isolation reduces the number of potential bugs in a system, thus guarding the core functionality from accidental alteration. However, given that (opaque) packages can themselves require other packages as dependencies, the full dependency graph of an application can be difficult for a developer to easily see. For example, if the functionality of a package you have implemented suddenly changes, how do you debug it? Is the error in the package? Is it in one of its dependent packages?

Understanding *what is going on* in your npm dependency graph is essential when you are deploying Node applications. In this section, we will look at ways to stay up to date on package updates, use Git to manage private packages, track the health of an *entire* dependency graph, and look at best practices to set version rules in your application's `package.json` file.

Understanding Semver

Semantic Versioning (Semver) is simply a set of rules that have been proposed to govern how dependencies in a system are declared. Npm enforces these rules in its package manager, so understanding how they govern dependency management is what will be discussed here.

Take for example the following npm package file:

```
"devDependencies": {
  "browserify": "^6.1.0",
  "gulp": "~3.8.8",
  "foobar": " >=1.2.3 <1.3.0"
}
```

Each dependency is given a version number corresponding to a version in the npm repository. Some of these numbers are further modified by tokens, for example, a caret (^) or a tilde (~), as well as version ranges. Let's look at what each segment of semantically versioned numbers signify and how various tokens are used to modulate those segments.

A version number is broken into three segments, which are shown here:

```
1.2.7
Major.Minor.Patch
```

Semver concretely describes allowable package version ranges as well as implying the current stability or state of a package—whether the package is stable, whether it is mature, and so on. The numbering proceeds in order: 1.0.1 precedes 1.0.2, which precedes 2.0.0.

The significance of the changes that Semver describes proceeds from left to right, where a change in the major version of a package typically describes changes that break compatibility with lower versions—2.0 is not compatible with 1.0. According to semver.org, you should use version numbers in this way:

> *"Given a version number MAJOR.MINOR.PATCH, increment the: MAJOR version when you make incompatible API changes, MINOR version when you add functionality in a backwards-compatible manner, and PATCH version when you make backwards-compatible bug fixes."*

Then, Semver allows you to set acceptable range limits on the versions of dependencies in your application with an eye toward providing useful indications of the level of impact implied by version changes. Some common usage examples are given here:

- "3" indicates that only the major version (3) must be satisfied, ignoring minor or patch values—3.0.0, 3.6.3, and 3.99.99 are all acceptable.

- "3.4.5" indicates that *only* that version is acceptable, with no variation.

- "<, <=, > and >=" range comparators work as expected in many programming languages and can be used to set controlled ranges. >= 3.0.1 <= 3.2.1 accepts 3.0.2 and 3.1.9 but not 3.0.0 or 3.2.2.

- 1.3.4 >= 3.0.1 <= 3.2.1 accepts the version range as described in the preceding point *or* the 1.3.4 version.

- Being equivalent to >= 0.0.0, "*" indicates that *any* version is acceptable.

- Hyphen ranges (-) describe inclusive sets. The hyphen range 1.0.0 - 2.0.0 matches any package with a major version of 1.

- x-ranges provide a shorthand for minor and patch ranges; 1.2.x is equivalent to >= 1.2.0 <= 1.3.0 and 1.x is equivalent to >= 1.0.0 <= 2.0.0.

- Tilde(~) ranges allow patch-level changes if a minor version is specified and minor-level changes if it is not. ~1.3.2 is equivalent to >= 1.3.2 < 1.4.0, ~1.3 is equivalent to >= 1.3.0 < 1.4.0, and ~1 is equivalent to >= 1.0.0 < 2.0.0.

- Caret(^) ranges allow changes that do not modify the leftmost nonzero digit. ^1.2.0 is equivalent to >= 1.2.0 <= 2.0.0, ^0.2.1 is equivalent to >= 0.2.1 <= 0.3.0, and ^0.0.2 is equivalent to >= 0.0.2 < 0.0.3.

> For more details, visit `https://github.com/npm/node-semver` and `https://docs.npmjs.com/misc/semver`. A useful tool to check versions for specific packages against Semver tuples can be found at `http://semver.npmjs.com/`.

As we saw when we were using the `npm install <packagename> --save` construct, npm defaults to caret prefixing—npm will assign the newly installed dependency a version of `^<latest version>` in `package.json`. If you'd like to have a default tilde prefix, use `npm config set save-prefix="~"`.

Another important feature of Semver for maintainability is prerelease tags. These tags allow you to release a package version that is not ready for production (prerelease), which you might do in order to get it in the hands of other people on your team, beta testers, and so on, while ensuring that the default version will be installed on a "normal" install.

When you publish an npm package, you can use the `--tag` argument to tag that release. The published package is now no longer tagged as "latest" but as whichever tag you've assigned it. Let's say we tagged the **alpha.7** package (and changed the version field of the package with `npm version <version>-alpha.7`).

Now, consider the case where that package is being listed as a dependency somewhere in *userland*:

```
"my-package" : ">=1.03-alpha.1"
```

When this package is installed, npm will install the alpha.7 package—Semver ranges would apply as alpha.7 is greater than alpha.1.

Let's define our package in this way:

```
"my-package" : ">=1.03"
```

In the preceding case, the alpha.7 package will *not* be installed. In this way, we can see that by the Semver rule, prerelease tags only apply if the comparator (what you've set as the version of the package) also contains a prerelease tag. In this way, you can safely release experimental breaking changes in tagged packages as only someone who is fully aware of the tag name (and its alpha nature) would do the work required to be done to use it, while others continue to use production versions.

Managing packages with npm

One of the most important (and tricky) application management strategies you will deploy is choosing packages and updating package versions. In this section, good strategies to maintain your npm packages will be discussed—how to keep your packages up to date, how to lock dependencies, how to load packages from Git repositories rather than npm, and so on.

Generally, you'll want to balance the relative safety of the rigid Semver constraints with the need to stay as up to date as possible with the latest version of an important package and to keep your dependency tree predictable and clean. Developing a good strategy here will help with application maintenance.

Take a look at the following six aspects of package maintenance:

- Maintaining awareness of the full npm dependency tree
- Tracking divergence between the latest version and the installed version of a package
- Removing unused packages defined in your package file

- Ensuring that all needed dependencies are installed
- Ensuring that the dependencies you need are the ones you have
- Using private or other modules not held in the npm repository

Other package management systems enforce the rule that a single version of a package exists across all dependencies; npm does not. Packages typically require other packages, so multiple versions of the same package can enter into an npm build. An application may have A and B dependencies, with the A package requiring version 1.0.1 of the C package, and with the B package requiring version 2.0.1 of the C package.

Think about what it means to say that, on every npm install, there is limited (often barely thought out) control over the package versions inserted into a dependency tree—there is no guarantee that your application will run the same code at any given time. What's been installed at one moment may fundamentally change if you reinstall one hour later or even one second later. That's an extraordinary level of risk to introduce into production systems—similar to a software manager being indifferent to who makes changes, where, or when.

The first step is getting a full breakdown of what has been installed. Use npm ls for this, which returns something like the following:

```
...
├─┬ mocha@1.21.5
│ ├── commander@2.3.0
│ ├─┬ debug@2.0.0
│ │ └── ms@0.6.2
│ ├── diff@1.0.8
│ ├── escape-string-regexp@1.0.2
│ ├─┬ glob@3.2.3
│ │ ├── graceful-fs@2.0.3
│ │ ├── inherits@2.0.1
│ │ └─┬ minimatch@0.2.14
│ │   ├── lru-cache@2.5.0
│ │   └── sigmund@1.0.0
│ ├── growl@1.8.1
...
```

If you want this tree to be represented as JSON, use the `--json` flag: `npm ls --json`. To include the contents of each package's `description` field in the output, use `npm ls --long`. You can use `npm ls -g` to get this tree for *globally* installed packages. If you'd just like to know which packages are installed globally, try `ls ` npm root -g`.

Keeping up to date on the current versions of the installed packages is something you should be doing regularly. It doesn't take long for the version of a package to become outdated. Npm provides the `npm outdated` tool for this purpose (here, it is used with the `--long` "extended information" argument). The following screenshot shows this:

Package	Current	Wanted	Latest	Location	Package Type
hiredis	0.1.14	0.3.0	0.3.0	hiredis	dependencies
redis	0.8.2	0.12.1	0.12.1	redis	dependencies
formidable	1.0.11	1.0.17	1.0.17	formidable	dependencies

Here, we see that the `package.json` file within the `node_modules/redis` folder of our application is at version 0.8.2 (**current**), that the **latest** version is 0.12.1, and that the **wanted** Semver for *redis* in the root `package.json` file will match up to version 0.12.1. This indicates that it has been quite a while since `npm install` was run within this application. A very useful global tool to perform these sorts of checks is `npm-check` (`https://github.com/dylang/npm-check`), which delivers more detailed information, as shown in the following screenshot:

Additionally, this tool offers an interactive UI that will automatically update the packages you choose.

Another type of residue that accumulates over time is unused packages. These can be installed in `node_modules` but no longer linked, or these can be defined for a package but not required anywhere in the application's code.

To remove packages that are *installed* but no longer listed in `package.json`, you can use `npm prune`. Note that this is simply a technique for cleaning up the `node_modules` folder within an individual package's folder; it is not a smart, global tool to remove unused packages across the entire tree.

The `dependency-check` module (`https://github.com/maxogden/dependency-check`) is another tool to find unnecessary packages. Assuming that such an unused dependency exists, dependency-check will find it:

```
dependency-check package.json --unused
Fail! Modules in package.json not used in code: express
```

Conversely, packages may be required in the application code but not listed in a package file. This happens occasionally, when a necessary package is installed during development but not saved to `package.json`, possibly because the user forgets to use the `--save` option or for some other reason. The `dependency-check` command will walk all files in your codebase and find such cases, as shown here:

```
dependency-check package.json
Fail! Dependencies not listed in package.json: express
```

Note that it is expected that the entry point to your application is listed in `package.json` as `dependency-check` needs to know where your application tree is rooted. You should, therefore, ensure that your packages all have a `main` attribute pointing to an existing file. If you need to add further files to check, use the `--entry` argument as follows:

```
dependency-check package.json --entry a.js b.js [...]
```

To have a `main` entry point to your application is an important general practice that you should follow.

One final tool that can help speed up your npm builds is `npm dedupe`. When triggered, npm attempts to reduce the number of redundant package installs, "flattening" the tree somewhat, and, therefore, reducing install time. Consider this dependency tree:

```
A
└─┬ B
│ └─ C
└─┬ D
  └─ C
```

Here, the A package depends on the B and D packages, which each depend on the C package. Normally, C would be installed twice, once for each parent. However, if the Semver that B and D use to target C matches a single version of C, npm will reduce the tree in a way that both B and D pull from pull from the same, single, installed version of C. Note that Semver rules still apply—npm will not break version requirements solely to reduce the number of installs required.

It should be clear that many of the tools we've been looking at would fit nicely into a build/deploy process, issuing a warning if, for example, a given package is not used or is out of date. npm is itself an npm package (`https://github.com/npm/npm`)—try using npm programmatically within your build process to perform some of these checks.

Designing a dependency tree

All dependencies are not created equal. Some are necessary when in development mode but are not meaningful in production. The location and versions of dependencies can also vary as you may not always use packages in the npm repository, or you may want to use specialized versions.

There are three types of dependencies used in npm package files: **dependencies**, **devDependencies**, and **peerDependencies**. Let's look at the differences.

Simple dependencies are likely what you're most familiar with. These dependencies are *always* installed, regardless of context. You should place dependencies that *must* exist in this collection, typically the packages your production build will need.

When you are developing and building, you will often use tools, such as Mocha or gulp. Once a validated build is ready to be placed in production, however, there is no need for those packages to accompany it. The packages you do not need in production should be placed in the devDependencies collection. While npm will always install both dependencies and devDependencies, you can (and should) exclude devDependencies from the deploy install using the `--production` flag, which is as follows:

```
npm install --production
```

Usefully, if you run the `npm config set production` command, the `~/.npmrc` file will be updated such that all future installs will automatically set the `--production` flag. For example, your provisioner can do this configuration.

Finally, peerDependencies deals with the case of plugins. You're familiar with various Grunt plugins. While these are loaded via the npm ecosystem, they need their host program (Grunt) in order to function. You might think that each of these plugins should just `require('grunt')` — but which version of Grunt? Any one of these plugins may depend on a specific version of its host program, but those host programs are also direct dependencies of the package. So, consider this declaration:

```
"dependencies": {
  "grunt": "1.2.3",
  "gulp-plugin": "1.0.0" // requires grunt@2.0.0
}
```

The preceding declaration leads to a dangerous conflict:

```
└── grunt@1.2.3
└┬ gulp-plugin@1.0.0
  └── grunt@2.0.0
```

So, peerDependencies should be used in plugin-type packages that have specific host-program needs, allowing the plugin to "carry along" their needed host. If npm attempts to install a different version of that host program, an error is thrown. This, of course, leads to another problem — any given plugin can cause an install to fail if its required host program is not version-compatible with the one the main application is demanding. The complexities of peerDependencies remain an ongoing discussion in the Node community (`https://github.com/npm/npm/issues/5080`).

As mentioned, npm does not put many limits on package versions, allowing multiple versions of the same package to exist simultaneously and, indeed, for versions (and, therefore, package functionality) to change unexpectedly.

One way to secure your application's state is to lock a dependency tree using `npm shrinkwrap`. This command will trigger npm to generate the `npm-shrinkwrap.json` file containing explicit references to specific versions. The file generated contains definitions such as the following:

```
"moment": {
  "version": "2.8.4",
  "from": "moment@^2.8.3",
  "resolved": "https://registry.npmjs.org/moment/-/moment-2.8.4.tgz"
},
"node-uuid": {
  "version": "1.4.2",
  "from": "node-uuid@^1.4.1",
  "resolved": "https://registry.npmjs.org/node-uuid/-/node-uuid-1.4.2.tgz"
}
```

It should be clear how this syntax ensures that future installs will be identical. Note that this is a heavy-handed approach that you probably don't need very often. However, in production situations where you are deploying identical code across multiple machines, shrinkwrapped "bundles" may be exactly what you need.

Another option to ensure visibility in the behavior of your packages is to control them in their entirety. You are able to link dependencies to Git repositories, either public or private. For example, you can load Express directly from its GitHub repository:

```
dependencies : {
   "express" : "strongloop/express"
}
```

npm assumes GitHub, so you are able to use the compressed syntax, as shown in the preceding code.

You can also link to a private Git repository using `https/oauth`:

```
"package-name": "git+https://<github_token>:x-oauth-basic@github.com/<user>/<repo>.git"
```

You can also use SSH as follows:

```
"package-name": "git+ssh://git@github.com/<user>/<repo>.git"
```

The npm package manager is an essential part of the Node ecosystem, and Node applications are typically composed of dozens, even hundreds, of packages. Developing a strategy around package management is an important consideration if you plan to release and maintain a large-scale Node application.

Summary

In this chapter, you learned how to deploy a local build into a production-ready environment. The powerful Git webhook tool was demonstrated as a way of creating a continuous integration environment, and this knowledge was carried forward into the creation of a full build/deploy pipeline that connected a GitHub repository to a Heroku deployment via a CI environment configured using Jenkins. We also covered the semantic versioning system that npm uses and even how to use Semver, npm methods, and some helper libraries to keep our package trees clean and predictable.

From basic JavaScript programs to the deployment of full applications, in this book, we took a tour of Node's design and goals. We've worked through ways in which Node's event-driven architecture influences how we design networked software by building on the foundational concept of streams. With an eye toward the creation of fast, deployable systems, we worked through virtualization strategies, compiler optimizations, load balancing, and vertical and horizontal scaling strategies. Additionally, the power of composing software out of small, focused programs was considered by introducing the power of micro services, interprocess messaging, and queues as one way to build distributed systems.

Keeping in mind that software is written by fallible humans, we also covered strategies for testing and maintaining running applications, learning to expect failure, and planning for it, with the help of both native and third-party logging and monitoring tools. We learned debugging techniques and optimization strategies aimed at reducing bottlenecks at the local and network levels and also how to find their source when they inevitably appear. With the goal of making development simpler, we looked at how to make effective use of integration tools and versioning systems, provision virtual machines and test with headless browsers, enable developers to work freely and take risks, and push changes with the confidence that smart deployment strategies confer. Constructing a smart build pipeline, you learned about the power of full-stack JavaScript, transpilation, live updates, and continuous testing and integration.

You are encouraged to modify and extend the example code to improve it or, otherwise, change it to your needs. The hope is that, as you come to appreciate the power of Node.js, the npm ecosystem, and open source software, you will begin to naturally design your applications so that they will require few changes when pushed into production, and that you will share your discoveries so that others can do the same thing.

Index

A

add-ons, Heroku 33
Advanced Message Queuing Protocol
     (AMQP)
  about 80
  URL 84
alpha.7 package 234
Ansible
  deployed application, provisioning 219-222
  roles 220
  URL 222
Apache Bench tool
  URL 164
application development
  expensive technical realities 167
  with Browserify 168
  with Gulp 168
  with Handlebars 168
Application Programming Interface (API) 9
assert module
  about 186-188
  methods 187, 188
asynchronous execution 8
automated browser testing
  with CasperJS 199
  with PhantomJS 199
autopilot repository
  about 212
  URL 212

B

backup directive 77

bind command, arguments
  address 84
  callback 84
  port 84
Bit Operations (bitops) 105
bitwise operations
  bitmasks 108, 109
  bits, counting 106-108
  bits, getting 106-108
  bits, setting 106-108
  results, filtering 108, 109
  used, for analyzing user actions 105
bitwise operators 105
bluebird library
  about 120
  URL 120
bouncy module
  URL 79
Browserify
  about 20, 21, 168
  references 21
  URL 177
  using 178
BrowserSync
  about 168, 179
  URL 179
Brunch
  URL 181
build/deploy system
  implementing, webhooks used 212-215
  URL 212
Bunyan
  about 144
  URL 144

O

Object.create method
about 104
URL 104
Object-oriented (OO) language 102
OpenShift
Cartridges 40
Gears 40
installing 39, 40
MongoDB, installing 41
Node application, deploying 42, 43
Node application, installing 41

P

package 17
package management
about 231
aspects 234
with npm 234-237
with Semantic Versioning
(Semver) 232-234
parallelism 5-7
peerDependencies
about 238
reference link 239
performance optimization 113
PhantomJS
URL 199
used, for automated browser testing 199
used, for headless testing 199-201
playbooks 219
PM2
about 155-158
commands 156
monitoring 158, 159
port redirection
URL 51
process errors
catching 136-138
process ID (PID) 63
Procfile 33
production build 208
profiling processes
about 151-155
references 155

prototypes
reference link 105
using 102-105
proxy 69

R

RabbitMQ
about 80
URL 80
Read-Eval-Print-Loop (REPL) 145
Redis
about 105
bitwise operations, using 105
HyperLogLog, using 110-112
npm module, URL 94
pub/sub 94-97
used, for caching 119-122
remotely monitoring
about 144, 147-151
with Node REPL 145-147
Remote Procedure Calls (RPC) 20
reverse proxy 70
rhc tool
delete command 43
force-stop command 43
reload command 43
restart command 43
show command 43
start command 43
stop command 43
tidy command 43
using 43
routing keys 81
Rule of Modularity 16
Rule of Simplicity 7
runtime_function
about 115
URL 115

S

Sass CSS preprocessor
about 176
URL 176
scalability 53

Thank you for buying
Deploying Node.js

About Packt Publishing

Packt, pronounced 'packed', published its first book, *Mastering phpMyAdmin for Effective MySQL Management*, in April 2004, and subsequently continued to specialize in publishing highly focused books on specific technologies and solutions.

Our books and publications share the experiences of your fellow IT professionals in adapting and customizing today's systems, applications, and frameworks. Our solution-based books give you the knowledge and power to customize the software and technologies you're using to get the job done. Packt books are more specific and less general than the IT books you have seen in the past. Our unique business model allows us to bring you more focused information, giving you more of what you need to know, and less of what you don't.

Packt is a modern yet unique publishing company that focuses on producing quality, cutting-edge books for communities of developers, administrators, and newbies alike. For more information, please visit our website at www.packtpub.com.

About Packt Open Source

In 2010, Packt launched two new brands, Packt Open Source and Packt Enterprise, in order to continue its focus on specialization. This book is part of the Packt Open Source brand, home to books published on software built around open source licenses, and offering information to anybody from advanced developers to budding web designers. The Open Source brand also runs Packt's Open Source Royalty Scheme, by which Packt gives a royalty to each open source project about whose software a book is sold.

Writing for Packt

We welcome all inquiries from people who are interested in authoring. Book proposals should be sent to author@packtpub.com. If your book idea is still at an early stage and you would like to discuss it first before writing a formal book proposal, then please contact us; one of our commissioning editors will get in touch with you.

We're not just looking for published authors; if you have strong technical skills but no writing experience, our experienced editors can help you develop a writing career, or simply get some additional reward for your expertise.

Node.js Blueprints

ISBN: 978-1-78328-733-8 Paperback: 268 pages

Develop stunning web and desktop applications with the definitive Node.js

1. Utilize libraries and frameworks to develop real-world applications using Node.js.

2. Explore Node.js compatibility with AngularJS, Socket.io, BackboneJS, EmberJS, and GruntJS.

3. Step-by-step tutorials that will help you to utilize the enormous capabilities of Node.js.

Mastering Node.js

ISBN: 978-1-78216-632-0 Paperback: 346 pages

Expert techniques for building fast servers and scalable, real-time network applications with minimal effort

1. Master the latest techniques for building real-time, big data applications, integrating Facebook, Twitter, and other network services.

2. Tame asynchronous programming, the event loop, and parallel data processing.

3. Use the Express and Path frameworks to speed up development and deliver scalable, higher quality software more quickly.

Please check **www.PacktPub.com** for information on our titles

Node Web Development
Second Edition

ISBN: 978-1-78216-330-5   Paperback: 248 pages

A practical introduction to Node.js, an exciting
server-side JavaScript web development stack

1. Learn about server-side JavaScript with Node.js
   and Node modules.

2. Website development both with and without the
   Connect/Express web application framework.

3. Developing both HTTP server and client
   applications.

Instant Node.js Starter

ISBN: 978-1-78216-556-9   Paperback: 48 pages

Program your scalable network applications and web
services with Node.js

1. Learn something new in an Instant! A short,
   fast, focused guide delivering immediate
   results.

2. Learn how to use module patterns and Node
   Packet Manager (NPM) in your applications.

3. Discover callback patterns in NodeJS.

4. Understand the use Node.js streams in your
   applications.

Please check **www.PacktPub.com** for information on our titles